# PUBLIC
# EMPLOYEE
# ORGANIZING
## and the law

# PUBLIC EMPLOYEE ORGANIZING and the law

## Michael T. Leibig
## Wendy L. Kahn

The Bureau of National Affairs, Inc.
Washington, D.C.

**Library of Congress Cataloging-in-Publication Data**

Leibig, Michael T.
  Public employee organizing and the law.

  Includes index.
  1. Collective labor agreements—Government employees—United
States.  2. Trade-unions—Government employees—Law and
legislation—United States.  I. Kahn, Wendy L.  II. Title.
KF3409.P77L45    1987      344.73′0189041353      87-18398
ISBN 0-87179-499-3           347.304189041353

Printed in the United States of America
International Standard Book Number 0-87179-499-3

This book is dedicated to
Abraham L. Zwerdling (1914–1987)

# Preface

Two people deserve special mention as the motivators of this book.

Stephen I. Schlossberg, since September 1, 1987, Director, Washington Branch Office, International Labor Organization, and the author of *Organizing and the Law*, wrote the basic text for private sector organizing which served as the model for this book. Before joining the United States Department of Labor in 1985 as Deputy Undersecretary of Labor for Labor Management Relations and Cooperative Programs, Steve Schlossberg was our partner in the Washington, D.C., law firm of Zwerdling, Schlossberg, Leibig & Kahn. Before that, he served both as General Counsel and Director of Governmental Affairs for the United Automobile Workers. Steve got this book off the ground.

Abraham L. Zwerdling was, until his death in May 1987, the senior partner of Zwerdling, Paul, Leibig, Kahn & Thompson, P.C., in Washington, D.C. During the 1970s Mr. Zwerdling served as national General Counsel to the American Federation of State, County and Municipal Employees, AFL-CIO (AFSCME). This was the period when the AFSCME grew to be the largest public sector union for nonteaching employees and one of the leading forces in the American labor movement as well as the formative period for the law of state and local labor relations. Abe Zwerdling trained both of us as public sector labor attorneys and guided this work to completion. This book is dedicated to him.

This book arises out of the joint recognition by Mr. Schlossberg, Mr. Zwerdling, and its authors of the clear need for a basic guide to the rules of the game in organizing state and local employees both in the academic training setting and in the practical organizing campaign.

A number of individuals have contributed a great deal of work to this presentation of public sector organizing. They include Sue Scheider, who did most of the initial work in developing the comparative state-by-state analysis of over 75 state and local statutes; and Dennis Orke, Chris Wood, and Kathy Pirri, who also worked on that

vii

project. Ms. Kahn's and Mr. Leibig's graduate public sector labor law class at the Georgetown University Law Center during the Fall 1985 term reviewed, corrected, and updated that analysis. The attorneys on that project included Frederic Brandes, Kevin Brodar, Jeanne Carroll, Joseph Dombrosky, Chuck Goldner, Edward Hughes, Brian Meyers, and Catherine Powers.

A number of labor officials and leaders helped either by sharing their experience or by imparting practical advice and comments. They included Secretary-Treasurer William Lucy of the American Federation of State, County and Municipal Employees, AFL-CIO; President Robert Kliesmet of the International Union of Police Associations, AFL-CIO; President Ray Benton and Vice President Jim Hicks of Virginia Public Employees Council 30, AFSCME, AFL-CIO; Cephus Newton of AFSCME Local 2407; Judy Scott of the United Mine Workers; Maggie Rock of the AFL-CIO's Lawyer's Coordinating Committee; Dave Baker, Director of Public Sector Division of SEIU, AFL-CIO; and Steven Weissman of the Communication Workers of America, AFL-CIO.

Ingrid Coney and Kathy Jasper prepared and revised the text endlessly and tirelessly.

Finally, we appreciate the help we received from the staffs of various state and local labor boards. Personnel from the California, Iowa, Massachusetts, Michigan, New Jersey, New York, Pennsylvania, Washington, D.C., and Wisconsin boards all offered helpful comments. Gary Altman, then Counsel to the Massachusetts Labor Relations Commission, was particularly helpful.

Naturally, any inaccuracies or errors, as well as the expression of any opinions in these materials, are the sole responsibility of the authors.

# Foreword

There are over 13,600,000 American state and local public employees; state and local salaries and wages are 21.3 billion annually.[1] The growth in public employment and the extent of organization in the public sector have been steady over the past two decades. While the percentage of private sector workers belonging to unions or associations has been declining over the past decade—from over 30 percent to less than 21 percent of the eligible work force—the percentage of public sector workers joining unions has been increasing constantly. The Census Department reports that close to 50 percent of eligible public workers belong to labor unions or related employee associations.[2] In 1956, there were 16,575,000 union members in the private sector and 915,000 in the public sector. By 1978, private sector union membership had grown to 16,613,000—by 10 percent—while public sector membership had grown to 3,625,000—by 296 percent.[3]

The Public Employee Department of the AFL-CIO reported in February 1987 that there are approximately 10.5 million state and local government employees in the United States who are in jobs that are generally considered to be eligible for collective bargaining. But, because employees of our states and local governments traditionally have been excluded from the protection of national labor laws, it has been left to the individual states to determine whether to extend such rights to the public workers within the states. Today, 27 states and the District of Columbia have enacted comprehensive collective bargaining laws for their public employees. Six and one-half million employees in these states are protected. There are 4 million employees in the 23

---

[1] *See* BNA, GERR, 71:2111, RF-49 (Nov. 24, 1986).

[2] In 1980, 5,031,000 state and local employees—48.8 percent of the total work force—belonged to employee organizations. *See* Bureau of the Census, U.S. Department of Commerce & Labor Management Services Administration, *Labor Relations in State and Local Government, 1980* (Washington: 1981), 1.

[3] *Id.*

states without such laws, amounting to 40 percent of the 10.5 million total.[4]

The organization of public workers is a vital, even central feature of labor organizing in America. This is a handbook for public sector union organizers, designed as a companion to Schlossberg and Scott's *Organizing and the Law: A Handbook for Union Organizers.*[5] *Organizing and the Law* opens with a quotation from Charles Evans Hughes, Chief Justice of the Supreme Court of the United States, in *NLRB v. Jones & Laughlin Steel Corp.*:[6]

> Long ago we stated the reason for labor organizations. We said that they were organized out of the necessities of the situation; that a single employee was helpless in dealing with an employer; that he was dependent ordinarily on his daily wage for the maintenance of himself and family; that if the employer refused to pay him the wages that he thought fair, he was nevertheless unable to leave the employ and resist arbitrary and unfair treatment; that union was essential to give laborers opportunity to deal on an equality with their employer.[7]

Supreme Court Justice Potter Stewart, in *Abood v. Detroit Board of Education*,[8] pointed out that: "Public employees are not basically different from private employees; on the whole, they have the same sort of skills, the same needs, and seek the same advantages."[9] Public workers, like private workers, are "organized out of the necessities of the situation."

This book concerns the law of public sector union organizing— not a debate as to its merits or demerits—but what the law is and how it works.[10] Like its companion volume, *Organizing and the Law*, it sets out, in usable and readable form, the major legal principles affecting union organization. It is important that organizers have a grasp of some basic principles of labor, constitutional, personnel, state and local finance, and administrative law. Public sector organizers must also have the ability to determine the specific rules which vary among employers and organizing drives.

This book will not make lawyers out of organizers, but if carefully followed, may permit organizers to make intelligent choices under the

---

[4]Public Employee Department, AFL-CIO, *One Country . . . Two Different Worlds: How the Absence of Collective Bargaining Laws Limits Employee Bargaining Rights* (February 1987) (*See* Appendix G).

[5]3d ed. (1983).

[6]301 U.S. 1, 1 LRRM 703 (1937).

[7]*Id.* at 33.

[8]431 U.S. 209, 95 LRRM 2411 (1977).

[9]*Id.* at 229–230.

[10]Organizing federal employees is not expressly covered in this book. The concentration is on organizing state and local workers.

law and to know when they need lawyers. No organizer should assume that this volume can substitute for legal advice.

Unlike the private sector where there is one basic source of law which governs organizing (the National Labor Relations Act (NLRA) as it has been interpreted by courts and by the National Labor Relations Board (NLRB)), there is no single source of law that governs organizing for state and local employees. There is no federal statute providing for collective bargaining for state and local employees, and while some states have collective bargaining laws covering some, or most, public employees, other states do not. The laws that do bear on public sector organizing include state bargaining laws, where they exist; federal and state constitutions; open meeting and freedom of information acts; civil service laws; and other personnel rules and regulations. We hope to provide a basic source of laws and legal principles which apply to public sector organizing.

The job of the organizer—professional or amateur—will always be tough, and no quick and easy gimmicks are available to change that. To the unorganized and unrepresented, organization and representation may seem impossible. This is especially true in the public sector where NLRA policies favoring unionization may be absent. However, the United States Constitution itself protects organizing. In *Atkins v. City of Charlotte*,[11] the court found that public employees "are granted the right of free association by the First and Fourteenth Amendments of the United States Constitution; that right of association includes the right to form and join a labor union—whether local or national. . . ."[12]

Effective organizing lays the foundation for effective collective bargaining. Only through effective organizing can the political basis for collective bargaining legislation be laid in the public sector. This has been the experience in the states that have enacted broad collective bargaining statutes modeled on the NLRA; it is also true in those states that have not reached that stage.

In *Abood v. Detroit Board of Education*,[13] Supreme Court Justice Potter Stewart recognized that: "There can be no quarrel with the truism that because public employee unions attempt to influence governmental policymaking, their activities . . . may be properly termed political."[14] The political nature of collective bargaining in the public sector, including basic legislation, and the importance of organizing

---

[11]296 F. Supp. 1068, 70 LRRM 2732 (D.C.N.C. 1969).
[12]*Id.* at 1076.
[13]*Abood v. Detroit Bd. of Educ.*, above, note 8.
[14]*Id.* at 231.

in the political process, only serve to intensify the fact that effective union organizing is vitally important to public employees everywhere.

*Public Employee Organizing and the Law* is divided into two parts. Part I consists of six chapters which are intended to provide the organizer with an overview of organizing drive issues. Chapter 1 compares private with public sector organizing and discusses the basis of public sector labor relations policy. Chapter 2 outlines a series of public sector employment relations models. Chapter 3 presents a series of tools for the organizer including how to target an employer; how to analyze management structures, budgets, and wage and benefit packages; how to do an employee survey; and how to know your union. Chapter 4 discusses certain constitutional and statutory rights of public employees. Chapter 5 discusses the right of public employees to organize, with a focus on constitutional considerations. Finally, Chapter 6 outlines questions raised by, and strategies used in, organizing in the absence of a collective bargaining statute.

Part II presents (1) an analysis of state and local statutory public sector collective bargaining structures; and (2) a state-by-state overview of collective bargaining statutes and their organizing rules, which guides the organizer to specific statutory provisions in each jurisdiction.

Finally, seven appendices offer a series of resource materials including—

A. BNA's Digest of State Public Employee Statutes;
B. State Open Meeting and Freedom of Information Laws;
C. Analyzing Budgets and Proposals;
D. Guide to Costing Out Public Wage and Benefit Packages;
E. Sample Dues Deduction Form;
F. Sample Election Agreement; and
G. AFL-CIO Public Sector Bargaining Law Report

# Contents

# Part One

# The Tools of the Public Sector Organizer

# 1

# The Public Sector Organizing Drive: Getting Started

Because no statute dominates public sector organizing in the way the National Labor Relations Act (NLRA) governs private sector organizing,[1] it is impossible to set out "most of the law" of public employee organizing in a single chapter. This chapter and the ones that follow seek to provide some basic tools and suggestions for approaching the myriad customs, statutes, ordinances, regulations, and legal precedents that establish the rules of public employee organizing.

---

[1]The possibility of national legislation concerning state and local government bargaining ebbs and flows. Between 1976 and 1986, it was generally accepted that the U.S. Congress did not have authority under the commerce clause to regulate public employment. That belief was based on the Supreme Court's 1976 *National League of Cities* decision striking down congressional application of the federal fair labor standards minimum wage and overtime law to public employees. On February 19, 1985, the Court reversed *National League of Cities* in *Garcia v. San Antonio Metropolitan Transit Auth.*, 469 US 528, 27 WH Cases 65 (1985). On February 24, 1987, Rep. William Clay (D.-Mo.) introduced in the U.S. House of Representatives, H.R.1201, a bill to guarantee the right of firefighters to organize and bargain collectively. *See also National League of Cities v. Usery*, 426 US 833, 22 WH Cases 1064 (1976); *Transportation Union v. Long Island R.R.*, 455 US 678, 109 LRRM 3017 (1982); *EEOC v. Wyoming*, 460 US 226, 31 FEP Cases 74 (1983). *See also* D. Alfange, "Congressional Regulation of the 'States Qua States': From *National League of Cities* to *EEOC v. Wyoming*," 1983 *Sup. Ct. Rev.* 215; D. La Pierre, "The Political Safeguards of Federalism Redux," 60 *Wash. U.L.Q.* 779 (1982); D.E. Elisburg, "Legislative Outlook for Public Sector Labor Relations," in *Labor Relations Law in the Public Sector*, 21–29 (A.S. Knapp, ed. 1977); M. Lieberman, *Public Sector Bargaining: A Policy Reappraisal* (1980); R. Chanin, "Can a Federal Collective Bargaining Statute for Public Employees Meet the Requirements of *National League of Cities v. Usery?*" 6 *J.L. & Educ.* 493 (1977); W. McCann & S. Smiley, "The National Labor Relations Act and the Regulation of Public Employee Collective Bargaining," 13 *Harv. J. on Legis.* 479 (1976); H. Williams, "Public Employees Collective Bargaining: The Need for a Federal Presence," 1 *Okla. City U.L. Rev.* 85 (1976); E. Shaller, "The Consitutionality of a Federal Collective Bargaining Statute for State and Local Employees," 8 *Cap. U.L. Rev.* 59 (1978).

The successful public sector organizer should do a preorganizing drive review of each *specific* organizing opportunity. The organizer should know six things before the drive begins. They are:

(1) *Know What Is Useful From the Private Sector:* What is special about this organizing drive? How different is it from a private sector organizing effort? What is the basic employee relations policy of the jurisdiction applicable to the employees?

(2) *Know the Labor Relations Model:* Is this a situation where traditional relationships are patterned after the private sector/NLRA model or does some other tradition dominate—"public servant," "public safety," patronage, civil service, or "modern professional management"? Is it a mixed bag?

(3) *Know the Employees:* What are the characteristics of the group to be organized? Are the employees blue collar workers, clericals, public safety or health care employees, social workers, teachers, or administrative professionals? Are there other special characteristics of the group? What is its age, outside interests, sexual, religious, racial, educational, and recreational make up? Is it a local "native" or a transitory work force? Look at employee gripes and needs.

(4) *Know Management:* What is management like? What are its traditions? Who is the employer? Who has what degree of discretion on employment-related questions? Is the employment relationship authority divided among different people? Who speaks for and represents management? What are their names? What are they like? What are the employer's likely responses to unionization? Analyze the employer's budget. Cost out the compensation package. Compare it.

(5) *Know the Background of Organization Among the Employees:* What is the history of employee organizing attempts? Are there established organizations to which the employees belong—fraternal groups, churches, sports clubs or leagues, civic societies, professional associations? Are any other types of labor organizations involved?

(6) *Know the Rules:* What are the technical rules controlling the organizing game? Who are the referees?

These six groups of questions should provide the basis for a predrive overview of public sector organizing.

## Lessons From the Private Sector

### *Public/Private Distinctions*

It is good practice to recognize that organizing workers in the public sector is a similar endeavor to organizing in the private sector, with similar problems and solutions.[2] Too often, the differences between the two sectors have been overemphasized both by people with broad experience in private sector union organizing[3] and by people with ideological objections to unionization in any form.[4] In *Abood v. Detroit Board of Education*,[5] Justice Stewart adopted Clyde Summer's insight:[6]

> The uniqueness of public employment is *not in the employees* nor in the work performed; the uniqueness is in the special character of the employer.[7]

The same is true of organizing. The uniqueness of public sector labor organizing lies not with the employees or even the organizing techniques, but with the special character of the employer and the bargaining process which follows organizing.

---

[2]*See Abood v. Detroit Bd. of Educ.*, 431 US 209, 227–229, 95 LRRM 2411 (1977), for a discussion of the "often-noted" differences in the nature of collective bargaining in the public and private sectors. Justice Stewart's conclusion from a review of extensive literature is that while the bargaining process is, in many cases, quite different, public employees "are not basically different" from private employees. Note 24 of the opinion reviews the literature and private/public sector differences.

*See, e.g.*, K.L. Hanslowe, *The Emerging Law of Labor Relations in Public Employment* (1967); H.H. Wellington & R.K. Winter, *The Unions and the Cities* (1972); G. Hildebrand, "The Public Sector," in *Frontiers of Collective Bargaining*, 125–154 (J. Dunlop & N. Chamberlain, eds. 1967); C. Rehmus, "Constraints on Local Governments in Public Employee Bargaining," 67 *Mich. L. Rev.* 919 (1969); L.C. Shaw & T. Clark, Jr., "Practical Differences Between Public and Private Sector Collective Bargaining," 19 *U.C.L.A. L. Rev.* 867 (1972); R. Smith, "State and Local Advisory Reports on Public Employment Labor Legislation: A Comparative Analysis," 67 *Mich. L. Rev.* 891 (1969); C.W. Summers, "Public Employee Bargaining: A Political Perspective," 83 *Yale L.J.* 1156 (1974); "Project: Collective Bargaining and Politics in Public Employment," 19 *U.C.L.A. L. Rev.* 887 (1972). The general description in the text of the differences between private- and public-sector collective bargaining is drawn from these sources.

[3]For example, see J. Goulden, *Jerry Wurf: Labor's Last Angry Man* (1982), especially Chapters 4–6 which highlight the many differences and similarities which Wurf understood.

[4]S. Petro, "Sovereignty and Compulsory Public Sector Bargaining," 10 *Wake Forest L. Rev.* 25, 63–139 (1974). For strong criticism of Petro's sovereignty and delegation of powers arguments, see "Developments in the Law: Public Employment," 97 *Harv. L. Rev.* 1611, 1677 n.4 (1984), *citing Knight v. Minnesota Community College Faculty Ass'n*, 571 F. Supp. 1, 3–4, 111 LRRM 3156 (D. Minn. 1982), *rev'd sub nom.* Minnesota State Bd. for Community Colleges v. Knight, 462 US 271, 115 LRRM 2785 (1984); H. Edwards, "The Developing Labor Relations Law in the Public Sector," 10 *Duq. L. Rev.* 357, 359–360 (1972).

[5]Note 2, above.

[6]"Public Sector Bargaining: Problems of Governmental Decision-Making," 44 *Cin. L. Rev.* 669 (1975).

[7]*Id.* at 670.

The organizational structure of government and operational scale of a public employer may resemble closely that of many private employers. The size and location of the work force are often comparable. Workplace issues of wages, hours, working conditions, and the problems of employment security and workplace discipline often converge.

However, significantly divergent forces must also be recognized. It is important that the public sector organizer have a clear idea of the differences between public and private employment. The principal goal of private enterprise is profit-oriented, while the principal goal of the public concern is generally determined politically. Measures of output and performance vary a great deal from private enterprise to public employment.

Sources of financing vary so greatly between the two sectors that in many situations they can alter the basic motivations operating in conflicts between labor and management. In most cases, an interruption in services or production generated by a private sector disruption in the workplace will have an immediate and negative impact on employer revenue. This is true because private enterprise income is usually tied directly to its provision of services or products.

But this is not usually the case in the public sector. Instead, the typical public concern is financed by taxation, and the flow of tax income is almost never interrupted by a disruption in the public workplace.[8]

The division of the functions of government among a legislature, which generally has primary authority over finance and budget, an executive, which "runs things," and a judiciary, which sees that rules are followed, is radically different from the division in a private concern among a board of directors, a chief executive, and line supervisors. The chain of command in the private concern is usually clearer and more direct than in the public sector. Usually the "boss' in the private sector is a person with *specific*, clear, and definite authority subject

---

[8]This financial reality has brought about the gradual shift in attitude on the part of many union leaders with regard to the "right to strike" in the public sector and has, in many cases, generated a preference for binding arbitration. One of public labor's first and, at times, most militant leaders, Jerry Wurf, was not a proponent of striking:

> Nobody ever prints this, but I say it to our staff and I say it to our membership. I am opposed to strikes. I don't want strikes. They're bad. They're hard on the city but they're harder on the workers.
> I fight bitterly for the right to strike—the *right* to strike. But I don't think there's any principle involved in striking. Striking is a tactic to persuade an employer to deal with us.
> If it can be avoided, almost any price ought to be paid in order to avoid a strike.

*See* J. Goulden, above, note 3, at 184; *but see* "Developments in the Law: Public Employment," above, note 4, at 1701–1718; D. Gallager, "The Use of Interest Arbitration in the Public Sector," 33 *Lab. L.J.* 501 (1982); A. Anderson, "Interest Arbitration," 51 *Lab. L. Rev.* 453 (1977); K.L. Hanslowe & J. Acierno, "The Law and Theory of Strikes by Government Employees," 67 *Cornell L. Rev.* 1055 (1982).

to concrete tests of success and progress. In the public sector, management is less clearly defined; its authority is subject to extensive restrictions, checks, and balances. The public budgeting, planning, and administrative implementation scheme will often be unique to the specific public employer involved.[9]

In government, the position and rights of the citizens are wholly different from those of the owner, stockholder, or consumer of the private organization. The public sector's responsibility to provide police or fire protection, to keep the schools operating, the trash collected, and public services flowing generates influences in public sector organizing which are not present in the private sector. Due to these concerns, a public strike is nearly universally recognized as something to be avoided.[10]

There are clear differences between the private and public sector. While the differences between the two sectors have been described as "fuzzy,"[11] they often play an important role in decision making with regard to organizing. Those who oppose unions generally use the

---

[9]*See* F.O'R. Hayes, "Collective Bargaining and the Budget Director," in *Public Workers and Public Unions*, 89–100 (S. Zagoria, ed. 1972); D. Stanley, *Managing Local Government Under Union Pressure* (1972); A. Anderson, "Local Government—Bargaining and the Fiscal Crisis: Money, Unions, Politics, and the Public Interest," 27 *Lab. L.J.* 512 (1976); J.P. Weitzman, "The Effect of Economic Restraints on Public-Sector Collective Bargaining: The Lessons of New York City," 2 *Employee Rel. L.J.* No. 3, 286 (1977).

[10]Both management and labor recognize the unique problems raised by at least some public strikes. *See* note 8, above, on the attitude of public unions. The Supreme Court has perhaps overemphasized the point in seeing strikes as exemplar of the private/public sector division:

The distinctive nature of public-sector bargaining has led to widespread discussion about the extent to which the law governing labor relations in the private sector provides an appropriate model. To take but one example, there has been considerable debate about the desirability of prohibiting public employee unions from striking, . . . .

*Abood*, above, note 2, 431 US at 280.

In 1985, the California Supreme Court discussed the current law on public sector strikes in great detail in its landmark finding that, at least in California, public sector strikes are not prohibited by common law. *County Sanitation Dist. No. 2, Los Angeles County v. Service Employees Local 600*, 119 LRRM 2433 (1985). The finding of the case is clearly a minority view. *See, e.g., Teachers Local 519 v. School City of Anderson*, 252 Ind. 558, 251 NE2d 15, 72 LRRM 2466 (1969), *cert. denied*, 399 US 928, 74 LRRM 2552 (1970). At the same time, the California decision is practically a textbook on developing modern legal and workplace attitudes toward public sector strikes.

*See also* A. Anderson, "Strikes and Impasse Resolution in Public Employment," 67 *Mich. L. Rev.* 943 (1969); J.F. Burton, Jr., & C.E. Krider, "The Role and Consequences of Strikes by Public Employees," 79 *Yale L.J.* 418 (1970); G. Hildebrand, above, note 2; T. Kheel, "Strikes and Public Employment," 67 *Mich. L. Rev.* 931 (1969); H.H. Wellington & R.K. Winter, "More on Strikes by Public Employees," 79 *Yale L.J.* 441 (1970); S. Spero, "The 1919 Boston Police Strike," in *Collective Bargaining in Government: Readings and Cases*, 178–192 (J. Loewenberg & M.H. Moskow, eds. 1972); J.H. Burpo, *The Police Labor Movement: Problems and Perspectives*, 3–5 (1971); B.D. Meltzer & C.R. Sunstein, "Public Employee Strikes, Executive Discretion, and the Air Traffic Controllers," 50 *U. Chi. L. Rev.* 731 (1983).

[11]See "The Fuzzy Dichotomy: Public and Private Sectors," in statement of R. Scott Fosler, Director of Government Studies, Committee for Economic Development, *Hearings Before Subcomm. on the City of the House Comm. on Banking, Finance and Urban Affairs, 95th Cong., 2d Sess.,* 397–402 *(July 26, 1978), reprinted in* H. Edwards, R. Clark, & C. Craver, *Labor Relations in the Public Sector*, 34–36 (2d ed. 1979).

differences to justify increased opposition to the public sector organizing.[12] Even in the minds of some union activists, the differences have been used as the basis for a myth that unionization of the public sector is doomed to failure or at least to a kind of second-class status—an inferior field for the union organizer.[13] This could not be further

---

[12]L. Kramer, *Labor's Paradox: The American Federation of State, County and Municipal Employees, AFL-CIO*, 41 (1962).

[13]Even AFSCME, the union least identified with this view, began as an association organized to protect and promote civil service, not collective bargaining. AFSCME's constitution did not contain a commitment to collective bargaining until 1968. *See* L. Kramer, above, note 12, at 27; and Art. 2(B) of AFSCME *Constitution* (as amended 1968). The National Education Association and the American Nurses Association are active public unions. However, some of their affiliates still emphasize their history as professional associations more than their identity as unions.

There has been a noticeable recent growth in the public sector of a number of traditionally private sector unions like SEIU, CWA, the Teamsters, LIU, MEBA, UAW District 65, Machinists, and the Steelworkers. *See* J. Wurf & G. Meany, "The Outsider Enters Labor's Inner Circle," in J. Goulden, above, note 3, at 184–189.

The AFL-CIO Public Employee Department is composed of the following 33 affiliates:

American Federation of Government Employees
American Federation of School Administrators
American Federation of State, County and Municipal Employees
American Federation of Teachers
American Postal Workers Union
Communications Workers of America
Graphic Communications International Union
Hotel and Restaurant Employees' and Bartenders International Union
International Association of Bridge, Structural and Ornamental Iron Workers
International Association of Fire Fighters
International Association of Machinists and Aerospace Workers
International Brotherhood of Firemen and Oilers
International Brotherhood of Painters and Allied Trades of the United States and Canada
International Chemical Workers Union
International Federation of Professional and Technical Engineers
International Plate Printers, Die Stampers and Engravers Union of North America
International Typographical Union
International Union of Electrical, Radio and Machine Workers
International Union of Operating Engineers
International Union of Police Associations
International Union, United Automobile, Aerospace and Agricultural Implement Workers of America
Laborers International Union of North America
Masters, Mates and Pilots of the International Longshoremen's Union
National Association of Letter Carriers
National Marine Engineers' Beneficial Association
Office and Professional Employees International Union
Seafarers International Union of North America
Service Employees International Union
Sheet Metal Workers International Association
United Association of Journeymen and Apprentices of the Plumbing and Pipe Fitting Industry of the United States and Canada
United Brotherhood of Carpenters and Joiners of America
United Transportation Union
Utility Workers Union of America

In addition, the Teamsters, the nation's largest union, is active in the public sector. NEA, the second largest, is a wholly public union. A large number of nonaffiliated organizations, including the American Nurses Association and the Fraternal Order of Police, have extensive membership in the public sector.

from the truth. The extent to which unionization has taken hold in the public sector and the fact that, as a percentage, twice as many public workers join unions as private sector workers, is strong and pragmatic testimony that the differences in the public sector present no impediment to successful union organizing.

## Statements of Basic Labor Relations Policy

The findings and policy statements included in the NLRA set a course for private sector employee relations on the basis of a national policy commitment to privately negotiated collective bargaining contracts. That commitment has dominated union activity in the United States for 50 years.

Section 1 of the National Labor Relations Act declares it to be the policy of the United States:

> to eliminate the causes of certain substantial obstruction to the free flow of commerce and to mitigate and eliminate these obstructions when they have occurred by encouraging the practice and procedure of collective bargaining and by protecting the exercise by workers of full freedom of association, self-organizing, and designation of representatives of their own choosing for the purpose of negotiating the terms and conditions of their employment or other mutual aid and protection.

The NLRA expressly finds that the denial of unionization rights injures not only workers, but the country and its economy as a whole. It emphasizes that "inequity of bargaining power" between workers and "employers who are organized in corporate or other forms of ownership association, substantially burdens" the economy. Further, it finds that "experience has proven" that the protection of the right to organize safeguards commerce, reduces workplace strife, and encourages the friendly adjustment of industrial disputes. The NLRA proposed, and today protects, private sector unions and strikes as the marketplace counter to concentrated corporate power.

The problem addressed by the NLRA is one of unequal economic power between employers and employees in a pre-NLRA economy in which the government had protected and nurtured corporations and other forms of organized joint ownership while discouraging the economic consolidation of workers into unions and enjoining concerted worker strike activity. Senator Robert Wagner and the other authors of America's national labor policies redressed this imbalance by protecting worker self-organization and "concerted activity" (including strikes), establishing a bargaining process, and then leaving the parties free to set wages, hours, and working conditions.

The basic model permits the private bargaining process to establish labor costs. If, under the NLRA model, management is unfair or pays insufficient wages, labor may withhold its services through a strike. The strike puts economic pressure on management because during the strike management cannot produce its service or product and thereby loses out economically. The strike puts economic pressure on workers because they are not paid while out on strike. Under the theory, sacrifices on both sides should lead the parties to a settlement acceptable to each. The government leaves it to management and labor to settle their disputes over the costs of labor through this private self-help mechanism.

The government protects the property rights of management through established contract law and corporate law. It protects the right to concerted labor activity and collective bargaining through the NLRA. It protects both through a national labor policy based on private decision making.

The NLRA theory is one of economic competition, power balancing, self-help, and protection of the concerted activity through strikes as vital to properly functioning labor markets.[14] The NLRA's statement of findings and policies in Section 1 makes no special or express reference to a need to increase cooperative communications, to merit principles, to the public as the third party at the bargaining table (although the benefits to society of a smooth, efficient economy and the free flow of commerce without interruption due to industrial strife is emphasized), to any damaging potential of protected strikes, or to protecting the public safety.

Compare this with the policy statements of state and local public employee labor management relations statutes. An examination of 10 state and local labor law policy statements leaves no question that the policy basis of union representation in the public sector varies not only from the central policy basis under the NLRA, but also varies greatly from jurisdiction to jurisdiction.

The basic statutes in Connecticut and Michigan—two states generally recognized to have based their public sector systems on the NLRA model—track much of the NLRA language but delete any reference to findings, policy, or broad strike protections.[15] Is this

---

[14]*See* notes 8 and 10, above. President Ronald Reagan has recognized the vital link between strikes, a free labor management, and freedom generally in his many comments on the Polish Solidarity Movement. The odd juxtaposition of those comments and the PATCO firing highlights the sharp contrast between American views on this subject. Of course, both the PATCO workers and the Polish strikers were public workers "pledged by honor" not to strike. *See* note 9, above; B.D. Meltzer & C.R. Sunstein, note 10, above; and G. Baum, *The Priority of Labor: A Commentary on Laborism Excrecens, Encyclical Letter of Pope John Paul II on Labor*, 22–41 (1982).

[15]State Employees Relations Act, *Conn. Gen. Stats.*, Title 5, Sec. 5-270–5-280 (1975, as amended 1982); *Michigan Compiled Laws, Annotated*, Secs. 423.201–423.216 (1974, as amended 1978).

because the policies behind the NLRA, which rely on strikes as the worker's self-help tool, do not really make sense in systems, like those in Connecticut and Michigan, which do not provide for a right to strike?

The two most recently enacted statutes—the 1984 Ohio and Illinois Acts—approach the policy question differently. Ohio follows the Connecticut/Michigan model and does not include a specific, separate policy statement. Illinois, on the other hand, recognizes the public as a third party and the use of arbitration as a substitute for the right to strike. Sec. 2 of the Illinois Public Labor Relations Act states in part:

> It is the purpose of this Act to prescribe the legitimate rights of both public employees and public employers, to protect the public health and safety of the citizens of Illinois, and to provide peaceful and orderly procedures for protection of the rights of all. To prevent labor strife and to protect the public health and safety of the citizens of Illinois, all collective bargaining disputes involving persons designated by the Board as performing essential services and those persons defined herein as security employees shall be submitted to impartial arbitrators, who shall be authorized to issue awards in order to resolve such disputes. It is the public policy of the State of Illinois that where the right of employees to strike is prohibited by law, it is necessary to afford an alternate, expeditious, equitable and effective procedure for the resolution of labor disputes subject to approval procedures mandated by this Act. To that end, the provisions for such awards shall be liberally construed.[16]

The Meyers-Milias-Brown Act in California, which applies to local employees, emphasizes the need to promote "full communications between public employers and their employees by providing a reasonable method of resolving disputes." It protects the right to organize but protects "merit, civil service and other methods of administering employer-employee relations".[17]

The basic Hawaiian statute finds that:

> joint decision-making is the modern way of administering government. Where public employees have been granted the right to share in the decision-making process affecting wages, hours and working conditions, they have become more responsive and better able to exchange ideas and information on operations with their administrators.

The statute declares it to be the policy of Hawaii to protect the right to organize, require negotiations, "maintain merit principles and the

---

[16]*Ill. Ann. Stat.*, Ch. 48, Secs. 1601–1627 (Smith-Hurd 1966, as amended 1984).
[17]Meyers-Milias-Brown Act, *Calif. Gov. Code*, Secs. 3540–3549 (West 1975, as amended 1981).

principle of equal pay for equal work," and to create a public labor relations board.[18]

The statute in Minnesota provides, in part, that:

> It is the public policy of this state and the purpose of the act to promote orderly and constructive relationships between all public employers and their employees, subject however, to the paramount right of the citizens of this state to keep inviolate the guarantees for their health, education and safety and welfare.

The statute expressly recognizes a "responsibility to the people served," and that the public sector's "need for cooperation and employment protection are different from employment in the private sector."[19]

The Wisconsin statute "recognizes that there are three major interests involved" (the public, the employees, the employer); emphasizes the need for "fair, friendly, and mutually satisfactory employee management relations"; protects the right to organize; and encourages collective bargaining "subject to the requirements of the public service and related laws, rules and policies governing state employment."[20]

New York's Taylor Law replaces the NLRA's central emphasis on the right to strike with a policy statement emphasizing the importance of a strike prohibition.[21]

The Florida statute's policy statement includes a reference to related protections in the state constitution, protects the right to organize, outlines a duty to negotiate, and restates a state constitutional strike prohibition.[22]

The Texas statute on public employee rights (except for police and firefighters) states flatly that public sector collective bargaining is against public policy and outlaws strikes. Texas does recognize that "no person shall be denied public employment in Texas by reason of membership in a labor organization," and grants the right to representation in grievances "individually or through a representative that does not claim the right to strike."[23]

---

[18]*Hawaii Rev. Stat.*, Ch. 89, Secs. 89.1–89.21 (1970, as amended 1982).

[19]Minn. Public Employment Labor Relations Act, M.S.A. Ch. 33, Secs. 179A.01–179A.25 (1982, as amended 1985).

[20]State Employment Labor Relations Act, W.S.A., Ch. 111, Subchap. II, Secs. 111.80–111.94 (1966, as amended 1982).

[21]Taylor Act, Civil Service Law, N.Y.C.A., Secs. 200–214 (1967, as amended 1983).

[22]*Florida Stats.*, Part II of Ch. 447.201–447.605 (1977, as amended 1983); see also Art. I, Sec. 6, Florida Constitution.

[23]*Texas Code*, V.A.C.S. Art. 5154C, L. 1947, Secs. 1–6. We comment here neither on the constitutional question raised by this language, nor on the reality of lively public sector unionism in Texas. The Lone-Star State is unique in ways far beyond the scope of this book.

It is clear that the differences between these policies and the national labor policy, as well as among the policies themselves, center around the use of a cooperative/communications model as distinguished from a self-help/competition NLRA model; the position of merit or civil service principles; the recognition of the public as a third party in governmental labor relations; and the legality of strikes.

## Conclusion

While the differences between the public and private sector do not stand as a "keep out" barrier to the union organizer, a "fuzzy dichotomy" between the two is a factor of which every public organizer should be aware. Most public organizing drives will be different from private sector drives. The specific differences and what impact they will have on the drive must be assessed separately. In each case what is useful from the private sector, and what is not, depends more on (1) the specific labor relations policy of the jurisdiction, (2) the organizing target's employee relations model, (3) the work force involved, (4) management's structure, and (5) the union involved, than it does on any general or fundamental difference between the public and the private sector. These variables are reviewed individually in the chapters that follow.

2

# Labor Relations Models

There are a number of different systems or models of public sector labor relations. Each model has its own history; each is organized on a separate principle; each employs a distinct decision-making mechanism; each sets and controls the conditions of employment differently; and each influences public sector organizing in a separate way.

Six basic public sector labor relations models can be distinguished in the United States today. They are:

(1) The public service/patrician model,
(2) The military/public safety model,
(3) The patronage model,
(4) The civil service model,
(5) The professional management/Japanese team model, and
(6) The collective bargaining/NLRA model.

It is helpful to the public sector organizer to know the basics of each of the various employment models. An organizing problem which arises in a collective bargaining/NLRA-like employment context can be wholly different from one arising in a public service, civil service, paramilitary/public safety, patronage, or professional management context. In the real world, organizers will face a series of problems which mix the elements of the six models. While a single model may be dominant in a given employment relationship, in most situations the models will be mixed—that is, a system modeled primarily after the collective bargaining/NLRA model will also be influenced by civil

14

service, patronage, and modern management considerations.[1] Each of the six methods of organizing public employment deserves separate review.

One method of organizing and understanding the six public employment models is to trace their development through an oversimplified but nonetheless instructive version of the history of public employment in the United States. This slightly condensed history will help to emphasize the key features of each model.

## The Public Service/Patrician Model

Just after the American Revolution, George Washington's Federalist view of a public duty to serve dominated policy discussions of public employment.[2] Washington, it is said, served throughout the Revolution without salary (although he was an inventive expense account writer[3]). Service to one's country was an avocation; it was rendered as a citizen's duty, requiring self-sacrifice and dedication, and finding its reward in communitywide appreciation.

This patrician view of government service emphasized a concern for fitness of character and a fear that government could not be trusted to the excesses of the masses. Stalwarts of the community should run the government. Volunteer service, community position, social access, and technical qualification were the primary criteria for public employment. Although government service became more professionalized during the subsequent Jeffersonian period, the idea of it as a privileged, sacrificial duty of the citizen remained dominant throughout the early years of the republic.

Toward the end of the Federalist/Jeffersonian period, many Americans became suspicious of self-sacrificing public servants. It was rumored that special interests were served too often and too well,[4] and

---

[1]*See* I.B. Helburn & N.D. Bennett, "Public Employee Bargaining and the Merit Principle," 23 *Lab. L.J.* 618, 623–626 (1972); Comment, "The Civil Service-Collective Bargaining Conflict in the Public Sector: Attempts at Reconciliation," 38 *U. Chi. L. Rev.* 826 (1971); *Pacific Legal Found. v. Brown*, 624 P.2d 1215, 172 Cal. Rptr. 487 (Cal. S.Ct. 1981).

[2]*See generally,* "Developments in the Law: Public Employment," 97 *Harv. L. Rev.* 1611, 1619–1932 for a historic discussion centered on the development of federal civil service employment law; H. Fish, *The Civil Service and the Patronage* (1905); and D. Rosenbloom, *Federal Service and the Constitution* (1971).

[3]M. Kitman, *George Washington's Expense Account* (1970).

[4]L. White, *The Jeffersonians: A Study in Administrative History, 1801–1829* (1951); B. Aronson, *Status and Kinship in the Higher Civil Service: Standards of Selection in the Administrations of John Adams, Thomas Jefferson and Andrew Jackson* (1967).

with the demands and needs of practical government, this idealistic model of governmental services came to dominate public employment less and less.

## The Patronage System

The election of Andrew Jackson to the presidency in 1828 effected a revolution in public employment, since the Jacksonians held the patronage principle as one of their central tenets.[5] Patronage is a system under which an employee's political affiliation and place in a political machine (and that of a political patron) serve as the primary bases of his or her employment. Jackson and his followers believed that in a democracy the electorate must have the power to remove government officials from office at the ballot box and to replace them with new servants of the people. Popularly elected leaders would thereby be able to carry out the will of the electorate unhindered by the entrenched forces of wealth and privilege that were beyond the reach of the ballot. The motto of the Jacksonians was "To the victors belong the spoils."

The promise underlying the patronage system was that by rotation in office and by appointment of public officers on strictly partisan grounds there would be an expanded class of persons in public positions, greater responsiveness to the public will, and limited corruption through entrenchment in office. Under the system, the political party, under leadership responsive to the masses, became the central force in organizing public employment.

In Mr. Justice Stewart's 1976 concurring opinion in the U.S. Supreme Court's decision in *Elrod v. Burns*, a leading case on the unconstitutionality of patronage-based terminations, the Justice discusses the history of the American spoils system:

> Partisan politics, as we know them, did not assume a prominent role in national politics immediately after the adoption of the Constitution. Nonetheless, Washington tended to confine appointments even of customs officials and postmasters to Federalists, as opposed to anti-Federalists. As the role of parties expanded, partisan considerations quickly influenced employment decisions. John Adams removed some Republicans from minor posts, and Jefferson, the first President of an opposing party, made significant patronage use of the appointment and removal powers. The administrations of Madison, Monroe, and John Quincy Adams provided no occasion for conspicuous patronage practice in em-

---

[5]J.W. Ward, *Andrew Jackson: Symbol for an Age*, 46–97 (1962); M. Meyer, *Jacksonian Persuasion: Politics and Belief*, 234–275 (1957); and A.M. Schlesinger, Jr., *The Age of Jackson*, 45–47 (1945).

ployment, as each succeeded a copartisan. Jackson, of course, used patronage extensively when he became the first President since Jefferson to succeed an antagonistic administration.

It appears that patronage employment practices emerged on the national level at an early date, and that they were conspicuous during Jackson's Presidency largely because of their necessary dormancy during the long succession of Republican Presidents. During that period, however, patronage in hiring was practiced widely in the States, especially in New York and Pennsylvania. This afforded a theoretical and popular legitimacy to patronage, helping to lay the groundwork for acceptance of Jackson's actions on the national level.[6]

The Justice goes on to discuss some of the benefits of the patronage system:

Patronage practices broadened the base of political participation by providing incentives to take part in the process, thereby increasing the volume of political discourse in society. Patronage also strengthened parties, and hence encouraged the development of institutional responsibility to the electorate on a permanent basis. Parties became "instrument[s] through which discipline and responsibility may be achieved within the Leviathan."[7]

The patronage system, once it became part of American public employment, continued dominant, even at the federal level, into the Civil War. Ultimately, however, the patronage system came to be viewed as corrupt and inefficient, and it was for this reason that later reformers became advocates for the civil service system and for restrictions on the political activities of government employees.

## The Military/Public Safety Model

Since the days of the Revolution, the citizen soldier had been widely seen as the ideal American military man. The elitist patrician Federalist and the yeoman farmer volunteer of the Jacksonians were represented, respectively, as the archetypal officer and militiaman. However, a separate, more professional tradition was also developing within the military. During the Revolutionary War, Baron Von Steuben had worked with Washington's troops at Valley Forge and built a well-drilled army where before there had been only a loose, poorly organized militia. Von Steuben followed the example of the Prussian professional military, with its emphasis on highly disciplined troops, a strict chain

---

[6]427 US 347, 379 (1976).
[7]Id.

of command, and general staff system. He replaced the farmer running from the field to muster and returning for planting and harvesting with the semiprofessional, disciplined foot soldier. Similarly, he replaced the class-conscious, elitist English officer with the Prussian professional staff officer. With the establishment of West Point as a national military academy, Von Steuben's concept of the professionally organized military was preserved throughout the War of 1812 and the Mexican War. But this professional understructure was always dominated by the volunteer soldier led by men who were part-time generals and part-time politicians. During the Civil War, however, such part-time civilian leadership as a core concept for military organization became impossible. It was increasingly recognized that the discipline and organized responses of a system built on a general staff, a chain of command, a code of military conduct, and a system of general orders was the superior form of military organization.[8]

After the Civil War, and into the early part of the 20th century, the paramilitary organization was presented as the answer to a need for reform of municipal police and fire protection services. Police and fire protection had, early on, been viewed as volunteer projects. As cities on the East Coast grew, a system manned by first generation immigrants and dominated by the patronage system governed the large police forces. With the progressive reformer's attention to police and fire reform, the military system, with its emphasis on the chain of command, general order, and a professional staff system, became an attractive model on which to base public safety organization.[9]

A system of police administration patterned after the military came to dominate most police departments. The International Association of Chiefs of Police's manual, *Managing Police Discipline*, introduced its treatment of the subject of police administration and discipline with a section entitled "Influencing Officer Behavior: The Military Legacy":

> Management's goals in any organization are not necessarily the inherent goals of employees. A basic tactic of sophisticated management is to bring these goals into harmony. A common approach to management which attempts to converge these goals can be called the "military model." This approach has been the dominant influence in the development of today's police organizations. The term "military model" is

---

[8] J.T. Flexner, *Washington: The Indispensable Man*, 118–121 (1974); B. Catton, *U.S. Grant and the American Military Tradition* (1954).

[9] R. Fogelson, *Big City Police* (1977); S. Walker, *A Critical History of Police Reform* (1977); R. Ayers & T. Wheeler (eds.), *Collective Bargaining in the Public Sector: Selected Readings in Law Enforcement* (1977).

used here to describe a management style, rather than to denote militaristic quality in the execution of law enforcement *per se*. This model comprises the total body of management philosophy and techniques used to achieve compliance to direct orders. This style reached the peak of its expression in most of the world's armed forces in the first half of this century. Several management principles, such as unity of command, clearly delineated authority, formal communications through channels, and standardization of roles, were applied to achieve control in these organizations.

This style of management was also adopted at an early date by private and public sector management to achieve control of employee conduct. While private industry has discarded many of the more visible and control-oriented features of the military model, the public sector in general and police organizations in particular have not.[10]

The manual goes on to emphasize that the pure military model "may not be the optimum choice for police management." The police chiefs' organization recognizes that modern management and public administration models also influence police organization. However, little doubt exists that a modified military model plays a vital role in public safety employee relations.[11]

In a study published in 1982, George Kelling and James Q. Wilson traced the development of the military model in modern police management. They see its attractions partly as a reaction to the corruption which grew up under the patronage model. According to Kelling and Wilson, the "reform police strategy" which grew up in America between 1930 and 1980 was likewise a reaction to the patronage departments of the late 19th and early 20th centuries.[12]

In an address to the 1984 convention of the International Union of Police Associations, Kelling explained that the modified-military "reform police strategy is an integral part of the culture of policing at the present time." That model emphasizes three elements. First, the "reform model" sought to remove the nation's police departments from politics and the political involvement with the community which was seen to dominate and corrupt the stereotypical cop on the corner. The "just the facts, ma'am" attitude typified by Joe Friday of the television show "Dragnet" replaced the jovial, beat-walking Officer Mickey. According to Kelling, "[P]olicing moved to limit its authority by defining the role of the police officer narrowly to criminal justice."[13]

---

[10]IACP, *Managing Effective Police Discipline*, 3 (1977).

[11]*Id.*, at 3–8; *see also* J.H. Burpo, *Police Labor Movement: Problems and Perspectives*, 3–20 (1971).

[12]J.Q. Wilson & G.L. Kelling, "Broken Windows: Police and Neighborhood Safety," *Atlantic Monthly*, March 1982, at 29–38.

[13]G.L. Kelling, Remarks at IUPA Convention, August 28, 1984, Memphis, Tenn.

Second, a system of very specific general orders and control from the top sought to minimize the discretion of the officer on the beat. Third, police work was moved from the street, with its close regular access to the community and its political pressures, to the squad car and the office. According to Kelling:

> That's been the model, that's been the organizational strategy that contemporary policing operates out of. You enforce the law. Discretion is not recognized. You're distant remote professionals. Strong chain of command—memos and orders flow down. Information that you have remains in your soul but in terms of the organization getting your ideas about what ought to be done in the community or neighborhood, that stays with you, maybe your sergeant, but essentially your organization does not set out to get information from you.[14]

Wilson, Kelling, and others, including the International Association of Chiefs of Police, have recognized to varying degrees the erosion of the military model in public safety employment. However, all recognize that a modified public safety model remains dominant today.

## The Progressives and Civil Service Reform

The Republican party so dominated American politics between the Civil War and 1900 that the Jacksonian patronage system, which Reconstruction and Republican political machines of the Gilded Age perfected, lost support on three fronts: (1) the most successful machines were based primarily on both Democratic and working-class support without sufficient national Republican political power to withstand attacks from business and middle-class reformers in both parties; (2) the machine's base became increasingly dependent on immigrants who were often attacked and looked down upon; and (3) long-tenured patronage power (without the rotation in office which the Jacksonian model saw as one of the internal reforming graces of the system), boodle, kickbacks, illicit spoils, and financial corruption came to dominate the machine system. The virtues of the patronage system—citizen participation, constituent service, and protection from elitist domination by "special" or patrician classes—were overwhelmed by their own success. Entrenched machine power ended the regular rotation in office which was a central virtue of the system. Ironically, just as the

---

[14]*Id.*

populist Jackson had forced out the patrician Federalists and Jeffersonians, patrician Progressives such as Theodore Roosevelt and Woodrow Wilson campaigned against the machine-dominated boss system.[15]

In place of the patronage system, the Progressive reformers offered the Civil Service model. In 1887 Woodrow Wilson, then a professor at Princeton, argued in the *Political Science Quarterly* that "a merit-based system, staffed by professional experts and freed from the corrosive influence of politics by formal legal constraints on appointment and tenure, would provide the most efficient, rational tool for achieving the aims of public policy."[16]

Merit principles, political neutrality, and the bureaucratic vision became the core of a system of organizing public employment under a new system of rules and regulations, competitive examinations, and job classifications based on "scientific management" principles.[17] In 1892, partially in response to President Garfield's assassination by a disappointed office-seeker, the Pendleton Act established the Federal Civil Service, which thereafter grew and came to dominate in federal employment. It also became the model for many state systems of employee relations.[18]

The U.S. Supreme Court's majority opinion in *Elrod v. Burns* explained the "demise" of American patronage:

> Indeed, only a few decades after Andrew Jackson's administration, strong discontent with the corruption and inefficiency of the patronage system of public employment eventuated in the Pendleton Act . . . , the foundation of modern civil service. And on the state and local levels, merit systems have increasingly displaced the practice. . . . Factors contributing to the declining use of patronage have not been limited to the proliferation of merit systems. New methods of political financing, the greater necessity of job expertise in public employment, growing issue orientation in the elective process, and new incentives for political campaigners have also contributed.[19]

A national movement for civil service reform spread throughout the country and affected public employment in nearly every jurisdiction.

---

[15]A.A. Hoogenboom, *Outlawing the Spoils: A History of the Civil Service Movement 1865–1883* (1968); J.G. Sproat, *The Best Men: Liberal Reformers in the Gilded Age* (1968).

[16]W. Wilson, "The Study of Administration," 2 *Pol. Sci. Q.* 197 (1887), summarized in "Developments in the Law: Public Employment," 97 *Harv. L. Rev.* 1611, 1629 (1984).

[17]*See* "Developments in the Law: Public Employment," note 16, above, at 1629–1633.

[18]L.D. White, *The Republican Era: 1869–1901: A Study in Administrative History* (1958); A.A. Hoogenboom, note 15, above.

[19]427 US at 354.

## Collective Bargaining/NLRA Model

During the Progressive Era (1890–1915), workers also sought union representation as a remedy to problems experienced under the patronage system. The Boston police strike of 1919, and Massachusetts Governor Calvin Coolidge's subsequent quick and popular anti-union reaction to it, caused public sector unionization a nearly 50-year setback. Public sector collective bargaining was not seriously offered as an alternative during the formative years of the civil service model.[20]

Over time, however, it became clear that the civil service system was itself not perfect. The bureaucratic strengths of that system became entrenched; its weaknesses were revealed. The merit protections, examinations, and classification procedures of civil service became stagnant with time. They lost the ability to respond to changing needs and specific individual problems. Enthusiasm, flexibility, and the recognition of individual needs were lost.

A civil-service-dominated institution often loses contact with the needs of its constituency and of its employees. As a recognition of the need for an employee voice becomes clear, pressure builds for alterations in the system. This often results in the formation of a civil service employee association.

Associations of civil service employees grew up at first as professional organizations of governmental employees which emphasized civil service reform, training, and professional and fraternal aid. The associations soon became representatives of employees, seeking to protect their rights to tenure and classification before merit boards of review. Since "nonpolitical" civil service systems establish all employee rights (including both the basic merit system rights and the terms and conditions of employment) through a mixture of bureaucratic and legislative action, the associations became both representatives of their members before civil service commissions and lobbyists before the legislature. They became very active in the legislature and in the rulemaking process. They grew during the first half of the 20th century in membership, expertise, and influence.[21]

The magna carta of American collective bargaining—the National Labor Relations Act (NLRA) or Wagner Act—was enacted in 1935.

---

[20]S. Spero, "The 1919 Boston Police Strike," in *Collective Bargaining in Government: Readings and Cases*, 178–192 (J. Loewenberg & M.H. Moskow, Jr., eds. 1972).

[21]J. Stieber, *Public Employee Unionism: Structure, Growth, Policy*, 15–50 (1973); A.Z. Gammage & S.L. Sachs, "Development of Public Employee/Police Unions," in *Collective Bargaining in the Public Sector: Selected Readings in Law Enforcement*, 90–92 (R. Ayers & T. Wheeler, eds. 1977).

It excluded public employees from coverage.[22] However, by a gradual process of statutory enactment and executive order at the federal, state, and municipal levels of government, collective bargaining rights based on the NLRA model have been extended to many workers in the public sector.

The basic NLRA model, as developed in the public sector, is one which:

(1) Protects the right of public employees to organize,
(2) Grants exclusive recognition to labor organizations when certified as the exclusive representative of employees in collective bargaining units, and
(3) Provides for some bargaining rights.

Usually, the law provides for an administrative agency of some type and procedures for enforcement. It does not usually protect the right to strike.[23]

In 1936, one year after the enactment of the NLRA, the American Federation of Labor chartered the first national union for state and local government employees—the American Federation of State, County and Municipal Employees (AFSCME). AFSCME had grown up as Wisconsin's civil service employee association. At the time of its charter, AFSCME had 9,737 members. In 1939, an AFSCME local union in Philadelphia negotiated a labor agreement with the city. That contract was almost unique at the time and stood as such for decades.[24]

By 1954, Robert Wagner (the son of the senator who sponsored the National Labor Relations Act) was mayor of New York City. His Executive Order 49 granted recognition to labor organizations of New York City municipal employees. The Wagner order, together with a strengthened system in Philadelphia, meant that by the mid-1950s two major cities backed the collective bargaining model for public employees.[25]

By the late 1950s, public sector labor organizations were fairly widespread in the country. State and federal employee associations were very active. In Minnesota, Wisconsin, New York City, and the

---

[22]See text of President Franklin D. Roosevelt's letter to the President of the National Federation of Federal Employees in C.S. Rhyne, *Labor Unions and Municipal Employee Law*, 436–437 (1946).

[23]See Chapter 1, n. 10 and accompanying text.

[24]See J. Wurf & M. Hennessy, "The American Federation of State, County and Municipal Employees," in *Collective Bargaining in Government: Readings and Cases*, 60–66 (J. Loewenberg & M.H. Moskow, Jr., eds. 1972).

[25]*Id.*, at 62, n. 42.

federal Post Office, they were also politically effective. In 1957, Minnesota enacted the first state employee collective bargaining statute modeled after the National Labor Relations Act.[26] Wisconsin followed with a statute based on the NLRA in 1959.

The 1960s marked the nationwide trend. In 1962, President John Kennedy granted some limited collective bargaining rights to federal employees with Executive Order 10988. By 1970, 22 states had enacted collective bargaining statutes. The collective bargaining model continued to spread in the 1970s, but slowed somewhat after 1978. In 1984, however, Ohio and Illinois, the only two major non-Southern states without statutes, each adopted complete systems patterned on the NLRA model.[27]

## Fiscal Crisis and Professional Management

With the increasing economic problems of the late 1970s and the resulting pressure placed on public finance, the importance of state and municipal fiscal constraint increased. This placed great pressure on public managers of employer and employee relations. In 1978, the city of New York faced a severe fiscal crisis. In spite of the widely perceived notion that New York's public employee unions were to blame for the fiscal crisis, it was the public unions' involvement which led the city to a solution of the immediate crisis.[28] However, the fiscal crisis in New York became the symbol for a whole series of crises in

---

[26]See Act of April 27, 1957, Ch. 789, Sec. 1, 1957 Minn. Laws 1073 (as codified at Minn. Stat. Secs. 179.61–.76) (1982).

[27]See Chapter 1, note 17 and accompanying text.

[28]The solution worked out by the New York teachers unions and AFSCME District Council 37 involved the investment in the city of employee pension assets and the enactment of a complicated package of state and federal legislation. See Note, "Public Employee Pensions in Times of Fiscal Distress," 90 Harv. L. Rev. 992 (1977).

The investments were a key element in a November 26, 1975, agreement to save New York City from default. Before approving the agreement, the teachers' fund trustees insisted on a sound overall package and a number of provisions designed to protect the fund: (1) the $860 million investment commitment was approximately equal to 2½ years of employer contributions to the plan, an amount reasonably expected to be lost in the event of default; (2) the bonds purchased were backed by the full faith and credit of the city, yielding 9% interest; (3) the investment was conditioned upon (a) the enactment of federal legislation providing for the seasonal financing needs of the city for 2½ years (the New York City Seasonal Financing Act of 1975, P.L. 94-143 U.S.C. 1051, et. seq.); (b) the enactment of state legislation indemnifying the trustees and modifying the state fiduciary standard to allow consideration of the impact of the investments of participants in the plan (Chapter 890 of the Laws of New York 1975, effective December 5, 1975); and (c) an Internal Revenue Service ruling, or act of Congress, providing that the bond purchase would not affect the tax status of the plan (P.L. 94-236, 90 Stat. 238); and (4) state legislation strengthening the state's commitment to funding the system. See, M.T. Leibig, "You Can't Do That With My Money," 6 J. Pension Plan. & Comp. 358, at n.52 (1980).

public finance which resulted in a national emphasis on increased fiscal and budgetary planning.[29]

Increased emphasis on managing the public budget coincided with a perceived crisis in American corporate management. This brought new attention to the "Japanese team" model of professional management, which utilized joint goal-setting, productivity guidelines, and a team approach to labor-management relations.[30] This "new approach" created a generation of public managers who operated on the basis of new classification guidelines, job studies, and goal-setting and budget-making mechanisms in their effort to modernize public employment practices. All of this occurred in a climate dominated by ballot initiatives in California, Massachusetts, and other states which called for simple but straitjacketing limits on tax rates and public financial decision making. Simultaneously, such factors as increased sophistication on both sides of the table in collective bargaining and in Civil Service rulemaking and job classification standards setting; changes in federal revenue sharing; new equal employment opportunity standards based on comparable worth studies and job title analysis; and anti-public employee and anti-union political rhetoric combined to generate a sixth model of employer-employee relations in the public sector—the professional management/Japanese team model. This model is based on "scientific" management and job studies and new management and team techniques, and it is marked by an increased emphasis on short-term budget planning. It emphasizes the view of the worker as "team member" or "partner" and presupposes a sensitive management that listens keenly for ideas and suggestions from workers. The system is keyed to worker satisfaction, "participation in achieving goals," and a leadership system which puts "everyone on one side." It is often dependent on the use of an outside consultant in developing and defining the employment relationship.[31]

## Labor Relations Models and the Organizer

Table 1 summarizes the six public sector labor relations models discussed in this chapter. For each model is listed: the central or key

---

[29]*See* R. Schnadig, "Public Sector Collective Bargaining in Times of Fiscal Crisis," and T. Sachs, "Public Sector Unions and Fiscal Crisis," in *Labor Relations Law in the Public Sector*, 203–214 and 215–223 (A.S. Knapp, ed. 1977).

[30]C. Johnson (ed.), *The Industrial Policy Debate* (1984).

[31]*See* "Labor-Management Consultants: A New Breed of Union-Busters," in S.I. Schlossberg & J.A. Scott, *Organizing and the Law*, 114–142 (3d ed. 1983) and J. Baird, J. Anderson, & S. Damas, *Practical Labor Relations for Public Employers*, 21–32, 168–176 (1978).

## TABLE 1.  PUBLIC SECTOR LABOR RELATIONS MODELS

| Model | Key to the Employment Relationship | Decision-Making Method | Terms and Conditions of Employment | Current Example | Historical Relationship | Dates | Employee Organizing Principle |
|---|---|---|---|---|---|---|---|
| Public Service/ Patrician Model | Honor/Duty/ Patriotism; Public Service | Elitist; Nonprofessional; Hierarchical | Unilaterally Set; Agreement to serve | Community Action and Poverty Programs | George Washington; Jeffersonian Leaders | 1774–1828 Federalist and Jeffersonian Leaders | Social Obligation; Fraternal; Expertise |
| Military/Public Safety Model | Service to Leader and Honor/Duty/ "Law Enforcement" | Hierarchical; Chain-of-Command "Downhill" Flow | General Orders | Police and Prison Guards | Baron Von Steuben's Prussian Chain of Command, Staff System | 1780– from Von Steuben's Reforms to present | Fraternal; Comrade-in-Arms; Service; Security; Economic Progress |
| Patronage Model | Politics | Political Compromises and Boss-Ruled Machine | Political Alliance and The Machine "Handshake" | Daley's Chicago and Rizzo's Philadelphia | Jacksonian Spoils System | 1828–1900 Jacksonian Democrats and Bossism | Political Club House; Economic Progress; Representation |
| Civil Service Model | Merit | Administrative; Bureaucratic | Rules and Regulations; Examination/ Classification | Federal Government | Progressive Merit Service Reform | 1900–1950 Progressives; Civil Service Reform | Service; Representation; Economic Progress |
| Professional Management/ Japanese Team Model | Production Goals and "Modern Management" Studies | Professional Management and "Uphill" Flow | Goal Setting and Employee Manuals | Toyota and Management Studies Movement | Management Studies; Fiscal Reform; Japanese Model | 1978– from New York Fiscal Crisis and Subsequent Response | Voice in Decision; Security Needs; Economic Progress |
| Collective Bargaining/ NLRA Model | Collective Bargaining | Mutual Negotiations Structure | Contract | 1984 Statutes in Ohio and Illinois | The NLRA: Labor Management; 1960s Reform | 1960– from Wagner's New York City and Kennedy's Executive Order 10 | Solidarity: Joint Decision Making; Economic Progress |

feature of the public employment relationship, its decision-making method, the mechanism for setting terms and conditions of employment, current examples of the model, historical examples of the model, the time period during which the system flourished, and the main principles motivating employee organizing under the particular model.

In reviewing the models and their history, it is important to keep in mind that in most real-life situations no one model will be found in its pure form. Actual employment practices are a combination of various facets from any number of the systems, the result of an employer's unique history. However, a few broad generalizations, and their implications for an organizing drive, can be made.

The public service model will often be found in community service agencies and poverty- or related programs. This model also influences any profession—for example, teaching, health care, public safety, or social work—where public service is at the heart of the job. Most often, the appeal in the model is to duty; its decision making tends to be hierarchical, with "professionals" controlling the nonprofessional "volunteer." The terms and conditions of employment are most often unilaterally set by the service-providing agency and are accepted, automatically at first, as part of the agreement to serve. The employees' interests extend beyond bread-and-butter issues. Employee organizations may be viewed, at times, as professional associations.

The military model will dominate public safety programs and agencies. The key to employment in these areas is often seen as service and loyalty to the organization's leaders, as well as a duty to enforce the law or "keep the peace." Decision making will be extremely hierarchical, following a strict chain of command. The terms and conditions of employment will often be controlled by a set of "general orders." "Not following the chain of command" and "conduct unbecoming an officer" are viewed as serious charges. Job pressures are high. Professionalism as a goal confronts a strictly hierarchical chain of command in this model. Employee organizations in such a military setting are often seen as fraternal, comrade-in-arms clubs. Employees often live in closed groups where, for example, police officers only socialize with other police officers and "the only real friend of a firefighter is a firefighter."

The patronage model will be centered about political relationships. Patronage employees often have alternative "volunteer" duties (whether as precinct captains, ward workers, or simply as voters and promoters of the political futures of their patrons). A series of Supreme Court decisions has, at times, been viewed as sounding the death knell of the old fashioned patronage system as it operated in Mayor Daley's Chicago, or, early on, in Mayor Rizzo's Philadelphia.[32] However, decision making by political compromise, boss rule, and power blocks remains very important today. Political allegiance, the machine "handshake," lobbying, and legislative work ultimately play a vital role in setting the terms and conditions of employment. Employees are voters, and friends and relatives of voters. Employees are often sophisticated about politics, but insecure in their ability to fight city hall when they have a problem which puts them at odds with the machine. Their employee organizations are often wheels in the political machine.

The civil service system relies on merit principles and bureaucratic decision making. It is dominant in the federal service and typical of public employment everywhere. The terms and conditions of employment are set by civil service rules and regulations, often controlled by

---

[32]*See Branti v. Finkel,* 445 US 507 (1980) and *Elrod v. Burns,* note 6, above.

a commission or similar agency. Employees are usually entitled to representation before such a commission, both with regard to rule-making and disciplinary and other job-related issues. Civil service associations vary in their makeup from those which are primarily fraternal, professional associations to those which behave as a traditional union. Employees under a civil service system often are more interested in job security and public service and may not be used to militancy.

The professional management/Japanese team model works on scientific management principles and uses outside management efficiency consultants, productivity goals, "team work" guidelines, and employee manuals. Employees are regarded as members of a team. Employee organizations may be nonexistent, may act as cheerleaders, or may be real representatives of worker concerns.

The full collective bargaining model—under which there is true, joint decision making; mutual control of wages, hours, and working conditions set by contract; and all of the worker protections of the NLRA—offers real advantages to public workers under any mix of these systems. Only in this system is the employee organization a vital partner exercising significant joint decision making.

The public organizer should be aware of the peculiar history and practice used to control employment at the agency targeted for an organizing drive. Some idea of the pre-organizing drive forces at work, the keys to employment, the methods of decision making, and the mechanism used to control terms and conditions of employment is vitally important. The strengths of one model may be the weaknesses of another. The fraternal, social obligation, comrade-in-arms, and expertise appeals which are likely to be old hat in the public service and public safety environment can strike a responsive chord with civil servants or "almost private sector" blue collar workers. The political appeals which are trite to the patronage worker can attract police officers or social workers who care about, but feel cut off from, policy decision making. Basic bread-and-butter and "control of the workplace" issues which are the staple of the collective bargaining model appeal to all public workers. The real key to a successful organizing drive is knowing the habits of the workplace and gearing the organizing drive accordingly. An organizer who seems not to understand "how things are done around here" may never get worker attention. The organizer who cannot see and explain better ways to do things may lose quickly.

# 3

# The Organizer and Union Advocacy

## The Target Employer

There is no substitute for competency. The organizer who knows how an employer's operations work, its financial and fiscal situation, its personnel policies and procedures and how they are set, its budget, and its labor relations personnel, as well as the problems and aspirations of the workers, has a tremendous edge. An organizing campaign will move with more assurance, be better received by the workers, and have a greater chance of employer acceptance, if the organizer knows what he or she is talking about in discussing employer operations. Even basic information readily available to the public can be very useful to the organizer in the campaign.

## Employer Operations and Management Structure

This section presents six tools designed to help organizers know the public sector organizing target. An organizer should know:

(1) Sources of information about the employer,
(2) The different types of public employers,
(3) The institutional structures which govern labor relations in the targeted agency,
(4) Methods for developing a statistical picture of the work force,
(5) How to review the employer's budget, and
(6) How to cost out the employer's wage and benefit package.

## Sources of Information

Finding out the facts about the workplace is in certain respects easier in the public sector than it is in the private sector. Freedom of information laws, public or open records laws, open meeting laws (sometimes known as sunshine laws), and right-to-know laws are among the laws in most states that require governments to put certain information and decision making on the public record.

### Freedom of Information Laws

While the state and municipal laws vary on exactly what records governments must make public, nearly every state has some disclosure requirements. A typical state freedom of information or public records law will require that the names, titles, departments, and salaries of all public employees be available for public inspection. Under some laws, the home addresses of employees must also be made public,[1] although in other jurisdictions home addresses are not considered public records or are protected from disclosure to the public on grounds of privacy.[2]

Other types of information which may be helpful in an organizing effort are also generally available under public information laws.[3] Personnel manuals, organization charts, operating manuals, classification standards, meeting minutes of legislative bodies and executive branch commissions, budgets and budget backup data, contracts of all kinds, and reports required to be filed with other governmental agencies are among documents which may be available.[4]

---

[1] For example, unions successfully obtained employees' names and addresses under state laws in *Michigan State Employees Ass'n v. Michigan Dep't of Management and Budget*, 428 Mich. 104, 404 N.W.2d 606 (1987); *Tobin v. Michigan Civil Serv. Comm'n*, 416 Mich. 661, 331 N.W.2d 184 (1982); *Webb v. City of Shreveport*, 371 So.2d 316 (La. App. 1979); *Warden v. Bennett*, 340 So.2d 977, 94 LRRM 2383 (Fla. Dist. Ct. App. 1976).

[2] *Government Employees Local 1923 v. Department of Health & Human Servs.*, 712 F.2d 931, 113 LRRM 3537 (4th Cir. 1983) (denying access to names and addresses under the federal Freedom of Information Act).

[3] Procedure under most public sector collective bargaining laws is similar to procedure under Taft-Hartley in the private sector whereby—in what is known as the Excelsior Rule—prior to a representation election, the employer provides the NLRB with a list of names and addresses of employees eligible to vote in the election, after which the list is available to all parties to the proceeding. In *Van Bourg, Allen, Weinberg & Roger v. NLRB*, 728 F.2d 1270, 115 LRRM 3374 (9th Cir. 1984), after a consent election, the court ordered the NLRB to disclose—under the federal FOIA—the Excelsior list to a union which was not a party to the election, but was interested in possibly attempting to decertify the incumbent.

[4] Much of the information which must be disclosed under state laws may also be helpful in preparing for bargaining. In *Hathaway v. Joint School Dist. No. 1, Green Bay*, 116 Wis.2d 388, 342 N.W.2d 682 (1984), a union obtained a computer printout listing the names and addresses of parents with children in the school system. The union wanted to inform parents about ongoing contract talks. In *Service Employees v. Internal Revenue Serv.*, No. 82-1081 (D.D.C. 1982), the union obtained the names of all hospitals that employed union members that had filed a notice to withdraw from the Social Security system.

One source of information on state freedom of information or public record laws is the list in Appendix B. Most public employers have a public information (or freedom of information) office which will provide a copy of the law and describe the procedures necessary to get the information.

The typical procedure requires a written request for the desired information, sets up a timetable for the agency to respond, and sets forth remedies if the agency fails to respond or responds inadequately. Under most laws, the agency must provide members of the public with a place to inspect the requested public records during regular business hours. The agency may charge a reasonable fee to copy any requested documents.

## Open Meeting Laws

Every state has some type of open meeting law under which at least some decisions must be made in meetings open to the public. A citation to each state's law can also be found in Appendix B.

The laws typically (though not always) exempt from the open meeting requirement such things as collective bargaining sessions; employment matters relating to individual employees; acquisitions of real property; parole board proceedings; and consideration of litigation. Other laws exempt other kinds of meetings as well.

While the laws vary, nearly all the laws require advance public notice of a public meeting and require that minutes be kept and made available to the public; most provide sanctions against officials who violate the law (e.g., misdemeanor) and render actions taken in violation of open meeting laws either void or voidable.

## Types of Public Employers

There are many different types of public employers—state governments, county and municipal governments, boards and commissions, and some publicly chartered corporations. It can be very helpful to know the type of employer that is the target of an organizing drive. More than the most obvious information is helpful.

If the target is a state government, what are the relative authorities and powers of the legislature? Where does the agency to be organized fit into the government structure? Who is the head of the agency that is targeted? What decision makers have what degree of authority? An organizer must not hesitate to ask the public information office of the government for explanations of the structure of the government. The legislative representatives who serve the leaders of the organizing drive can also be sources of information.

Organizers should take a look at the state statutes, especially an annotated code, for the jurisdiction. Important to check are provisions on public personnel, civil service, and any provisions controlling the operations of the organizing target. Annotations describe briefly the legislative history of the provisions and any disputes that have arisen as legal cases under them. Such annotations—available in a public library—can prove useful even to the nonlawyer. While no layman should consider reading the annotations as a reliable source of technical legal principles, the lay organizer can gain useful glimpses into both the structure and the specific history of the target agency.

If the organizing drive faces an employer other than the state government, it is important that the organizer understand the nature of the employer authority. What are the "home rule" provisions of the state government? How much independence does a county, a city, a school board, or a police department have to adjust the working conditions of its employees? What form of management is involved?

Wellington and Winter, in their classic 1971 study *The Unions and the Cities*, point out the difficulty in locating the ultimate source of managerial decision making in public employment:

> [T]he public sector alone faces the often frustrating question of deciding which branch or branches of local government should represent management, and what the internal allocation of management functions for collective bargaining should be.
>
> At common law, the identifying marks of an employer were that: (1) he selected and engaged the employee, (2) he paid the wages, (3) he had the power of dismissal, (4) and he had power and control over the employee's conduct. It might be supposed, therefore, that the executive branch responsible as it is for the administration of a city, would perform all four of these functions. This often is not the case. The legislative branch usually must approve all transactions with monetary consequences and sometimes there is an independent board of finance that also must give approval. Thus, at least one other part of the local government will share the wage-paying function of an employer. In addition, in many communities, independent commissions or boards rather than executive departments run important city services such as schools or parks. A commission may perform all the functions of an employer, or all except providing the needed money for wages and fringe benefits. Moreover, a municipal or county civil service commission may have an important role in fixing wages, hours and conditions of employment.
>
> Each branch of local government has different goals; each is subject to different pressures. And unless curative legislation can be enacted at the local or state level, each may participate in the collective bargaining

process in ways that vastly complicate the formation and administration of collective agreements between a city or county and its unionized employees.[5]

In every campaign, a first step should be to try to find out who has what authority. If a city is involved, what is the form of government? Is there a strong mayor? A weak mayor with a strong council? A city manager? A commission or series of boards and commissions?[6]

An organizer should know how decisions are made by the employer and who must be convinced to grant recognition, dues checkoff, and bargaining rights to the union. What entity of government has the authority to make the decision? What specific individuals must become convinced?

## Personnel Management and Bargaining Structures

In addition to knowing the general structure and authority of the government involved, the organizer should try to track down who specifically has authority, responsibility, and day-to-day contact assignments for dealing with personnel matters, with collective bargaining, and with unions. Are there clear responsibilities in these areas? What chain of command is involved? What are the general attitudes, histories, and personalities involved? Table 2, a chart from David Stanley's *Managing Local Government Under Union Pressure*, while developed in the early 1970s, still provides some idea of the diversity to be encountered in the assignment of responsibility for employee relations and collective bargaining.

Organizers should spend a few minutes thinking about management's structure. The constitutional, political, and bureaucratic makeup of the employer should be considered. The existence and degree of interest in local government of "citizens for better government" groups, taxpayer alliances, community associations, parent-teacher associations, police and fire auxiliaries, and similar organizations should be reviewed.[7]

It is important for the organizer to get to know personnel office employees and collective bargaining specialists. Any available organization charts should be studied to find relationships between line supervisors and management decision makers. The position of people

---

[5]H.H. Wellington & R.K. Winter, *The Unions and the Cities*, 117–118 (1971).

[6]E.C. Banfield & J.Q. Wilson, *City Politics* (1963).

[7]M. Derber, "Management Organization for Collective Bargaining in the Public Sector," in *Public Sector Bargaining*, 80–117 (B. Aaron, J.R. Grodin, & J.L. Stern, eds. 1979).

### TABLE 2.   OFFICIAL WITH PRIMARY BARGAINING RESPONSIBILITY IN THE 19 LOCAL GOVERNMENTS SURVEYED (1972)

| Government | Official with Primary Responsibility |
|---|---|
| *Governments with Collective Bargaining Agreements* | |
| Dade County | Chief executive (later changed to staff assistant) |
| Multnomah County | Chief executive |
| Tacoma | Chief executive |
| Boston | Labor relations specialist (heavy responsibility carried by a staff attorney) |
| Detroit | Labor relations specialist |
| Milwaukee | Labor relations specialist (responsibility formerly exercised by personnel director) |
| New York | Labor relations specialist |
| Cincinnati | Civil service or personnel director |
| Dayton | Civil service or personnel director |
| Hartford | Civil service or personnel director |
| New Castle County | Civil service or personnel director (initial agreements under collective bargaining negotiated by a consultant) |
| Philadelphia | Civil service or personnel director (long-term labor relations consultants retained before establishment of an office of labor relations) |
| Wilmington | Civil service or personnel director (jointly with city solicitor) |
| Binghamton | Executive assistant to mayor (later changed to corporation counsel) |
| Buffalo | Budget director (later changed to personnel director) |
| *Governments without Collective Bargaining Agreements* | |
| Los Angeles County | Personnel director (later made responsible for "meet and confer" sessions) |
| New Orleans | None |
| St. Louis | Personnel director (responsible for "meet and confer" sessions tantamount to bargaining) |
| San Francisco | None |

*Source:* David Stanley, *Managing Local Government Under Union Pressure* (1972), Table 2, p. 26.

in the budget-making process should be reviewed. Individuals responsible for the relationship between the legislative and the executive branch and community relations and press representatives of the employer are also individuals with whom the organizer should become familiar.[8]

In all of this, it is a good idea for the organizer to get to know management's representatives in the same way the employees to be organized are known—personally and by name and sight. It is wrong to make unwarranted assumptions about management attitudes: The organizer should assume from the beginning that management representatives are acting and speaking in good faith. The organizer must behave as though he or she wants to build a strong, sound relationship with management and improve employer-employee relationships. The organizer must be truthful. It is important that management representatives trust the organizer and recognize that what is said is meant.[9]

## The Statistical Picture

All states and local jurisdictions with 100 or more employees are required to file an annual report—form EEO-4—with the federal Equal Employment Opportunity Commission (EEOC). This report gives employment statistics by race, ethnic group, sex, occupation, and salary range. Elementary and secondary school systems must file a similar report, form EEO-5; and institutions of higher education must file form EEO-6. The information in these reports may be obtained, if necessary, from the EEOC through a federal Freedom of Information Act (FOIA) request. However, as a general matter, an employee or taxpaying citizen should be able to get a copy of the report simply by requesting it from the state or local employer and, at times, agreeing to pay the cost of producing a copy.

## Budgetary Review of the Public Employer

One of the most useful documents to a public sector union organizer is the employer's budget document. Not only do budget presentations supply a full review of the economic and fiscal position of

---

[8]J.F. Burton, Jr., "Local Government Bargaining and Management Structure," 11 *Indus. Rel.* 123 (1972).

[9]For an idea of the potential for and the value of a good relationship, *see* "Life With a Union," in Seyfarth & Shaw, *Practical Labor Relations for Public Employers*, Ch. 13 (1978). The authors' advice to employers is summarized as follows:

Formulation of a strategy for living with the Union is presented. The approach of constant conflict and the tactics used to implement this strategy are considered. Emphasis is on the approach of peaceful coexistence and the management techniques necessary to maintain this relationship.

*See also* R. Ayers, "Labor Relations: The Law Enforcement Administrator's Dilemma," in *Police Labor Relations and Collective Bargaining* (R. Ayers & W. Sirene, eds. 1984).

the employer, they also contain detailed descriptions of the employer's planning, policy, and administrative structures. A careful examination of the budget's expenditure projections will reveal clearly the employer's plans over the next year, as well as a great deal about the employer's internal decision-making process.

The organizer should have no trouble obtaining copies of the employer's budget documents. If any difficulty is found, a taxpayer request for the documents or a request made by a friendly legislator may be tried. If these methods fail, consider the state freedom of information route discussed above. The American Federation of State, County and Municipal Employees (AFSCME) has developed an extremely useful pamphlet, *Budget Analysis: A Guide For AFSCME Negotiations*, and a companion publication, *Justifying Proposals*. They are reproduced in Appendix C.

### Costing Out an Employer Wage and Benefit Package

Finally, an organizer should be able to cost out the wage and benefit package which applies to the employees being organized. The value of the package of wages and benefits should be understood. An organizer who can understand, discuss, and compare the costs of the package is at a real advantage in explaining the need for a union. A review of how to cost out such a wage package has been developed by the Midwest Center for Public Sector Labor Relations from a 1978 U.S. Department of Labor publication, *The Use of Economic Data in Collective Bargaining*.[10] The report is reproduced in Appendix D.

### The Organizer and the Work Force

Nothing is more important to the success of an organizing drive than knowing the employees. Without real personal contact and support, no organizing project can succeed.

It is extremely important that the organizer carefully evaluate both the group to be organized and their job-related concerns. No group is monolithic. There are individual concerns in every group. The organizer must recognize both group and individual needs.

This means that the organizer should be familiar with the employer's operations, structure, budget, and employee wage and benefit

---

[10]Originally republished in BNA *Government Employee Relations Report*, 61:3081, RF-195 (July 7, 1980). *See also*, C. Mulvaliy, "Costing the Economic Package," in *Collective Bargaining in the Public Sector: Selected Readings in Law Enforcement*, 131–149 (R. Ayers & T. Wheeler, eds. 1977).

package. The cost, value, and comparative worth of the employee's wages, hours, and working conditions will always interest them.

In addition to the big issues that affect everyone, the organizer should be familiar with the specifics of as many grievances and related employee discipline situations at the location as possible. The organizer should find out about actual past and current grievances. These grievances should be understood and explained. Their resolution, whether successful or not, should be reviewed.

The organizer should know how any civil service, employee bill of rights, or grievance procedure works. It is not enough to know technical requirements; the organizer should also assess how successful the procedure has been in resolving workplace problems.

The organizer should avoid the constant negative. The emphasis should be on making the workplace a better place, helping workers do a better job, and reinforcing the possibility that by working together and achieving collective negotiations with the employer, things really will improve. Specific comparisons are always a good idea.

## The Pre-Drive Evaluation

The concerns and interests of public workers will vary widely with the type of employment, recent on-the-job history, and the current economic and fiscal situation of the employer. Read the local press. What does it say, if anything, both about the employer and the workplace to be organized? Is there an employer or employee newsletter or monthly bulletin? If so, get it and read it. Look into basic economic, bread-and-butter concerns with wages, hours, and working conditions; check for job security issues relating to any recent changes in the work force or potential for reductions or expansion in force. Do any special work-related concerns worry the group to be organized? Have there been recent fiscal problems? What are the specific jobs done by the group? How are they done? What particular problems or concerns do they generate? The organizer should talk directly to individual workers about their problems.

In every job there are special concerns. In education, for example, the organizer should look into issues such as student discipline and curricula, the availability and content of instructional materials, the instructional methods used, teaching assignments and the methods for making them, questions of scheduling and school day and year, the structure of the school system, and decentralization. In health care, special concerns are the quality of health care, the medical equipment provided, and the availability of training. In police departments, important issues are shift and job assignment, the position of any civilian review board, departmental policies on deadly force and firearms use, and the department's attitude to officer discipline and liability. For sanitation workers, the assignment and working of routes are important issues.

Other types of concerns are common to many different kinds of employment situations. These include: the availability of equipment and training in its use; what happens to employees when something breaks or goes wrong; health, job safety, and equal employment opportunities; upward mobility in promotions, training, and income; job security, seniority protections, the loss of work through contracting out, bumping rights, and reduction-in-force procedures; and pay and benefit comparisons both within the employer's work force and with similarly situated workers (i.e., mobility, security, and comparability).

The pre-drive evaluation should include not only the basic information on the group itself—age, sex, race, educational level, job history—but also less formal information on sports league participation, church membership, credit union, and fraternal club participation. An evaluation of group leaders should also be part of the process.

Investigate every avenue of information to build a picture of the employees. Obviously, a list of names and addresses will be very helpful and should be a key aim of the pre-drive evaluation. Familiarity with, and access to, the work sites involved can be vital.

### The Employee Survey

The American Federation of State, County, and Municipal Employees' *Representation Campaign: A Guide for AFSCME Organizers* emphasizes the importance of knowing the target workplace. The *Guide* counsels the organizer to:

(1) Find out all the work sites and the number of employees at each;
(2) Review former organizing or union drives at the proposed site;
(3) Get a feel for the employees' attitudes toward unions in general;
(4) Find out how employees feel about their employer;
(5) Determine what issues concern the employees, such as wages, benefits, etc.;
(6) Discover the length of employment of employees at various work sites;
(7) Survey job satisfaction;

(8) Check on prior union membership or history of employees; and

(9) Look for interest among employees in joining a union.

AFSCME advises that ideally "an independent firm can be hired to conduct this research" but recognizes "that in smaller units, union people (staff and leaders) can do it themselves." The AFSCME *Guide* suggests a union survey of employees:

> A survey of all or a majority of employees at the targeted site should be completed by personal contact. Through initial contacts, the organizer should identify all the work areas and the leaders in each area. Then, make up a chart consisting of all employees broken down by work area and shift. Meet with the leaders individually and ask each one of them to introduce you personally to their co-workers. You will be able to determine through this process if these are the true leaders and if other employees want a union. Each employee you meet with should be able to introduce you to another employee who is interested or may be interested in the union. NO leaflets and NO cards are used at this stage.
>
> If the ingredients are there: employees have grievances; working conditions are considered bad and wages are not satisfactory, and employees believe there is not a vehicle to resolve these problems, then there is a good possibility for a successful union drive. However, a union will not succeed unless the employees have expectations that are not currently being met by the employer. ONLY if these criteria are met should the organizer recommend an organizing campaign.[11]

## *The Employer Survey*

As the employer becomes aware that a union organizing campaign is in progress, the employer will conduct an employee survey of its own. This may be a formal, written document distributed among all employees or it may be an informal, verbal solicitation for information from supervisors and employees. Both methods are intended to gauge employee dissatisfaction. The AFSCME *Guide* makes the following observation about employer surveys:

> At this stage, the employer will begin research on the union (locally and nationally), as well as researching wages and benefits of other employers in the area. This is all preliminary work before they officially

---

[11]Remember that this reference to the AFSCME guide is advice specifically designed to fit the national organizing problem of AFSCME International. All of the advice should be tailored to the situation. For example, in its initial section, the AFSCME guide says, "Do *not* organize a unit where you will not be able to get a contract." This may make sense in terms of AFSCME's national programs, but should not be viewed as a universal truth. In many jurisdictions without collective bargaining, public employee organizations have been very successful. In fact, historically, success in organizing drives has nearly always preceded the enactment of bargaining rights.

begin a campaign. When management decides that there is a union campaign of substance, they may hire the union-buster.[12]

A manual developed by the law firm of Seyfarth and Shaw for public employers seeking to resist public sector organizing drives, *Practical Labor Relations for Public Employers*, explained the causes of public employee unionism under two headings: (1) job-related dissatisfaction; and (2) predisposition to join a group that provides social or individual recognition and status.[13] The manual claims that dissatisfaction with unfair treatment, poor wages, low job security, unresolved grievances, poor working conditions, insufficient employer recognition for experience and seniority, inadequate fringe benefits, lack of communication about rules and goals, disregard for personal problems, insufficient attention to professionalism, and lack of individual recognition, in that order, are the primary "dissatisfactions" causing unionism. Employers also recognize that family and personal background, familiarity with the union movement, a need for peer solidarity, and a need for worker participation and status in control of their own affairs predispose workers to unions.[14]

The employer's position toward effective organizers highlights these same points. The law firm of Seyfarth and Shaw gives the following advice to employers:

> A skilled union organizer can make many, many promises to prospective union members or supporters. Indeed, he attempts to solve every employee's problem with a promise. The organizer can promise, directly or indirectly, that if the union is selected or designated as bargaining representative, it will gain for the employee such improvements as: (1) increased job security based on seniority; (2) higher pay; (3) shorter and more favorable working hours; (4) fairer treatment on the job through impartial grievance arbitration; (5) improved working conditions; (6) more paid holidays; (7) longer vacations; (8) improved sick leave benefits; (9) increased insurance benefits with decreased employee contributions; (10) new benefits such as dental care, group legal services, and employee paternity leave; (11) increased "professionalism" within the governmental unit; (12) a greater role in determining how things will be done; (13) an end to unfair treatment or favoritism by supervisors; and (14) a handwritten contract which can be enforced by each employee.
>
> In individual cases, the union organizer holds out the potential of recognition and individual status to various employees. He compares these things to the employee's perception of unkept promises by public administrators and disregard for the individual.

---

[12]*Id.*

[13]J. Baird, J. Anderson, & S. Damas, *Practical Labor Relations for Public Employers* (1978).

[14]*Id.*

It is relatively easy to play on an employee's dissatisfaction and predisposition. How successful the union organizer will be, in large part, depends on the extent of the employee's dissatisfaction and the strength of the employee's predisposition to join and support the union. Consequently, it is none too soon to take steps to decrease employee dissatisfaction, and to weaken any predisposition whenever and wherever it can be located.[15]

The organizer should focus on all of these "obvious" points. It is important in doing so that (1) the organizer's "promises" be based on fact, be realistic and achievable, and (2) the organizer present promises in a manner designed to appeal to specific workers and their needs. To do this, the organizer needs to get to know the workers by talking to them wherever and whenever the opportunity presents itself. Get to know names. Talk to workers about their interests and needs, especially their job, their need to participate in workplace decision making, and their wages, hours, and working conditions. When organizers talk about these things, the more specific and realistic the talk is, the more successful the organizing drive will be.

## The Organizer as Union Representative

It is very important that the organizer know as much as possible about the history, organization, constitution, membership, and dues structure of labor organizations. In some organizing drives, a specific labor organization seeks to organize and represent workers who had not previously been members of any organization. In other drives, the employees might have been members of a fraternal or other organization, but not of a union. In still others, the workers might be considering either forming a new organization or affiliating with an existing group.

Of course, organizers working for a union must understand and be able to answer questions clearly and directly about their own organization. Where another organization is in competition, it helps to know that organization's history and structure. Those who are "shopping" for an employee organization want to know all they can about all of the unions in the field. Finally, workers seeking to form a new organization will do well to review existing organizations as models.

---

[15]*Id.*; *see also* W. Sirene, "Labor's Most Effective Organizer," in *Police Labor Relations and Collective Bargaining*, 7–10 (R. Ayers & W. Sirene, eds. 1984).

## Types of Public Sector Labor Organizations

There are a number of different unions and employee organizations active in the public sector, ranging from large, active public employee unions, such as the American Federation of State, County and Municipal Employees[16] and the American Federation of Government Employees,[17] to small associations which represent only the workers in a single department of a single public employer, such as the Alexandria, Virginia, Sanitation Department Employees' Association.[18] Among the most active are organizations concentrating in specific fields such as education (the National Education Association[19] and the American Federation of Teachers[20]), firefighting (International Association of Firefighters[21]), and police (International Union of Police Associations and the Fraternal Order of Police[22]). A number of independent associations (the unaffiliated state and municipal civil service associations, American Nurses' Association, the National Association of Social Workers,[23] and the American Association of University Professors[24]) are active in the public sector, as are many private-sector-based unions (e.g., the Teamsters, the Communications Workers of America, the Service Employees International Union, the Laborers' International Union, and the United Auto Workers, especially its District Council 65).[25] Public sector craft and building trades workers belong to their craft or trade union in the private sector (the Carpenters, Plumbers, and others).[26] The literature is full of descrip-

---

[16]J. Baird, J. Anderson, & S. Damas, note 13, above, at 67.

[17]L. Kramer, *Labor's Paradox: The American Federation of State, County and Municipal Employees, AFL-CIO* (1962); J. Goulden, *Jerry Wurf: Labor's Last Angry Man* (1982); R. Billings & J. Greenya, *Power to the Public Worker* (1974).

[18]J. Neven & L. Neven, *AFGE-Federal Union* (1976). AFGE's membership is predominately but not completely in the federal work force; *see* J.L. Stern, "Unionism in the Public Sector," in *Public-Sector Bargaining*, 45–62 (B. Aaron, J.R. Grodin, & J.L. Stern, eds. 1979) for a discussion of federal unions including NAGE, NFFE, and NTEU.

[19]*See* J. Stieber, *Public Employee Unionism: Structure, Growth, Policy*, 8–9, 28–30, 42–44 (1973) and J.L. Stern, note 18, above, at 62–79.

[20]M.O. Donley, Jr., *Power to the Teacher: How America's Educators Became Militant* (1976); T. Herndon, *We, the Teachers: Terry Herndon on Education and Democracy* (1983); D. Rubin, *The Rights of Teachers* (1984).

[21]*Id.*, and M. Liberman & M.H. Moskow, *Collective Negotiations for Teachers: An Approach to School Administration* (1966).

[22]J. Stieber, note 19, above, at 51–53, 107–108, 120–123, 143–145, and 164–171, *citing* B. Klienast, *Policemen and Firefighter Employee Organizations* (1972); and W. Schweppe, *The Firemen's and Patrolmen's Unions in the City of New York* (1948).

[23]H. Juris & P. Feuille, *Police Unionism: Power and Impact in Public Sector Bargaining* (1973); J.H. Burpo, *Police Labor Movement: Problems and Perspectives* (1971); and A. Cory, "Police Unions Jockey for Position," *Police Magazine*, May 1983, at 12–18.

[24]J. Stieber, note 19, above, at 76–88; H. Edwards, R. Clark, & C. Craver, *Labor Relations in the Public Sector*, 10–12 (2d ed. 1979).

[25]F. Kemerer & J. Baldridge, *Unions on Campus* (1975).

[26]*See* note 13, above; and J. Stieber, note 19, above, at 1–50.

tions, histories, and comparative discussions of the various organizations. Nearly every public sector labor organization also has a newsletter, journal, or newspaper which can provide a wealth of information for organizers.

## Constitutions, Charters, and Bylaws

The basic governing document of most employee organizations is either a constitution or charter and a set of bylaws. The organizer should have a copy of the governing documents and should read through them thoroughly enough to at least understand the basic organizational pattern of the organization, its membership requirements, the nature of its leadership, and its basic dues structure. Preliminary questions can be answered by this knowledge. For example,

(1) Is the organization a corporation or a nonprofit organization?
(2) Is it chartered merely as a tax-exempt service group?
(3) Is it designated an ''employee organization''?
(4) Is the organization a multitier structure made up of local unions, state councils, and a national or international body?
(5) What are the relationships, obligations, and duties of each level of the union's structure?
(6) How much autonomy does the local have?
(7) How much service does a local get from a council or from the national?
(8) Is the organization affiliated with the AFL-CIO?
(9) Does it represent a specific type of employee?
(10) Is its membership composed entirely of public employees?
(11) Is its membership limited to teachers, sworn police officers, firefighters, registered nurses, or other professionals?
(12) How is the leadership of the organization selected?
(13) Will a new local be organized at the drive site?
(14) Will an organizing committee be used that can become a new local, if the drive is successful?
(15) How often are meetings held?
(16) How will bargaining proposals be developed?

## The Dues Structure

It is important for the organizer to have a clear understanding of the dues structure of the union. The organizer should be able to answer directly and clearly all questions about dues—how they work; how they are accounted for; and how, whether, and when they can be increased. Prospective union members will want to know what they will be getting for their dues and the manner of payment.

The advice to management offered in *Practical Labor Relations for Public Employers* suggests that employers use the cost of union membership as a theme in fighting an organizing drive. They advise

> Here the employer can point out the large amounts of money the union will cost employees in initiation fees and monthly dues required of union members, as well as the possibility of regular and special dues assessments. The employer also may wish to point out that many unions reserve the right to fine, discipline or expel members for disobeying union rules or directives, including initiating decertification petitions, trying to get rid of the union, or returning to work during a strike.[27]

An organizer will need to respond to the types of questions raised by a flyer used by the city of Tampa's Employee Relations Division in response to an organizing drive, reprinted as Exhibit 1 below. The

---

### EXHIBIT 1.   DO YOU NEED A UNION?

**Do you need the union?**
**or**
**Does the union need you?**

QUESTIONS FOR YOU TO ASK THE UNION SALESMAN

1. Can you guarantee that you will get us everything you say you will? Can you guarantee that you will get us *any* of the things you say you will?
2. Is it illegal for you to promise things and never get them for us?
3. Why is the City prohibited from promising things before the election?
4. If the union wins, will we be able to go to our supervisors as in the past to discuss our problems or will we have to go through the union?
5. Does the law require that we be represented by a union?
6. Where does all the money collected from dues go?
7. Will the union demand that all union dues be automatically deducted from members' paychecks if it wins the election?
8. Can the union collect fees and assessments over and above the regular monthly dues?

> *The answer to each question is important. Carefully consider the answers given to you by union salesmen. If you have any questions, feel free to talk with your supervisor. Above all, base your decision on the facts. . .*

City of Tampa Employee Relations Division

---

[27]*Id.*

organizer must be prepared to talk about union dues clearly and with assurance. He or she must know exactly what the dues are, how collection works, what portion of any dues goes to state or national organizations, and what services result from any per capita fees or charges. Exhibit 2, a flyer prepared by the Service Employees' International Union for use in an organizing drive in the city of West Palm Beach, addresses many of these issues.

---

### EXHIBIT 2.  LOOK WHAT YOU GET FOR $6.00.

#### Look What You Get For

#### $6.00 A Month

—LOCAL FULL TIME STAFF REPRESENTATIVE
—LOCAL ATTORNEY (Specializing in Public Employee Law)
—LOCAL ECONOMIST
—LOCAL BARGAINING AGENT
—SEIU, FULL-TIME STAFF REPRESENTATIVE
—INTERNATIONAL ATTORNEY (Specializing in Labor Law)
—INTERNATIONAL ECONOMIST
—INTERNATIONAL BARGAINING AGENT
—UNION CONTRACT

#### How Your Dues Dollar Is Spent

SEIU, AFL-CIO, WASHINGTON, D.C. ———————————————— $1.80

 (SEIU guarantees to return to West Palm Beach
 City Employees the full amount paid to the
 Washington office for a period of two (2) years.)

FLORIDA COUNCIL ———————————————————— .10
YOUR LOCAL TREASURY MAINTAINS ——————————— 4.10

            TOTAL ———— $6.00

### VOTE ☒ SERVICE EMPLOYEES
### INTERNATIONAL
### UNION AFL-CIO

STRONG AND RESPONSIBLE REPRESENTATION—
*SERVICE EMPLOYEES*
*INTERNATIONAL UNION AFL-CIO*

***Remember: Union Dues Are 100% Tax Deductible*

---

4

# Constitutional and Statutory Rights of Public Employees

Under our constitutional system, the government may not impermissibly interfere with freedom of speech and association, deprive people of life, liberty, or property without due process of law, or refuse to afford similarly situated groups equal protection of the law.

These constitutional limits on governments in their relationships to individuals also apply when the government functions as an employer. As a result, *public employees enjoy constitutional protections and rights which are not available to private sector employees*. Some of the constitutional rights are directly applicable to organizing public workers; others, though not as directly applicable, can provide important tools to the organizer.

Three important constitutional concepts derived from amendments to the U.S. Constitution provide important tools to the organizer. They are:

(1) The First Amendment rights to freedom of speech, expression, and association,

(2) The 14th Amendment protection against the government's depriving any person of life, liberty, or property without due process of law, and

(3) The 14th Amendment guarantee of equal protection of the law to any person.

Constitutional rights are particularly important in states without a public sector collective bargaining statute. For instance, under most state public sector bargaining statutes, it is unlawful to fire an employee for urging people to join a union, or to fire employees for joining.

46

That would be an unfair labor practice.[1] If there is no public sector bargaining law, however, there is no such thing as an unfair labor practice. Instead, one must look to the constitutional freedom of association to protect public employees from discharge for advocating unionism and for joining a union.

The beauty of the Constitution is that it sets forth in broad language basic rights that are essential to our system of government, balancing rights of the individual against rights of the government. As a result of its purpose and its broad language, however, it is not always possible to explain or predict precisely what activities are and are not protected. Those questions are ultimately raised and answered in court cases. The answers vary depending on the particular facts and interests involved in each situation; the answers vary with different courts; and the answers vary over time.[2]

This, of course, is not a textbook on constitutional law. However, this chapter does outline a few of the basic principles of constitutional law and describes how the principles can be helpful in organizing public workers. A lawyer may be needed if there appears to be a constitutional right or issue involved in a particular organizing situation.[3] In this chapter, we will focus on how the First Amendment and due process protections may apply in an organizing situation. We will also outline some federal and state laws—in addition to collective bargaining laws—that may be useful when organizing public employees.

---

[1]*See* S.I. Schlossberg & J.A. Scott, *Organizing and the Law*, 68–98 (3d ed. 1983).

[2]For a long time, courts viewed public employment as a "privilege" and held that governments could condition continued employment on public employees giving up their constitutional rights. For example, in *McAuliffe v. Mayor of New Bedford*, 155 Mass. 216, 29 N.E. 517 (1892), the court upheld the firing of a public employee for engaging in political speech ("the petitioner may have a constitutional right to talk politics, but has no constitutional right to be a policeman."). *See Adler v. Board of Education*, 342 US 485 (1952). But in more recent years, our highest court has rejected the idea that government employment is a privilege. Now it holds that even if there is no right to public employment, the government may not condition government employment upon the willingness of individuals to sacrifice their constitutional rights. *Keyishian v. Board of Regents*, 385 US 589 (1967); *Shelton v. Tucker*, 364 US 479 (1960).

[3]A very useful and fairly detailed guide to how principles and developments to constitutional law apply to public employees, especially teachers, can be found in D. Rubin, *Rights of Teachers: The Basic ACLU Guide to a Teacher's Constitutional Rights* (Rev. ed. 1984).

If a lawsuit involving constitutional issues becomes necessary in an organizing campaign, and the court finds a constitutional violation, the losing side may have to pay the winning side's attorneys' fees under § 1988 of the Civil Rights Attorneys' Fees Awards Act of 1976 (42 U.S.C.A. § 1988).

## First Amendment Rights of Speech and Expression

The First Amendment to the Constitution of the United States[4] protects public employees against unwarranted employer interference with their freedom of speech, expression, and association. The Amendment also protects:

- The right of public employees to join a union or to advocate joining,
- The right to speak out on matters of public concern, and
- The right of access to a public employer's property.

While First Amendment freedoms are not absolute, any limitations on the freedom of speech or association must be justified. Under the First Amendment, the interest of public employees in free speech is balanced against the interest of the state, as employer, in promoting the efficiency of the public services it performs through its employees.[5] Any limitations on freedom of expression must be narrowly drawn and directly related to the state's interest.[6]

### Speech Supporting the Union

For employees covered by a collective bargaining statute with unfair labor practices and procedures for handling such claims, it is an unfair labor practice to discipline someone for union activity or for advocating support of a union.[7] And under many such laws, disciplining people because they are seeking to improve conditions or pay for employees is an unfair labor practice even if no union is on the scene.[8]

---

[4]The First Amendment reads "Congress shall make no law . . . abridging the freedom of speech, or of the press; . . .". Laws enacted by state legislatures are also subject to this prohibition. *See Gitlow v. New York*, 268 US 652 (1925).

[5]*See Pickering v. Board of Educ.*, 391 US 563, 568 (1968); *Connick v. Myers*, 461 US 138 (1983); *McPherson v. Rankin*, 107 S.Ct. 1561 (1987). For a collection of the many U.S. Circuit Courts of Appeal cases applying *Connick v. Myers*, *see* Sachs, "The First Amendment Rights of Public Employees," AFL-CIO Lawyers Coordinating Committee (April 28, 1987). Copies of the paper are available through Maggie Rock at the AFL-CIO Coordinating Committee Office, AFL-CIO, 815 16th Street, N.W., Washington, D.C. 20006. *See also* Editorial Note, "The Public Employee's Right of Free Speech: A Proposal for a Fresh Start," 55 *Cin. L. Rev.* 449 (1986).

[6]T. Emerson, *The System of Freedom of Expression* (1969).

[7]Nearly every public sector law which covers unfair labor practices makes it an unfair labor practice for an employer to discriminate against an employee for union activity, that is, the laws prohibit "any discrimination with respect to hire or tenure of employment to encourage or discourage membership in a union." In interpreting this language, most states follow the interpretation of the identical language under the National Labor Relations Act. *See* S.I. Schlossberg & J.A. Scott, note 1, above, at 87 *et seq.*

[8]Under the sections of the NLRA applicable to the private sector, it is an unfair labor practice under 8(a)(1) "to interfere with, restrain or coerce employees in the exercise of rights guaranteed

Even in states without unfair labor practices, there is protection against discipline for union activity. Since the right to form and join a union is part of the freedom of association under the First and Fourteenth Amendments to the Constitution, public employers cannot discipline their employees for joining a union or advocating that others join a union.[9] State action whose purpose is to intimidate public employees from joining a union or taking an active part in its affairs, or to retaliate against those who do, violates the First Amendment.[10] Action which has a "chilling effect" on rights of free speech and association, such as reprimanding someone for being a zealous union advocate or assigning union advocates less desirable assignments, are also impermissible.[11]

What if it is not so clear that an employer discharged an employee solely for union activity, for joining a union, or for advocating others to join a union? What if the employee who is fired is indeed attempting to organize a union, but also has a record of habitual tardiness, and the employer claims the employee's tardiness, not union activity, was the cause of the firing?

The general rule established by the Supreme Court,[12] is that if the employer can prove the employee would have been fired even if the employee had not engaged in union activity, then the discharge will be upheld. The Court's rationale is that the employee should not be in a better position because of engaging in union activity than if the employee did not engage in union activity; in other words, an employee is not insulated from justifiable adverse action just because of being active in the union. Thus, the fact that a person is an advocate

---

by Section 7." Section 7 gives employees the right to engage in union activity and "in other concerted action for the purpose of collective bargaining or other mutual aid or protection." Section 7 covers combined employee action for mutual aid, even if there is no union in the picture. Some but not all public sector statutes contain language similar to the Sections 7 and 8(a)(1) language in the NLRA. If a state statute does contain such language or similar language, combined employee action for mutual aid is protected even if there is no union around.

[9]*See, e.g., McLaughlin v. Tilendis*, 398 F.2d 287, 71 LRRM 2097 (7th Cir. 1968); *State, County, & Municipal Employees v. Woodward*, 406 F.2d 137, 70 LRRM 2317 (8th Cir. 1969); *Lontine v. VanCleave*, 483 F.2d 966, 84 LRRM 2445 (10th Cir. 1973).

[10]*Professional Ass'n of College Educators, TSTA/NEA v. El Paso County Community College Dist.*, 730 F.2d 258, 116 LRRM 2150 *and* 3454 (5th Cir. 1984), *cert. denied*, 469 US 881, 105 S.Ct. 248 (1984), citing *Smith v. Arkansas State Highway Employees Local 1315*, 441 US 463, 101 LRRM 2091 (1979); *Alabama State Fed'n of Teachers v. James*, 656 F.2d 193 (5th Cir. 1981).

[11]*Columbus Educ. Ass'n v. Columbus City School Dist.*, 623 F.2d 1155, 105 LRRM 201 (6th Cir. 1980); *Reichert v. Draud*, 511 F. Supp. 679 (E.D. Ky. 1981).

[12]*Mount Healthy Bd. of Educ. v. Doyle*, 429 US 274 (1977). Once the employee shows that conduct which is constitutionally protected was a "substantial" or "motivating" factor in the employer's adverse action, the burden shifts to the employer to show by a preponderance of the evidence that it would have reached the same decision on the adverse action, even in the absence of the constitutionally protected conduct.

for the union and is protected in that advocacy by the First Amendment will not prevent the employer from being able to fire the employee for other legitimate reasons, such as bad attendance or insubordination.[13]

## Speech About Working Conditions

It is common at all stages of the organizing process for employees to complain about working conditions and the impact those working conditions have on their work—the delivery of public services. Generally, the complaints are kept "inside the office," consisting of grumbling between employees or raising the complaints to the employer; sometimes, however, the complaints surface outside the office—to the city council or to the media, for example.

People do not lose their First Amendment rights to criticize the government by becoming public employees; but that does not mean that the First Amendment protects public employees in saying anything they want to anybody at any time or in any context.[14]

Employers may try to stop or to stifle the complaints by disciplining the complainers. The employer may either genuinely believe that the complaints are disruptive to the work site and undermine the employer's authority, or the employer may really just be trying to discourage complaints, or—when union organizing is going on—the employer may be trying to discourage the employees from joining the union.

What are the ground rules? Can public employees be disciplined for complaining or speaking out? Is the answer different if union activity is going on?[15]

Rules by legislative bodies that prohibit employees, their representatives, or organizations of employees from appearing before them on matters relating to employment are generally impermissible. Of course, legislatures may govern what items reach the agenda, sign-up procedures for speaking, and so on, as long as the rules are not applied differently to different people. The legislative body should have any such procedural rules available in writing for public distribution.

---

[13]Examples of cases upholding the discharge of employees who happened also to be union advocates are *Ramsey v. Leath*, 706 F.2d 1166, 114 LRRM 2537 (11th Cir. 1983) (upholding discharge for violation of departmental rules); *Parker v. Cronvich*, 567 F. Supp. 1073 (E.D. La. 1983) (upholding discharge for act of insubordination).

[14]*Pickering v. Board of Educ.*, note 5, above.

[15]A more detailed treatment of the First Amendment rights of teachers (and public employees generally) can be found in D. Rubin, note 3, above, at Ch. 11.

What about complaints on employment-related matters made to the legislative body or to the media or to one's superiors? Can a public employee be disciplined for speaking out in this context?

There is no single or simple answer to this question. The courts look very closely at the facts of the particular case: What was said? By whom? To whom? When? In what context? What was the subject? Some generalizations can be made, however. The general rules are:

(1) *Public Concern.* If the speech is not primarily a matter of public concern, it won't be given First Amendment protection. Matters that are primarily internal grievances about employment or personnel are unlikely to be held matters of public concern.[16]

(2) *The Balance.* A balance must be struck between the interest of a public employee, as a citizen, in commenting on issues of public concern and the interest of the state as an employer, in promoting the efficiency of its public services via its employees.[17]

(3) *The "But For" Test.* If the disciplined employee did engage in speech protected by the First Amendment, the discipline will be upheld if the employer can prove that the employee would have been disciplined for other, legitimate reasons.[18]

A number of facts are very important in these cases. Each of the three general rules—public concern, the balance, and the "but for" test—deserves a separate review.

## Issues of Public Concern

Is the subject on which the employee speaks out a matter of "public concern" or "public importance"? Or is the matter more an employee grievance concerning internal office policy? The more the subject concerns a matter of public concern, the more the speech is protected so that the speaker cannot be disciplined for the speech.[19]

This test causes many difficulties. Often a complaint about some aspect of public employment not only reflects an employee's dissatisfaction but also involves matters of public concern. In deciding how

---

[16]*Connick v. Myers*, note 5, above.
[17]*Pickering v. Board of Educ.*, 391 US 563 (1983); *Connick v. Myers*, note 5, above, at 145.
[18]*Mount Healthy Bd. of Educ. v. Doyle*, note 12, above.
[19]*Connick v. Myers*, note 5, above.

to characterize the speech, the courts look to "the content, form and context of a given statement, as revealed by the whole record."[20]

Sometimes it is relatively easy to characterize the speech. For example, in a case where a teacher appeared before the school board and the city council, charging that robberies and assaults were being committed in his school, the court found that society's interest in information about the operation of its schools in this serious area "far outweighs any strain on the teacher-principal relationship" which was created by the statement.[21] In a case involving employees' peaceful distribution of leaflets on and near hospital premises disputing the layoffs proposed by the hospital's board of trustees, and the effect of the proposed cuts on the level of public health care, a court found this to be a matter of public concern, even though layoff decisions also involve internal concerns.[22]

On the other hand, the court found no matter of public concern when a deputy sheriff in a small department gave the sheriff a letter he planned to send to the press complaining that a newspaper article based on an interview with an officer was inaccurate in reporting that a burglary had been solved by the interviewed officer when, in fact, three others had been equally involved.[23] The court characterized the case as involving "personal pique."

---

[20]*Id.*

[21]*Lusk v. Estes*, 361 F. Supp. 653, 663 (N.D. Tex. 1973). Similarly, in a case where a teacher sent a press release to the media stating that a principal (unnamed) had exposed children to the risks of serious physical harm by making them go outside in a thunderstorm for a tornado drill, the court found the "press release involved matters of public concern and was not merely a petty personal attack." *Swilley v. Alexander*, 629 F.2d 1018, 1021 (5th Cir. 1980). *And see Czurlanis v. Albanese*, 721 F.2d 98 (3d Cir. 1983).

[22]*Woodruff v. Board of Trustees, Cabell Huntington Hosp.*, 116 LRRM 3482 (W. Va. Sup. Ct. App. 1984). *See also Postal Workers v. U.S. Postal Serv.*, 762 F.2d 715 (2d Cir. 1985), *cert. denied,* _____ U.S. _____ , 106 S.Ct. 1262 (1986) (letter from union president to large customer that postal service has deteriorated due to recent layoffs is in part a matter of public concern); *Anderson v. Central Point School Dist. No. 6*, 746 F.2d 505 (9th Cir. 1984) (letter written by assistant coach to members of school board concerning athletic policies which had become a matter of public debate was a matter of public concern protected by First Amendment even though not every word of the letter was of interest to the public); *Bowman v. Pulaski County Special School Dist.*, 723 F.2d 640 (8th Cir. 1983) (statements by assistant football coach concerning corporal punishment imposed on students by head coach is protected); *Leonard v. Columbus*, 705 F.2d 1299, 31 FEP Cases 1441 (11th Cir. 1983), *cert. denied,* 468 US 1204 (1984) (black officers' removal of American flag from their uniforms in an effort to emphasize a widely held perception of racial discrimination in the police force is a matter of public concern); *Wilson v. Littleton*, 732 F.2d 765 (10th Cir. 1984) (police officer's wearing of black shroud across his badge to express his personal feeling of grief over death of a policewoman from another town is not a matter of public concern, though police officers' deaths would be of public concern if officer were shot during an ongoing public controversy over whether to purchase bulletproof vests).

[23]*Cooper v. Johnson*, 590 F.2d 559 (4th Cir. 1969). *See also Yoggerst v. Hedges*, 739 F.2d 293 (7th Cir. 1984) (comment about agency's director made to fellow employee spoken in role as employee about her personal feelings and not in her role as citizen on qualification of the director).

The line between matters of public concern and personal internal concern is not, however, always easy to draw. *Connick* was a case involving an assistant attorney general who was disgruntled over a job transfer and circulated a questionnaire soliciting the view of co-workers on the desirability of a grievance committee, office morale, the level of confidence in superiors, office transfer policy, and pressure to work in political campaigns. The U.S. Supreme Court held in a 5-4 decision that although the questionnaire touched on a matter of public concern in a limited sense (pressure to work in political campaigns), it was "most accurately characterized as an employee grievance concerning internal office policy."[24]

On the other hand, where there is no evidence that the person circulating the questionnaire has a pending grievance, a questionnaire seeking the views of faculty on a broad range of issues, such as the degree of mutual confidence existing between administration and faculty, the extent to which good teaching and good research were rewarded, the extent to which faculty opinions were listened to and respected, the effectiveness of the administration in dealing with grievances, and the accuracy and completeness of information used to evaluate teachers may be more likely to be considered of "public concern."[25]

A court considered it a matter of "public concern" when, at a city council meeting, and later on a television interview, a representative of a labor organization criticized the council's decision not to give police officers their annual raise. The court found that by focusing on compensation, the speech dealt directly or indirectly with the ability of the city to attract and retain qualified police personnel and the competency of the police force. By generally dealing with the working relationship between the police union and elected city officials, the speech was related to "the agency's efficient performance of its duties."[26]

One court has tried to define matters of public concern as follows:

> Speech by public employees may be characterized as not of "public concern" when it is clear that such speech deals with individual personnel disputes and grievances and that the information would be of no relevance

---

[24]*Connick v. Myers*, note 5, above.

[25]*See Lindsey v. Board of Regents*, 607 F.2d 672 (5th Cir. 1979). *See also Knapp v. Whitaker*, 757 F.2d 827 (7th Cir.), *cert. denied*, _____ US _____ , 106 S. Ct. 36 (1985) (issues of a teacher's classroom assignments and the content of his personal evaluation are not matters of public concern; issues of inequitable mileage allowance, liability insurance for coaches and volunteer parents who transport student athletes, and functioning of the grievance procedure when grievance procedure was subject of ongoing collective bargaining negotiations are matters of public concern).

[26]*See Connick v. Myers*, note 5, above.

to the public's evaluation of the performance of governmental agencies. . . . On the other hand, speech that concerns "issues about which information is needed or appropriate to enable the members of society" to make informed decisions about the operation of their government merits the highest degree of first amendment protection.[27]

## Balancing Employee Interests and Employer Rights

Did the speech affect the maintenance of discipline in the office or harmony among co-workers? Assuming the speech does contain an element of public concern, the less disruption caused by the speech, the more likely that the speech will be protected.

In the Supreme Court's *Connick* decision, the supervisor, a district attorney, believed the circulation of a questionnaire would disrupt the office, undermine his authority, and destroy close working relationships. The disruption factor is given more weight in cases (such as with attorneys) where close working relationships and loyalty and trust with supervisors are important.[28] Further, the more the speech deals with matters of public concern, the greater the degree of disruption that will be tolerated.[29] For instance, despite the disharmony created, an employee's speech informing of misbehavior (padding of mileage claims) by public officials was held protected.[30]

The First Amendment right to criticize policies or practices of the public employer on matters of public concern covers remarks communicated privately to the employee's superior as well as remarks communicated publicly.[31] In determining whether speech is a matter of public concern, the fact that the speech was addressed to the public is sometimes a factor,[32] although communicating to the public cannot convert something which is not a matter of public concern into such a matter. Depending on the manner, time, and place in which the criticism is delivered, the speech may so interfere with institutional efficiency as to become unprotected.[33]

---

[27]*McKinley v. City of Eloy*, 705 F.2d 1110, 1114 (9th Cir. 1983).

[28]For cases involving but rejecting claims that a close working relationship made the speech unprotected, *see Potner v. Califano*, 595 F.2d 770 (5th Cir. 1979); *Swilley v. Alexander*, note 21, above; *Allen v. Autauga County Bd. of Educ.*, 685 F.2d 1302 (11th Cir. 1982).

[29]Courts recognize that expression of criticism or an unpopular view inevitably causes some tension between the speaker and the object of his/her speech.

[30]*Atcherson v. Siebenmann*, 458 F. Supp. 526 (S.D. Iowa 1978), *rev'd in part on other grounds*, 605 F.2d 1058 (8th Cir. 1979); *see O'Brien v. Caledonia*, 748 F.2d 403 (7th Cir. 1984).

[31]*Givhan v. Western Line Consol. School Dist.*, 439 US 410, 18 FEP Cases 1429 (1979).

[32]*McKinley v. City of Eloy*, note 27, above; *Czurlanis v. Albanese*, note 21, above.

[33]*Connick v. Myers*, note 5, above. The U.S. Supreme Court shed additional light on the scope of First Amendment protections in *McPherson v. Rankin*, 786 F.2d 1233 (5th Cir. 1986), *aff'd*, 107 S.Ct. 1561 (1987), in which a clerk-typist in a constable's office commented to a fellow worker after the attempted assassination of President Reagan, "I hope they get him next

## The "But For" Test

As is true with the discharge of a person who is outspoken in support of the union, discharge of a person who speaks out about working conditions that are of public concern will not be a constitutional violation if the employer can prove that the individual would have been fired even in the absence of speaking out. In general, the Supreme Court has said that if the individual would not have been fired "but for" his or her speaking out, then the discharge was illegal and must be overturned; however, if the employer can prove it would have taken the same action even if the employee had never spoken out, then the discharge will stand.[34]

## Statutory Protection for Whistleblowers

Several states have passed laws specifically protecting employees from reprisals for speaking out. These laws are usually called "whistleblower protection laws."[35] This statutory protection is in addition to whatever protection exists under the Constitution. The laws vary a great deal in the type of communication that is protected and the available remedies.

Disclosure of the employer's violation of a law, rule, or regulation is the most commonly protected information. Some state laws cover disclosure of mismanagement, abuse of authority, waste of public funds, and/or dangers to public safety. Many states protect the disclosure only if it is made to certain entities, such as to legislative bodies or in testimony to courts or administrative bodies. Under such limits, disclosure to the media, for example, would not be protected.

## The Due Process Clause and Unjust Discharge

The due process clause of the 14th Amendment[36] helps protect public employees in many situations from arbitrary discharge. If the

---

time." The Fifth Circuit held that plaintiff's expression of her political opinion addressed a matter of public concern which outweighed the interest of the constable's office in efficient operation. The Court upheld the Fifth Circuit in a 5 to 4 decision. The Court held "given the function of the [Constable's office], McPherson's position in the office, and the nature of her statement, we are not persuaded that Rankin's interest in discharging her outweighed her rights under the First Amendment." (Slip Opinion, at 13)

[34]*Mount Healthy Bd. of Educ. v. Doyle*, note 12, above.

[35]The statutes at least in the states listed below give "whistleblower" protection to some, if not all, public employees: Connecticut, Delaware, Illinois, Indiana, Iowa, Kansas, Louisiana, Maine, Maryland, Michigan, New Hampshire, New York, Oklahoma, Oregon, Rhode Island, Texas, Washington, Wisconsin.

[36]The 14th Amendment provides that no state shall "deprive any person of life, liberty or property without due process of law."

due process clause applies, the employer must give the affected employee notice of the reason for the adverse action, a meaningful opportunity for the employee to respond to the charges and to present evidence, and the right to an impartial decision maker.

The due process clause, when it applies, puts a damper on a public employer's ability to claim an employee is being fired for one reason (e.g., tardiness) when the real reason is something else (e.g., union activity).

As a general matter, the nonprobationary public employee may not be disciplined or discharged without reason. Even a decade ago, the U.S. Department of Labor reported that more than 70 percent of state and local bargaining agreements provided for grievance arbitration on discipline.[37] These agreements nearly universally provide that discipline may be imposed only for just cause.[38] More importantly, insofar as the unorganized are concerned, civil service protection against non-just-cause discipline is both widespread and growing.[39] In 1955, only 23 states had civil service laws covering approximately 65 percent of all full-time state employees. In 1974, 84 percent of the cities, 83 percent of the counties, and 96 percent of the states had adopted some type of merit system.[40] These protections, whether through a grievance or civil service procedure, provide for an avenue of appeal in situations in which employees are disciplined.

The public sector organizer should know how to represent employees using any and all existing contractual or civil service protections afforded employees.[41] Such representation is important (1) because it is useful in protecting employees involved in the organizing target from unjust discipline; (2) because it may be vital in providing a pre-contract, and even pre-collective bargaining basis for public employee organizations; and (3) because the law of the jurisdiction with regard to the nature of the public employment "contract" affects the constitutional right of employees to due process.

The public employee's constitutional right to due process, as explained above, gives the public organizer a tool to fight injustice in

---

[37]"Grievance and Arbitration Procedures in State and Local Agreements," at 18, 40 (U.S. Dept. of Labor, Bureau of Labor Statistics, Bull. No. 1833, 1975).

[38]See C. Craver, "The Judicial Enforcement of Public Sector Grievance Arbitration," 58 Tex. L. Rev. 329 (1980); F. Elkouri & E.A. Elkouri, How Arbitration Works. 165–167 (4th ed. 1985).

[39]R. Vaughn, Principles of Civil Service (1976); and 15A Am. Jr.2d, "Civil Service" (grounds for dismissal) §§ 61–67 (procedures) §§ 68–77 (1976).

[40]See H. Pettitt, Termination of Employment Dismissal Law and Practice, at 226 n.54 (1984).

[41]See R. McMaster, "Defending Civil Service Employees From Discharge," in 24 Am. Jurisprudence Trials 421 at §§ 1–91.

the workplace which is not available in the private sector. In applying constitutional due process protection to public employees, at least three issues must be addressed:

(1) Does the employee have a "property interest" in the job?
(2) Does the employee have a "liberty interest" which the employer threatened by unjust employer discipline?
(3) What process is due the employee?

The law on each of these issues is in development and often confusing. In most cases, its application will require the aid of an attorney. However, the public organizer should know something about the basics found in a line of U.S. Supreme Court decisions.[42]

The first question an employee must face in establishing an entitlement to constitutional due process is whether the employee has a constitutionally protected interest. Under *Roth* and *Sindermann*, the employee will have to show either that the specific employment situation is one in which the employee has a "property" interest, or that the acts of an employer in terminating or disciplining the employee threatened a "liberty" interest. The simplest way to put the issue is by application of a set of five questions:

(1) Is the employee a probationary employee? If so, the property interest is likely to be absent.
(2) Is the employee formally a "tenured" employee? If so, the property interest is likely to be present.
(3) Is the employee protected by a contract or by a civil service system from noncause discipline? If so, the property interest is likely to be present.
(4) Has the employer by the totality of its employment policies and actions created an expectation of continued employment and a protection from unjust discipline in its employees? If it has, the basis for showing a property interest may be present.
(5) Has the employer taken unjust disciplinary actions which do serious injury to the reputation of the employee or to the employee's expectation of finding continued employment? Has the employer worked to see that the employee "never works again"? If so, then the basis of a liberty interest case may be present.

---

[42] Among the most prominent cases in that line are *Board of Regents v. Roth*, 408 US 564 (1972); *Perry v. Sindermann*, 408 US 593 (1972); *Arnett v. Kennedy*, 416 US 134 (1974); *Bishop v. Wood*, 426 US 341 (1976); *Codd v. Velger*, 429 US 624 (1977); and, most recently, *Cleveland Bd. of Educ. v. Loudermill*, 470 US 532, 118 LRRM 3041 (1985).

There is no easy test of whether a protected interest is present. Extensive litigation throughout the federal court system over two decades has not settled the matter.[43] If it looks like the basics are there, the organizer should check with an attorney.

## The Loudermill Decision

If a constitutional property or liberty interest does exist, what protections must be supplied?[44] A review of the Supreme Court's most recent decision in this area will be helpful. On March 19, 1985, the Court decided *Cleveland Board of Education v. Loudermill*. The Court ruled that all public employees who are entitled to good cause protection from discharge may not be discharged without a pre-discharge opportunity to hear and respond to the charges involved, coupled with a post-discharge administrative hearing. The *Loudermill* decision is a major clarification and extension of the due process protection afforded public employees.

*Loudermill*'s new requirement of a pre-termination hearing requires major changes in some public employee discipline procedures. The decision, especially its concurring opinions, may also have a substantial impact on the current practice of placing public employees in extended periods of nonpay status awaiting the outcome of post-termination review processes.

Since the Supreme Court's 1972–1974 decisions in *Roth*, *Sindermann*, and *Arnett v. Kennedy* clearly established constitutional due process protection for public employees, a line of cases has struggled with what procedural protections are required by the Constitution— what kind of hearing must be held, when must it be held, and what representation will be allowed.[45] Many of the cases seemed to follow the theory espoused by Justice Rehnquist (though not by a majority of the Court) in *Bishop v. Wood*. Under this approach, a statute or regulation creating a public job or any right in continued public employment could also control what *procedures* were applicable to a discharge. Under these cases, the lower courts typically approved the various formal and informal procedures governments established unless they provided no meaningful opportunity to respond to charges. Under this

---

[43]G. Frug, "Does the Constitution Prevent the Discharge of Civil Service Employees?" 124 *U. Pa. L. Rev.* 942 (1976); "Developments in the Law: Public Employment," 97 *Harv. L. Rev.* 1611, 1780–1800 (1984); P. Simon, "Liberty and Property in the Supreme Court: A Defense of Roth and Perry," 71 *Calif. L. Rev.* 146 (1983); R. Glennon, "Constitutional Liberty and Property: Federal Common Law and Section 1983," 51 *S. Calif. L. Rev.* 355 (1978).

[44]H. Friendly, "Some Kind of Hearing," 123 *U. Pa. L. Rev.* 1267 (1975).

[45]*See* note 42 above.

approach, sometimes called the "bitter with the sweet" theory, if the procedures contained in general orders, personnel regulations, or elsewhere in state law were followed, any discharged public employee, by definition, received all the process which was promised and due. But in *Loudermill*, a decision in which every justice except Rehnquist joined, the Supreme Court specifically and clearly rejects the "bitter with the sweet" approach. Justice White wrote in the majority opinion

> In light of these holdings, it is settled that the "bitter with the sweet" approach misconceives the constitutional guarantee. If a clearer holding is needed, we provide it today. The point is straightforward: the Due Process Clause provides that certain substantive rights—life, liberty, and property—cannot be deprived except pursuant to constitutionally adequate procedures.[46]

Under *Loudermill*, a pre-termination notice of charges and opportunity to respond must be afforded any discharged public employee who shows a liberty or property interest. It is clear from *Loudermill* that some form of pre-termination hearing must take place. It is also clear that a notice and opportunity to respond will be sufficient pre-termination protections only if coupled with significant post-termination protections. The decision makes clear that the level of post-termination protection has a direct bearing on the adequacy of limited pre-termination rights. In his concurring opinion, Justice Marshall placed heavy emphasis on the length of time required to complete the post-termination review process and whether the officer involved goes without pay. Justice Marshall explained

> I continue to believe that *before the decision is made to terminate an employee's wages*, the employee is entitled to an opportunity to test the strength of the evidence "by confronting and cross-examining adverse witnesses and by presenting witnesses on [their] own behalf, whenever there are substantial disputes in testimonial evidence."[47]

However, no other justices joined Marshall in this.

The exact outline of the type of post-hearing procedure with which a pre-termination notice and opportunity to respond must be coupled is a question left open by the Court. It is clear that even when a termination is preceded by a notice of the charges and an opportunity to respond, significant additional due process protections must be afforded the terminated employee. The courts are left to struggle with

---

[46]*Cleveland Bd. of Educ. v. Loudermill*, 470 US 532, 118 LRRM at 3044.
[47]*Id.* at 3047; for basic law review comments on the *Loudermill* decisions and its impact, see 71 *A.B.A.J.* 114–115 (June 1985), 18 *Akron L. Rev.* 631–648 (1985), and 1985 Army L. 1 (1985).

the full requirements of those procedures in future cases. Related questions involving lesser forms of discipline, the adequacy of remedies, the burden of proof, requirements of *impartial* review, the right to call and cross-examine witnesses, and access to counsel remain unresolved.

## Guarantee of Equal Protection

The equal protection clause of the 14th Amendment to the U.S. Constitution provides that no state shall "deny to any person within its jurisdiction the equal protection of the laws." It requires the government to treat similarly situated persons in a like manner. The equal protection clause does not require that the government treat everyone the same, but it does mandate that it treat similarly situated groups similarly unless it can establish a legitimate reason for not doing so. State constitutions typically contain an equal protection clause or similar language. Many state equal protection clauses have been interpreted to give broader rights to public employees than employees have under the federal equal protection clause. Employer limitations on, or preferences for, one group over others in collective bargaining, in dues check-off, or in access to government property all may be tested against the equal protection clauses. Chapter 5 discusses the practical implications of the equal protection clause for organizing.

## The Right to Political Participation

### Politically Motivated Hirings and Firings

The patronage system of employment still exists in many places, as described in Chapter 2. In a "pure" patronage system, where jobs are filled (and promotions given) with an eye to the political party affiliation of the applicants or employees, people are also fired for having the wrong political affiliation—if only to make room to hire people with the right political affiliation.

Unions are often tugged from at least two directions in jurisdictions with patronage systems of employment. A union which already represents employees does not want those employees to be subject to patronage firings (even though the employees might originally have obtained their jobs as a result of patronage hiring). On the other hand, if a union actively campaigns against the incumbent and its candidate wins, the union may want the newly elected official to be able to make changes.

As a result of recent court decisions, it seems quite clear that a patronage *dismissal* of a nonpolicymaking, nonconfidential employee is an unconstitutional interference with the employee's freedom of association and freedom of political belief.[48] But patronage dismissals of policymaking and confidential employees are not unconstitutional. While the distinction between the "policymaking" and "nonpolicymaking" is not always clear, it is clear that most people represented by unions or who are eligible to be represented by unions are in nonpolicymaking positions and could challenge a patronage dismissal.[49]

Of course, actions less drastic than dismissal may be patronage-based as well, such as demotions, promotions, transfers, and reassignments. These too may be subject to legal challenge.[50]

Despite these cases, patronage hiring, firing, promotions, and transfers are still the practice in many jurisdictions. While patronage hiring is not easily challenged, adverse actions based on patronage are more easily challenged.

In a particular jurisdiction, patronage dismissal may be challenged on grounds in addition to—or other than—constitutional grounds. If the jurisdiction has a civil service system, and the employee involved is in the civil service, it is unlikely that a patronage dismissal would be legal under the civil service statute. And, of course, if there already is a collective bargaining agreement in place, the agreement undoubtedly limits the employer's discretion to discharge on grounds of political affiliation.

Thus, a successful legal challenge may be possible in situations where an organizing campaign is ongoing and the employer discharges or otherwise adversely affects the union advocates for patronage reasons. As previously discussed in this chapter, the Constitution also protects public employees from discharge because of union activity. Thus, if an individual is told that he or she is fired for patronage, but the real reason is that person's union activities, the person has two grounds to challenge the discharge.

---

[48]*Elrod v. Burns*, 427 US 347 (1976); *Branti v. Finkel*, 445 US 507 (1980); *Parker v. Wallace*, 596 F. Supp. 739 (M.D. Ala. 1984).

[49]Courts differ on whether deputy sheriffs are in a policymaking or confidential position; see *Jones v. Dodson*, 727 F.2d 1329 (4th Cir. 1984); *McBee v. Jim Hogg County*, 730 F.2d 1009 (5th Cir. 1984); *Joyner v. Lancaster*, 553 F. Supp. 809 (M.D. N.C. 1982); *Parker v. Cronvich*, note 13, above; and *Cerjan v. Fasula*, 539 F. Supp. 1226 (N.D. Ohio 1981).

[50]*Delong v. United States*, 621 F.2d 618 (4th Cir. 1980). *See* Note, "First Amendment Limitations on Patronage Employment Practices," 49 *U. Chi. L. Rev.* 181 (1982).

## Hatch Act and Derivatives

Probably more common than systems which are heavily patronage-based are systems in which employers impose rules limiting political participation. These rules are theoretically aimed at preventing employees from being coerced on political grounds.

Limits on permissible political activities of public employees exist in the Hatch Act and acts patterned after the Hatch Act. The U.S. Congress and every state legislature have passed legislation aimed generally at eliminating or reducing partisan political activity among covered employees. The federal law, the Hatch Act,[51] is aimed primarily at federal employees, and prohibits covered employees from taking "an active part in political management or in political campaigns." It is intended to prevent the party in power from using government workers to promote the continued dominance of the party. (Certain high level officials are permitted to take an active part in campaigns but are prohibited from attempting to coerce others.) The Hatch Act also applies to employees who work for state or local agencies and whose activities are "financed in whole or in part by loans or grants made by the United States or Federal agency,"[52] but it only prohibits those employees from candidacy for elective public office in partisan elections and from attempting to coerce others to support a party or person for public office. The federal Hatch Act does not prohibit covered state and local employees from taking an active part in political management and political campaigns.[53] Much criticism has been leveled at the Hatch Act, although the Supreme Court has upheld its constitutionality.[54]

Most state and local employees are not covered by the federal Hatch Act, but are covered by a state or local "little Hatch Act." What is permitted and what is not permitted varies a great deal under the laws, and the laws themselves are changed quite often. Many, though not all, of the state laws are less restrictive than the federal Hatch Act and permit state and local employees to engage in more

---

[51]Act of Aug. 2, 1939, ch. 410, 53 Stat. 1147 (1939); Act of July 19, 1940, ch. 640, 54 Stat. 767. Codified throughout 5 U.S.C. and 18 U.S.C., *see* especially 5 U.S.C. § 7324(a). The current regulations describing permissible activities and impermissible activities can be found at 5. C.F.R. 733.11 and 5 C.F.R. 733.122.

[52]Examples are programs in public health, public welfare, housing, urban renewal, employment security, and public works.

[53]U.S.C. § 1502(a)(3), as amended in 1974. The Office of the Special Counsel, U.S. Merit Systems Protection Board, 1120 Vermont Avenue, N.W., Washington, D.C. 20419, publishes a pamphlet "Political Activity and the State and Local Employees" outlining the federal Act's applicability to nonfederal employees.

[54]*United States Civil Serv. Comm'n v. Letter Carriers*, 413 US 548 (1973).

political activity than federal employees are allowed.[55] It is important for organizers to check current local laws and regulations to see what restrictions apply.[56]

## Other Areas of Employee Rights

Four additional areas of worker protection are likely to become issues in an organizing drive. These are:

(1) Public worker rights under the federal Fair Labor Standards Act;
(2) Employee protections in the occupational safety and health area;
(3) Employee rights with regard to the use of lie detector tests; and
(4) Employee rights to protection against unreasonable searches of their person, property, desk, or office.

In each of these areas, public employee rights differ somewhat from those of private sector employees.

### *Fair Labor Standards*

On February 19, 1985, the Supreme Court ruled, in *Garcia v. San Antonio*, that the minimum wage and overtime provisions of the federal Fair Labor Standards Act are applicable to state and municipal employers and their employees. The ruling was a major reversal of the Court's 1976 *National League of Cities* decision in which the Court held that congressional regulation of the wages and hours of state and local employers was an unconstitutional use of power to regulate commerce.[57]

*Garcia's* imposition of the federal minimum wage of $3.35 per hour will have little impact as such, since wage rates for most public employees already exceed that level. However, renewed application of a rule which requires time and one-half pay for all hours worked

---

[55]The Minnesota Court of Appeals has, for example, upheld the constitutional right of a nonprobationary, non-policy-making public employee to run for office without taking an unpaid leave of absence. *AFSCME Council 65 v. Blue Earth County*, 389 N.W.2d 244 (Minn. Ct. App. 1986).

[56]The Public Employee Department of the AFL-CIO prepared a Summary of Little Hatch Acts in September 1982, with the assistance of BNA. Copies may be available through the Department. State Little Hatch Acts are amended frequently so the summary is somewhat out of date. It is a useful starting point for anyone interested in an overview and comparison of the state laws. Organizers in a particular locality should check local laws.

[57]*Garcia v. San Antonio Metropolitan Transit Auth.*, 460 US 226, 27 WH Cases 65 (1985); *see* Chapter 1, n.1.

by nonexempt employees beyond 40 hours a week (and by law-enforcement personnel beyond 42.75 hours in a 7-day work period, 85.5 in a 14-day work period, and 171 hours over a 28-day work period) may require major changes. New rules on compensatory time, standby time, court time, and volunteer time may also be called for in many situations.

There are a whole series of exceptions to the wage and hour law involving executive, administrative, professional, and other special classes of employees. The mere payment of salary rather than hourly wages is not itself an exception. Furthermore, an employer's designation of a position will not be accepted at face value. All exceptions must be tested against specific rules issued by the U.S. Department of Labor.

An organizer should be aware of the applicability of federal wage and hour rules in the public sector. Their application is recent and can be confusing. When an issue arises, the Department of Labor's Wage and Hour Division can be helpful. Private enforcement is also available and, in some situations, an attorney should be consulted.

### Occupational Safety and Health

The federal Occupational Safety and Health Act (OSH Act) covers private sector employers and does not directly apply to state and local employees. While responsibility for enforcement of the act is given to the federal Occupational Safety and Health Administration (OSHA), states meeting certain requirements may take over enforcement. States doing so must have in place, among other things, a safety and health program covering public sector employees that includes protections "as effective" as those afforded private sector workers. More than 20 states have such federally approved plans covering public as well as private employees. OSHA's regulations also permit states to submit plans that cover only public employees. Once such plans are approved by OSHA, the federal government will pick up 50 percent of the enforcement costs. By April 1985, only Connecticut and New York operated under this program. If a state does not have a federally approved program, there still may be a local occupational safety and health law—the District of Columbia, Maine, Ohio, and Wisconsin are among the jurisdictions with programs which cover some or all public employees. All states have a designated agency to address public employee safety and health concerns. Many unions have negotiated additional protections. Health and safety in the workplace can be important organizing issues. Where an organizer can demonstrate that public workers must work under conditions that would be illegal for private sector workers covered by the federal OSH Act, worker interest in the issue and methods of dealing with it will increase.

About 20 states have passed right-to-know laws which require employers to provide workers—including public employees—with information about hazardous chemicals in the workplace.[58] The laws vary a great deal but generally require employers to make available to employees information on chemicals and other toxic substances, and prohibit employers from retaliating against anyone who exercises a right under the right-to-know law.

## Lie Detector Tests

Employers' relatively recent attempted escalation in the use of lie detectors, searches, and testing for substance abuse has been of great concern to employees. Dissatisfaction with management's initiatives and attempts to respond to such initiatives often provide a catalyst for organizing employees. Employees should be aware that there are numerous state laws and constitutional rights which may limit an employer's ability to require such tests. Developments regarding lie detector tests and tests for substance abuse are occurring so quickly that the organizer should review recent state court decisions and laws before deciding on strategy.

Many jurisdictions have laws dealing with the use of lie detectors, or polygraphs. Some states completely prohibit the use of polygraphs in employment; others forbid employers from "requiring or suggesting" that employees take a polygraph (presumably tests can be used if employees voluntarily take them); others prohibit employers from requiring a polygraph test as a condition of getting or keeping a job; some states regulate the subjects examiners can inquire into; and still other states contain no laws at all on polygraphs. Other variations also exist.

Courts differ on whether the Constitution gives public employees additional protection against the use of polygraphs. Some courts have ruled that it is unconstitutional to condition continued employment or advancement on submitting to a polygraph examination, while other courts find no violation.[59]

---

[58]As of 1984, Alaska, California, Connecticut, Delaware, Florida, Illinois, Iowa, Maine, Maryland, Massachusetts, Minnesota, New Hampshire, New Jersey, New York, Oregon, Pennsylvania, Rhode Island, Washington, West Virginia, and Wisconsin have right-to-know laws.

[59]*Compare Farmer v. Fort Lauderdale, Fla.*, 427 So.2d 187 (Fla.), *cert. denied*, 464 US 816, 52 USLW 3262 (1983); and *Kaske v. City of Rockford*, 96 Ill.2d 298, 450 N.E.2d 314, *cert. denied*, 464 US 960, 52 USLW 3369 (1983) (finding polygraphs impermissible), *with Kersey v. Shipley*, 673 F.2d 730 (4th Cir. 1982) (discharge upheld); *Gulden v. McCorkle*, 680 F.2d 1070, 29 EPD ¶32931 (5th Cir. 1982); and *Brown v. Tennessee*, 693 F.2d 600, 30 FEP Cases 459 (6th Cir. 1982) (polygraph test upheld as precondition to promotion). *And see Hester v. City of Milledgeville*, 777 F.2d 1492 (11th Cir. 1986).

## Unreasonable Searches and Drug Testing

The Fourth Amendment to the U.S. Constitution bars unreasonable searches and seizures. It was designed to "safeguard the privacy and security of individuals against arbitrary invasion by government officials."[60] Employer policies requiring searching of employees, including testing for drugs, can raise serious issues.[61]

Recently, public employer efforts to impose universal or random drug testing without a finding of good cause to test an individual based on evidence of impairment have been successfully challenged. This is particularly so where the employer is unable to demonstrate a strong need to test based on the sensitivity of the job in question.[62]

---

[60]*Camara v. Municipal Court of San Francisco*, 387 US 523, 528 (1967).

[61]In March 1987, the U.S. Supreme Court decided *O'Connor v. Ortega*, ___ US ___, 55 USLW 4405 (1987) holding that a public employee doctor had a reasonable expectation of privacy in his office (desk and file cabinets) but that an employer's reasonable search of these areas for work-related purposes or for investigations of work-related misconduct was permissible without a warrant or probable cause to believe wrongdoing. The question of whether an employee has a reasonable expectation of privacy must be addressed on a case-by-case basis.

Earlier cases on this issue include cases listed below which were gathered by C. Becker, "Public Employees' Constitutional Rights to Privacy: Search, Interrogation and Disclosure," AFL-CIO Lawyers Coordinating Committee (March 27, 1985).

a. Employee's privacy interest at work. *Mancusi v. De Forte*, 392 US 364, 367–370, 68 LRRM 2449 (1968) (standing to challenge search of common office); *Berger v. New York*, 388 US 41 (1967) (phone conversation in office); *United States v. McIntyre*, 582 F.2d 1221 (9th Cir. 1978) (phone conversation in office); *Gillard v. Schmidt*, 579 F.2d 825 (3d Cir. 1978) (desk); *United States v. Speights*, 557 F.2d 362 (3d Cir. 1977) (locker); *United States v. Hagarty*, 388 F.2d 713 (7th Cir. 1968) (conversation in other's office); *United States v. Blok*, 188 F.2d 1019 (D.C. Cir. 1951) (desk); *United States v. Kahan*, 350 F. Supp. 784 (S.D.N.Y. 1972) (wastebasket in office); *State v. Ferrari*, 141 N.J. Super. 67, 357 A.2d 286 (App. Div. 1976) (desk); *Commonwealth v. Gabrielle*, 269 Pa. Super. 388, 409 A.2d 1173 (locker) (1979).

b. Employer notice regarding search cannot eliminate or render unreasonable employees' expectations. *Chenkin v. Bellevue Hosp.*, 479 F. Supp. 207 (S.D.N.Y. 1979); *Smith v. Maryland*, 442 US 735, 740 n.5 (1979).

c. Search for work related reason. *United States v. Bunkers*, 521 F.2d 1217 (9th Cir. 1975), *cert. denied*, 423 US 989 (1975) (locker in post office); *United States v. Collins*, 349 F.2d 863 (2d Cir. 1965), *cert. denied*, 383 US 960 (1966) (jacket in post office); *Shaffer v. Field*, 339 F. Supp. 997 (C.D. Cal. 1972), *aff'd*, 484 F.2d 1196 (9th Cir. 1973) (locker in police station); *United States v. Donato*, 269 F. Supp. 921 (E.D. Pa.), *aff'd*, 379 F.2d 288 (3d Cir. 1967) (locker in mint).

d. Employer policy of search employees. (1) Prison guards. *Security & Law Enforcement Employees Dist. Council 82, State, County & Municipal Employees v. Carey*, 737 F.2d 187 (2d Cir. 1984) (no random searches; reasonable suspicion for strip searches; warrant for visual body cavity searches); *McDonnell v. Hunter*, 746 F.2d 785 (8th Cir. 1984) (preliminary injunction) (reasonable suspicion for strip searches; less intrusive searches, uniform or by automatic random selection); *Armstrong v. New York State Comm'r of Corrections*, 545 F. Supp. 728 (N.D.N.Y. 1982) (suspicion based on articulable facts). (2) Hospital employees. *Chenkin v. Bellevue Hosp.*, 479 F. Supp. 207 (S.D.N.Y. 1979) (warrantless search of packages upheld).

[62]See *Patchogue–Medford Congress of Teachers v. Board of Educ.*, No. 1987-156 (N.Y. Ct. App. June 7, 1987); *NTEU v. Von Raad*, 816 F.2d 170 (5th Cir. 1987); *Louvoir v. City of Chattanooga*, 647 F. Supp. 875 (E.D. Tenn. 1986); *McDonnell v. Hunter*, 809 F.2d 1302 (8th Cir. 1987); *National Ass'n of Air Traffic Specs. v. Dale*, No. A 87-073 (D. Alaska March 27, 1987); *Mulholland v. Dept. of Army*, No. 87-0317A (E.D. Va. April 20, 1987); *AFGE v. Weinberger*, 651 F. Supp. 726 (S.D. Ga. 1986); *Rushton v. Nebraska Public Power*, 653 F. Supp. 1510 (D. Neb. 1987); and *Turner v. FOP*, 500 A.2d 1005 (D.C. Cir. 1985).

# 5

# The Rights of Public Employees to Organize

## The Right to Join a Union

The constitutional freedom of association includes the right to form and join unions;[1] and employees cannot be fired for exercising this right.[2] However, the right of public employees to join a union is not without restriction. Such restrictions may be imposed if it can be shown that they are the least drastic means of achieving a substantial and legitimate governmental interest.

In an organizing drive, a public employer may try to prevent employees from joining a union affiliated with a national union; or—as often happens with police—contend that the employees may only join a union made up of employees who do the same kind of work; or bar supervisors from being affiliated with the same union which represents the people they supervise. Whether the employer can impose these limitations depends partly on how the courts have interpreted the meaning of the freedom of association and partly on the employer's own actions.

---

[1]*Atkins v. Charlotte, N.C.*, 296 F. Supp. 1068, 70 LRRM 2732 (W.D.N.C. 1969). Public employees "are granted the right of free association by the First and Fourteenth Amendments of the United States Constitution; that right of association includes the right to form and join a labor union." *See, e.g., Lontine v. VanCleave*, 483 F.2d 966, 84 LRRM 2445 (10th Cir. 1973); *State, County & Municipal Employees v. Woodward*, 406 F.2d 137, 70 LRRM 2317 (8th Cir. 1969); *Police Officers Guild v. Washington*, 369 F. Supp. 543, 85 LRRM 2203 (D.D.C. 1973). *See Federation of City Employees v. Arrington* (CV 82 500–274) (10th Cir. 1982).

[2]*Lontine v. VanCleave*, note 1, above; *State, County & Municipal Employees v. Woodward*, note 1, above; *McLaughlin v. Tilendis*, 398 F.2d 287, 71 LRRM 2097 (7th Cir. 1968).

In this area more than many others, courts differ a great deal in their interpretations. For example:

- Prohibitions against public employees joining a union with national or international affiliation are generally, though not always, struck down.[3]
- Prohibitions against police joining an organization not exclusively limited to full-time law enforcement officers are sometimes upheld[4] and sometimes struck down[5] (upheld on the ground that such a limitation is necessary to insure that police officers can be impartial and neutral in handling labor disputes; and to avoid possible conflict of interests).
- Prohibitions against supervisors belonging to the same unions as employees they supervise are usually, though not always, upheld on the ground that such prohibitions maintain discipline by supervisors and preserve their undivided loyalty to management.[6]
- Prohibitions on membership in a union affiliated with a union asserting the right to strike are usually struck down.[7]

Even though a public employer may not be constitutionally prohibited from putting some limitations on the kind of unions employees can join, the employer may have acted in a way to make such limitations impermissible. For example, if the employer has not objected to sanitation supervisors being in the same union as employees they supervise, the employer will not likely be able successfully to restrict recreation department supervisors from being in the same union as the employees they supervise.[8]

---

[3]*Atkins v. Charlotte, N.C.*, note 1, above. Mere apprehension that affiliation with a national labor union might increase chances of public employee strikes is not enough to justify interference with employees' rights. Problem can be addressed by outlawing strikes. *Levasseur v. Wheeldon*, 112 N.W.2d 894, 49 LRRM 2525 (S.D. Sup.Ct. 1964).

[4]*Brennan v. Koch*, 564 F. Supp. 322 (S.D.N.Y. 1983). In *Brennan*, the court upheld a challenged statute under which police were free to join unions which admitted nonpolice to membership; however, such nonpolice unions could not be certified to be the exclusive representative for police.

[5]*Mescall v. Rochford*, 655 F.2d 111 (7th Cir. 1981).

[6]*Key v. Rutherford*, 645 F.2d 880, 107 LRRM 2321 (10th Cir. 1981); *Elk Grove Firefighters Local 2340 v. Willis*, 400 F. Supp. 1097, 90 LRRM 2447 (N.D. Ill. 1975), *aff'd*, 539 F.2d 714, 93 LRRM 2019 (7th Cir. 1976)(unpublished order); *Firefighters Local 2263 v. Tupelo*, 439 F. Supp. 1224, 96 LRRM 3098 (N.D. Miss. 1977); *Police Ass'ns Local 189 v. Barrett*, 111 LRRM 2728 (N.D. Ga. 1982); *Federation of City Employees v. Arrington*, note 1, above.

[7]*Police Officers Guild v. Washington*, note 1, above; *Atkins v. Charlotte, N.C.*, note 1, above; *Brennan v. Koch*, note 4, above; *Postal Clerks v. Blount*, 325 F. Supp. 879, 76 LRRM 2932 (D.D.C. 1971).

[8]The equal protection clause requires that the government treat similarly situated employees alike.

In one case, *Mescall v. Rochford*, an employer claimed restriction of police to a police-only union was necessary to insure police neutrality in labor disputes of other workers and to avoid conflicts of interest.[9] The facts were, however, that police were allowed to moonlight in other jobs and were free to join unions in those other jobs. In a decision siding with the police officers, the Court of Appeals for the Seventh Circuit pointed out that if one of those unions went on strike, the police would have at least as much conflict of interest as if a nonpolice affiliate of the local police union went on strike. Furthermore, police officers were free to join civil, fraternal, ethnic, and other organizations which held frequent demonstrations and other activities, and in such cases they might have to enforce the law against members of an organization to which they themselves belonged. While acknowledging that the restrictive rule might avoid some potential conflicts of interest, the court struck down the limitation. The court held the restriction to be unreasonable, arbitrary, and an impermissible limitation on the police officers' freedom of association.

When faced with a situation where restrictions exist on which union or type of union the employees may join, an organizer should first check the statute to see if the restrictions are spelled out there and whether or not anyone has challenged any restrictions in court.[10] Find out why the employer claims the restriction is necessary. If the employer gives no reason or gives a reason that cannot stand up to scrutiny, the union may be able successfully to challenge the restriction.

## Nonemployee organizers

Establishment of a union does not just happen. It takes hard work by everyone—from the organizer to the employees at the workplace being organized. Generally, the most experienced organizers are full-time organizers; they probably do not work for the city, county, or state whose employees are being organized. While a public employer may not prohibit public employees from discussing union or organizational business among themselves outside working time (e.g., lunch or breaks),[11] the employer may try to put limits on who can organize by prohibiting "outside" (nonemployee) organizers.

---

[9]*Mescall v. Rochford*, note 5, above.

[10]A few collective bargaining statutes contain limits on the types of unions certain employees can join. Just because the limitations are in the statute, however, does not necessarily mean they are constitutional.

[11]Any employer policy that seeks to restrict such conversation would be unconstitutional. *Hall v. Board of School Comm'rs, Mobile County*, 681 F.2d 965 (5th Cir. 1982); *McGill v.*

Whether such a limitation is permissible will depend in part on what other actions the employer has taken. Are there other groups of the employer's employees who are also organized or attempting to get organized? Did that other group use outside organizers? If the employer allows one group of employees to be organized by an outside organizer, the employer will have to offer a very persuasive reason why outside organizers should be banned for another group.[12]

What if no other employees are organized? Or what if other employees who are organized did it without an outside organizer? Does the First Amendment guarantee of freedom of association allow public employees (or their union) to select the spokesman of their choice without limitation?

To the extent the organizer is meeting with employees *off* the employer's property, the employees are free to have whomever they want as their organizer. In addition, an employer's rule preventing nonemployee organizers from meeting with employees on their breaks on government property may be improper depending on whether the facility is considered a "public forum."[13]

In general, any rule by the employer attempting to restrict the choice of an organizer only to employees should be scrutinized carefully. An organizer should find out the employer's practices, see if they are applied uniformly, and check the employer's justification for such action.

In cases in which an employer agrees to meet or bargain with a union even though not legally required to do so, the employer is severely restricted in its ability to limit the union's representatives to employees only.

The following justifications for restrictions against nonemployee or outside organizers have been rejected by the courts:

(1) Discussion with professional union representatives encourages strife and discord; and
(2) Direct discussions with employees are more efficient in finding mutually acceptable solutions.

These reasons are insufficient when balanced against the facts that none of the local employees is experienced or skilled in presenting

---

*Board of Educ.*, 602 F.2d 774 (7th Cir. 1979); *see Pickering v. Board of Educ.*, 391 US 563 (1968); *Tinker v. Des Moines Indep. Community School Dist.*, 393 US 503 (1969).

[12]Under the equal protection clause, the employer must have a good explanation to justify treating similarly situated employees differently.

[13]*Garland Indep. School Dist. v. Texas State Teachers' Ass'n*, 107 S.Ct. 41, 123 LRRM 2592 (1986), *aff'g without opinion*, 777 F.2d 1046, 123 LRRM 2533 (5th Cir. 1985). See discussion of "public forums" at 72.

employee grievances or discussing employment matters and that non-employee representatives are less subject to intimidation and harassment and are therefore more effective advocates.[14]

## Access to Employer Property

In the early stages of organizing, it is important to check what written rules, if any, the government employer has. Who can come on to public property? Who can use rooms for a meeting? What time limits are there for meetings? What sign-up procedures exist? Who can use any internal mail system or bulletin boards? It is also important to check what rules exist governing demonstrations or picketing on public property, for example, sidewalks.[15] Sometimes the rules—especially on such things as demonstrations—are part of the statutes or ordinances of the jurisdiction.[16] The rules on trespass to public property should be checked as well.

In addition to learning what written rules there are, the organizer should check on the actual practice. If there are no written rules, actual practice is important. Even if there are written rules, it is important to know if actual practice deviates from official policy. For example, if official rules say that the rooms of the government office building are not available for use by any group that is not conducting official government business, and yet many organizations hold regular meetings in the building without conducting official government business, then the employer may not be able to close the meeting rooms for union organizing meetings.

As in many other areas, the government employer may have by its own actions made itself more "accessible" than required. As described below, the employer may have a legitimate policy of limiting access to its meeting rooms, but if it breaks the policy for one group, it may have to break it for other groups.

---

[14]*O'Brien v. Leidinger*, 452 F. Supp. 720, 98 LRRM 2998 (E.D. Va. 1978). *See also Kenai Peninsula Borough School Dist. v. Kenai Peninsula Borough School Dist. Classification Ass'n*, 590 P.2d 437, 100 LRRM 3116 (Alaska S.Ct. 1979).

[15]Permit requirements are not uncommon. However, a permit or license requirement is not permissible if it may be granted or withheld at the discretion of an official. *Shuttlesworth v. Birmingham, Ala.*, 394 US 147 (1969). In *Teamsters Local 391 v. Rocky Mount, N.C.*, 672 F.2d 376, 109 LRRM 3114 (4th Cir. 1982), the court struck down a city ordinance which prohibited all picketing on city streets without a prior permit, since the law was an overly broad restriction of First Amendment free speech.

[16]One source of information is the police department's public information office, if the circumstances are appropriate for making such inquiry. Such an office can point out any limits on demonstrations or parades, where there are any criminal penalties for unauthorized entry to public buildings, etc.

What kind of limits may the public employer constitutionally put on access to its property and facilities? While the right to inform workers about the advantages of joining a labor union is constitutionally protected by the First Amendment,[17] governments do have the right to preserve their property for its intended use, and do not have to let all comers use the public facilities for any purpose they desire.[18] There are a number of general guidelines on what kind of restrictions on access to a public employer's property are permissible. These guidelines are the result of a series of court decisions and depend upon whether the employer's facility is regarded as a public forum, limited public forum, or nonpublic forum.

## Public Forums

If the property is a traditional "public forum,"[19] such as a park, sidewalk, or street, the government's ability to constitutionally restrict "expressive activity" such as solicitation, speaking out, and leaflet distribution is quite limited. In public forums, an attempt to restrict expression because of its message, ideas, subject matter, or content is generally unconstitutional. An example of a rule which is not "content neutral" is a rule that prohibits solicitation or picketing by a labor organization but permits solicitation or picketing by other groups. This type of rule is not permissible in a traditional "public forum."[20]

A rule (or practice) of a county council which routinely permits individuals and representatives of organizations to present their views during regularly scheduled meetings, but attempts to prevent its employees from expressing views on employment matters, or prevents a representative of a labor organization from presenting the collective views of its members at one of its meetings is content-based and is not constitutionally permissible.[21] The only time a content-based re-

---

[17]*Thomas v. Collins*, 323 US 516, 532, 15 LRRM 777 (1945).

[18]*Adderly v. Florida*, 385 US 39 (1966); *Members of City Council v. Taxpayers for Vincent*, 466 US 789 (1984).

[19]Public forums are "places which by long tradition or government fiat have been devoted to assembly and debate." *Perry Educ. Ass'n v. Perry Local Educators' Ass'n*, 460 US 37, 112 LRRM 2766 (1983).

[20]Similarly, a rule permitting labor picketing in public forums but prohibiting other kinds of picketing is not permissible. *Police Dep't of Chicago v. Mosely*, 408 US 92 (1972); *Grayned v. City of Rockford*, 408 US 104 (1972); *Carey v. Brown*, 447 US 455 (1980).

[21]*Madison Joint School Dist. No. 8 v. Wisconsin Employment Relations Comm'n*, 429 US 167, 93 LRRM 2970 (1976); *Firefighters Local 2653 v. Hickory, N.C.*, 656 F.2d 917, 108 LRRM 2096 (4th Cir. 1981); *Firefighters Local 1568 v. Board of Supervisors, Henrico County*, 549 F.2d 237, 107 LRRM 2432 (4th Cir. 1981); *Firefighters Local 2106 v. Rock Hill, S.C.*, 660 F.2d 97, 108 LRRM 2383 (4th Cir. 1981).

striction is permissible is if the restriction is narrowly drawn and necessary to serve a compelling state interest.[22]

Reasonable restrictions regulating the time, place, and manner of expressive activity in a public forum which are "content-neutral" and are not geared to restricting a message, ideas, or subject matter are acceptable as long as they are narrowly tailored and leave open ample alternative channels of communication.[23] Thus, although a rule requiring permits or licenses before marching in public forums is generally permissible,[24] conditioning use of public forums on payment of large administrative fees and obtaining expensive insurance more than necessary to protect the government's interests is not.[25] A rule prohibiting displaying any flag, banner, or device (including leafletting and picketing) on the sidewalk around the Supreme Court building was struck down by that Court.[26]

## Limited Public Forums

Sometimes public property becomes a public forum because the government has opened it for use by the public or part of the public as a place for expressive activity. Even though the government did not have to open the property for expressive use by the public in the first place,[27] once it does open it and as long as it keeps it open, it is bound by the same constitutional limits that apply to a traditional public forum.[28] For example, in *Ysleta Federation of Teachers v. Ysleta Independent School District*, in a situation where the employer had opened the school's internal mails to all employee organizations, the employer's policy of prior clearance of messages to insure that the use did not interfere with school use as determined by the superintendent was found to be unconstitutionally vague because it did not set forth "clear precise standards capable of objective determination" to limit the superintendent's discretion. In its decision, the Court of Appeals

---

[22]*See also, U.S. S.W. Africa/Namibia Trade & Cultural Council v. United States*, 708 F.2d 760 (D.C. Cir. 1983) (advertising areas at publicly owned airport are public forums. Government ban on political versus commercial or public service advertisements is a content-based restriction; because it does not narrowly serve a compelling state interest, it is impermissible).

[23]*Perry Educ. Ass'n v. Perry Local Educator's Ass'n*, note 19, above; *United States Postal Serv. v. Council of Greenburgh Civic Assocs.*, 453 US 114, 132 (1981).

[24]*Cox v. New Hampshire*, 312 US 569 (1941).

[25]*Eastern Conn. Citizens Action Group v. Powers*, 723 F.2d 1050 (2d Cir. 1983).

[26]*United States v. Grace*, 461 US 171 (1983).

[27]The courts call these "limited" or "designated" public forums.

[28]Regulations based on *content* are permissible only if the regulation is necessary to serve a compelling state interest and is narrowly drawn to achieve that end. Regulations on the *time, place, and manner* of speech which are not based on the content of the speech are permissible if they are narrowly tailored to serve a significant government interest and leave open ample alternative channels of communication.

for the Fifth Circuit held the superintendent's practice of refusing to give clearance to statements that opposed official school policy not permissible. It also found that the employer's rule providing that organizations could only put union recruitment literature in the mails one time each year, when the school term began, was impermissible unless the employer could prove the policy was narrowly drawn to further a compelling state interest.[29]

In these "limited" or "designated" public forum situations, it is important to look at to whom the government has given access, since the constitutional right of access only extends to other entities of similar character.[30] Thus, a state university which makes its facilities available for registered student groups cannot constitutionally prohibit a registered student religious group from using its facilities.[31]

## Nonpublic Forums

Public property which is not by "tradition" or "designation" a forum for public communication is treated by the courts as a nonpublic forum. Nonpublic forums are governed by different standards of access than public forums. Just because a government-owned building or grounds is public property does not make it a "public" forum. Nor does the fact that the public is permitted to freely enter and leave the grounds at practically all times and the public is admitted to the building at specified hours transform the building into a "public forum."[32]

The government, like private property owners, has the right to preserve its property for its intended use. As long as the government has not by its own actions opened its property to the public as a place for expressive activity, it does not have to allow public access to its property for expressive purposes. The constitutional limitation on the government's power to curtail the public's expressive activity on property that is not a public forum is that the regulation on speech should be reasonable and should not be an effort to suppress expression because public officials oppose the speaker's view.[33] In nonpublic for-

---

[29]*Ysleta Fed'n of Teachers v. Ysleta Indep. School Dist.*, 720 F.2d 1429, 115 LRRM 2096 (5th Cir. 1983).

[30]*Widmar v. Vincent*, 454 US 263 (1981). In *Perry Educ. Ass'n v. Perry Local Educators' Ass'n*, note 19, above, the Court held that even if civic and church organizations had been given access to school mailboxes thereby transforming them into "limited" public forum, the purposes of a rival union's communications were entirely different from those of the civic organizations that had been granted access, so the rival union was not entitled to the limited public forum.

[31]*Widmar v. Vincent*, note 30, above.

[32]*See Greer v. Spock*, 424 US 828 (1976).

[33]*United States Postal Serv. v. Council of Greenburgh Civic Assocs.*, note 23, above. *See Jones v. North Carolina Prisoners' Union*, 433 US 119 (1977) (upholding ban on certain union activity of inmates); *Lehman v. Shaker Heights*, 418 US 298 (1974) upholding ban on political advertising from "car cards" on city buses).

ums, the government may make distinctions concerning access on the basis of subject matter and speaker identity if they are "reasonable in light of the purpose which the forum at issue serves."[34]

In *Perry Education Ass'n v. Perry Educator's Ass'n*,[35] the Supreme Court upheld a public employer's restriction on use of school mail facilities to the exclusive representative but not to any other union. In this case, the Court found the school had not made the school mail system a limited public forum, because it had restricted the system's use to those who participated in the school's official business. Under this approach the union, as the exclusive representative of the employees, was not a part of the public, but an organization with special responsibilities related to school business. Therefore, the Court found the exclusion reasonable because of the need to insure "labor-peace within the schools" and because there were substantial alternative channels of communication for the many rival unions.[36]

Acknowledging that even in situations where no public forum is involved, "the government cannot suppress expression merely because the public officials oppose the speaker's view," the Court found that limiting use of the internal mail system to the exclusive representative was not a distinction based on the *views* of the organizations, but on the *status* of the organizations.[37]

An important factor in deciding whether or not a restriction is aimed at the views of an organization (and is therefore impermissible) is the availability of alternate channels of communication to the excluded group. In *Perry*, the rival union had access to school property after hours, access to the school bulletin boards, and with permission,

---

[34]*Perry Educ. Ass'n v. Perry Local Educators' Ass'n*, note 19, above, 460 US at 49. *NAACP Legal Defense & Educ. Fund v. Devine*, 727 F.2d 1247 (D.C. Cir. 1984).

[35]Note 19, above.

[36]*Id.* at 52. One difference between the *Perry* case and the *Ysleta* case is that since the school in *Ysleta* had indeed opened its mail system to all employee organizations, it had made the mails into a limited public forum. In *Perry*, since the school had not opened the mail system to all employee organizations, but only to the exclusive representative, the school had not made the mails into a public forum. In *Texas State Teacher's Ass'n v. Garland Indep. School Dist.*, 777 F.2d 1046, 123 LRRM 2533 (5th Cir. 1985), *aff'd without opinion*, _____US _____, 107 S.Ct. 41, 123 LRRM 2592 (1986), the court upheld regulations which denied an outside union representative access to school grounds during school hours and use of school mail facilities, despite the fact that the employer permitted selected groups of educators, textbook salesmen, and representatives of civic and charitable organizations to meet with students and faculty during nonclass school hours.

[37]On the other hand, in a state which did not have a collective bargaining law for faculty, a university policy was impermissible which prohibited use of university facilities (including the use of the campus mail system) to faculty organizations that had as their goal the organization of university employees for purposes of collective bargaining while permitting access to those facilities by faculty organizations which did not advocate the right to bargain collectively. This restriction was designed to suppress expression because the administration opposed the views expressed by the advocates of collective bargaining. *Professional Ass'n of College Educators, TSTA/NEA v. El Paso County Community College Dist.*, 730 F.2d 258, 116 LRRM 2150 (5th Cir. 1984), *cert. denied*, 469 US 881, 105 S.Ct. 248 (1984).

use of the school's public address system. In addition, the rival union could communicate by mouth, telephone, and the U.S. mail.[38]

The same principles that apply to school mail systems apply to school bulletin boards, public address systems, and meeting rooms. The public employer does not have to open these facilities to any outside groups,[39] but once it does, it not only may not exclude similar groups, but it is also limited in the restrictions it can put on the communications.

This discussion of the constitutional principles bearing on access to government property applies to all jurisdictions, whether or not they have a public sector collective bargaining law. If there is a collective bargaining law, there may be more access to government facilities by virtue of such law than the Constitution requires.

## Solicitation and Distribution of Literature

Although rules on solicitation and distribution of literature under the applicable public sector collective bargaining law may differ somewhat from rules that have developed in the private sector, the private sector rules are a good starting point.[40]

In the private sector, different rules have evolved covering distribution of union literature and solicitation of membership on the employer's property. Furthermore, there is one set of rules for employee organizers and another for nonemployee or professional organizers. In both the public sector and the private sector, organizers are free to hand out literature and solicit workers on public property such as sidewalks. And if the public employer has opened property which is otherwise not open to the public for literature distribution and/or membership solicitation at any time, the employer may not deny the same rights to distribute literature and/or solicit membership relating to a union. Assuming the employer has not opened its property for unlimited distribution and solicitation, however, the following general rules, modeled after the rules that have evolved in the private sector, may well apply:

---

[38]*See Houston Fed'n of Teachers Local 2415 v. Houston Indep. School Dist.* (D.S. Tex., CA No. H-83-719, 1983) upholding a restriction on union organizers' access to teacher's lounge where lounge was closed to parents, students, and vendors and when alternative channels of communication existed.

[39]Even if an employee organization cannot get access to a meeting room, if the employer permits employees to use meeting rooms, a group of employees should be able to get a meeting room without the sponsorship or auspices of the employees' organization.

[40]*See* S.I. Schlossberg & J.A. Scott, *Organizing and the Law* 48–55, 261–263 (3d ed. 1983).

(1) An employer may ban outside (nonemployee) union organizers from distributing or soliciting on the employer's property, except where the employees may not reasonably be reached otherwise or where the ban is applied discriminatorily.

(2) An employer also may prohibit workers from union distribution and solicitation during their working hours, unless it is shown that the rule was adopted for a discriminatory purpose or was unfairly applied.

(3) An employer normally may not bar employees from engaging in distribution or solicitation on company property during their nonworking time, unless there are special circumstances making such rules necessary in order to maintain production or discipline.

# 6

# Organizing in the Absence of Statutory Protections

A great many of the nation's most successful unions were organized without the benefit of statutory protection. Many collective bargaining statutes are on the books only because employees organized out of the needs of the workplace and worked to achieve contracts and protective legislation from that organizing base. Whether organizing or statutory protection comes first is almost a chicken-and-egg question.

Chapters 4 and 5 covered some of the constitutional and other protections public sector unions can use, even without a collective bargaining statute. However, where no protective bargaining statute exists, two questions are centrally important to the organizer. They are:

(1) If a group of employees is organized, will they be able to stay together and develop the resources necessary to support a real labor organization?
(2) Will employer recognition and bargaining be achievable at the target even without a statute?

Even if there is no collective bargaining statute, union representation of some sort is always possible. In determining whether to attempt to organize employees in a state without a collective bargaining statute, it is important to know not only the ground rules for organizing, but also how much the union will be able to do for the employees once they have expressed their desire for union membership and/or representation.

## The Importance of Dues Checkoff

The availability of voluntary dues checkoff is a very important consideration in the context of organizing without statutory protection. In many situations, it will be the minimum needed to develop an effective organization in the event of organizing successes. Voluntary, unfunded associations can get off the ground. Hand collection of dues, combined with "bake sales" and voluntary contributions may help get an organization moving, but without the stable, assured financial support of employer checkoff of dues from members' payroll, it is difficult for an organization to sustain itself over the long run.

Dues checkoff occurs when an employer deducts an amount from employees' paychecks for union dues and transmits that amount to the union. Checkoff is at the member's request. Normally, the amount checked off is a pro rata share of annual dues each pay period and is deducted from the employee's gross pay just like federal and state taxes, Social Security taxes (FICA), pension contributions, or charity contributions. With union dues checkoff, it is easier for the union to collect dues since it does not have to hand collect them from each member; it is also easier for the union member, who needs to do nothing but sign a card to authorize the employer to check off the amount.

In many states, there are laws which address whether and under what circumstances union dues can be checked off.[1] It is not uncommon to provide that union dues can be checked off upon a written authorization from the employee even before any union has been selected as the exclusive bargaining representative. Appendix E contains a sample form authorizing dues checkoff. Union dues checkoff is sometimes expressly authorized by law even though there is no collective bargaining law in the jurisdiction.[2] And in still other places, the laws and regulations say nothing about dues checkoff.

---

[1]Challenges are often made to dues checkoff even when there is a statute expressly providing for dues checkoff. *Morial v. Council of New Orleans*, 413 So.2d 185 (La. App. 1982) (upholding dues checkoff ordinance against claim by Mayor that formulation of a dues checkoff policy was prerogative of the executive branch).

[2]Under some of these statutes, if the employees are already represented by a union as an exclusive representative, the employer may not be free of checkoff dues to any other labor organization. In a few states, dues checkoff to a nonexclusive representative is permitted. Compare *Bauch v. City of New York*, 21 N.Y.2d 599, 237 N.E.2d 211, 67 LRRM 2994, *cert. denied*, 393 U.S. 834, 69 LRRM 2435 (1968); *Service Employees Local 22 v. County of Sacramento*, 28 Cal. App. 3d 424, 81 LRRM 2841 (1972) (upholding limiting dues checkoff to the exclusive representative) with *Milwaukee Fed'n of Teachers Local 252 v. Wisconsin Employment Relations Comm'n*, 266 N.W. 2d 314, 98 LRRM 2870 (Wis. Sup.Ct. 1978) (finding it an unfair labor practice for a municipal employer to refuse dues checkoff for a minority union when it checks off dues to the exclusive representative).

The first places to look to see if dues checkoff is authorized are the statutes, ordinances, and regulations. Even if there is no express authorization for dues checkoff and even if there is no collective bargaining, it may be possible to get dues checkoff if the employer is checking off dues to other unions. Since the equal protection clause of the Constitution requires public employers to treat similar entities in the same way unless the employer has a legitimate reason to treat them differently, once the employer checks off dues to one union, it may have to check off dues to other unions.[3]

What if the employer does not currently check off dues for any union, but does check off or deduct from employees' paychecks amounts for charities, a credit union, pension programs, or optional insurance programs? Can the union insist on having checkoff on the ground that the employer checks off money to similar groups? The union can always try to insist—and may be successful. However, unless the employer is checking off to other membership organizations, the union probably will not be able to get the courts to force the employer to check off union dues.[4]

If the employer does agree to check off dues, the employer may impose reasonable requirements, uniformly imposed.[5] However, there is always the risk where the employer is checking off dues voluntarily without compulsion of statute or contract that the employer will stop doing so. As long as the employer treats all similar unions the same the employer probably is free to stop dues checkoff in these circumstances.[6]

---

[3]Employers may successfully argue that police and fire unions are different enough to be treated differently from other unions; however, if the city checks off dues to the firemen's union, it will most likely have to check off dues to the police union and vice versa. *Teamsters Local 728 v. City of Atlanta*, 468 F. Supp. 620, 101 LRRM 2335 (N.D. Ga. 1979).

[4]*City of Charlotte v. Firefighters Local 660*, 426 US 283, 92 LRRM 2597 (1976) denying the union's attempt to force dues checkoff, accepting the city's explanation that it allows withholding or deduction only for programs (like insurance, pension, charities) which benefit all employees of a city or a department. Since union dues checkoff would only benefit certain employees of a department who join the union, it did not qualify.

[5]*Brown v. Alexander*, 718 F.2d 1417, 115 LRRM 3085 (6th Cir. 1984) (upholding Tennessee's requirement that an organization must have at least 20 percent of the employees in the executive branch as members before it can obtain dues checkoff; but striking down the provision that dues checkoff is unavailable to an organization that is affiliated with any other organization, as impermissibly limiting employees' freedom of association; however, upholding requirement that checkoff is only available to a wholly domestic (Tennessee) organization as rationally related to a state interest in favoring a domestic state organization over a foreign organization).

[6]*See Arkansas State Highway Employees Local 1315 v. Kell*, 628 F.2d 1099, 105 LRRM 2304 (8th Cir. 1980).

## Jurisdictional Differences

The answer to the question of what the union can do in the absence of a collective bargaining law varies a great deal from place to place so it is important for the organizer to check his or her jurisdiction. The state-by-state listing in Part 2 of this book indicates which employees are covered by collective bargaining statutes. In some places, there is no collective bargaining law for any employees in the state; in other places, nearly all public employees are covered by a collective bargaining statute. In still other states, some groups of employees (e.g., police, firefighters) are granted collective bargaining rights by statute, while other groups in the same state do not have such rights.

In only a few states is it against the law or public policy for public employers to enter into collective bargaining agreements with public employee unions. Even in some of those places—for example, in many Virginia localities—public employee unions play a significant role, though short of collective bargaining. Absent collective bargaining, unions can represent their members in whatever appeal procedure the employer has established (often a civil service commission procedure); can lobby the legislative body on measures of concern to employees including—but surely not limited to—budget matters; can file complaints (e.g., equal employment opportunity) with administrative agencies or courts on behalf of their members; and can take many other actions on behalf of the employees. Chapter 2, in discussing the different employee relations models, highlights some of the diverse roles of employee organizations.

In fact, except in the few places where it is against the law for public employers to bargain collectively, most public employers have the authority to enter into an enforceable collective bargaining agreement, even in the absence of a collective bargaining law.

The difference between jurisdictions with a collective bargaining law and those without a law is that in the latter, no matter how much the employees support a union and let the employer know of this support, the employer does not have to deal with any union, except if the employer chooses to do so. And the employer can pretty well establish the ground rules on which it will deal with unions. For example, the employer can decide whether it will voluntarily recognize a union or will require an election. The employer can decide whether it will deal with the union as a representative of its members only or as an exclusive representative of all people in a "bargaining unit." Also the employer can unilaterally define the appropriate bargaining unit if there is no statute.

## Past and Present Employer Practice

Once the employer does choose to deal with a union for some of its employees, however, it may not be able to refuse to deal with a union for others of its employees. In a jurisdiction without a collective bargaining law, it is important to find out if the employer has met with, bargained with, or agreed to hold a representation election involving any union. In such a jurisdiction, the answer to whether an employer must bargain with a union depends in part on what the employer is already doing.

While there is a constitutional right to join a union, as outlined in Chapter 5, there is no constitutional duty to bargain collectively.[7] If there is no statute or ordinance providing for bargaining, and the employer is not already dealing with any union for any of its employees,[8] courts will almost certainly not impose an obligation to bargain on a public employer. In these situations, unless the employer is willing to bargain with a union even in the absence of legislation, employee organizations must apply their efforts to achieving legislation or an executive order.

If a particular employer has decided to recognize a union for some employees, the employer may not be completely free to refuse to recognize a union for others of its employees. Since the Constitution requires the government to treat similar groups in a similar fashion, the public employer cannot without reason agree to let some of its employees be represented while refusing other similar employees representation.

In practice, the courts will usually either find enough difference between types of employees to hold that the groups are not "similar" or find that the employer does have a legitimate reason for treating different groups of employees differently. Thus, courts have upheld an employer's granting bargaining rights to police, but not to any other groups of employees;[9] upheld an employer's granting bargaining rights

---

[7]Courts uniformly have found that an employer's refusal to bargain collectively does not impair freedom of association. *See, e.g., Smith v. Arkansas State Highway Employees Local 1315,* 441 US 463, 465, 101 LRRM 2091 (1979); *Hanover Township Fed'n of Teachers Local 1954 v. Hanover Community School Corp.,* 457 F.2d 456, 79 LRRM 2299 (7th Cir. 1972).

[8]*See Chapter 5.*

[9]*State, County & Municipal Employees v. Jefferson County,* 110 LRRM 2372 (W.D. Ky. 1982).

to nonacademic employees of a board of education but not to police;[10] upheld granting bargaining rights to teachers but not to noncertified school employees;[11] upheld denying bargaining rights to teachers, while granting them to firefighters;[12] and upheld denying bargaining rights to police, while granting them to firefighters.[13]

Different treatment of police, firefighters, and teachers from each other and from other types of employees will almost always be justified by the courts—at least on the question of whether the employer must bargain collectively. However, the courts are more likely to find non-uniformed, noncertificated employees to be similar and to require similar treatment. Therefore, if the employer is already bargaining for sanitation workers and recreation aides, the courts may well require the employer to deal with a union representing the secretaries or other nonuniformed, noncertificated employees.

## Union Recognition Procedures

Public sector collective bargaining laws typically contain procedures for choosing an exclusive representative. What are the procedures if no law spells them out?

An employer that is willing to deal with a union, even though no collective bargaining law requires it, can pretty well spell out whatever procedures for recognition it wants, as long as it does not treat similarly situated groups differently. The employer may agree to voluntarily recognize a union or may require an election. The employer's rules may be explicit on how the election shall be conducted and by whom; the rules may be general; or the employer may have no rules at all. Often the organization seeking to represent employees has (or can take) a significant role in deciding how the election will be conducted. Some questions union organizers will want answered include:

- Who will be eligible to vote?
- What notification of the scheduled election will occur?

---

[10]*Confederation of Police v. City of Chicago*, 529 F.2d 89, 91 LRRM 2195 (7th Cir.), *vacated on other grounds*, 427 US 902, 92 LRRM 2918 (1976).

[11]*Charles County Supporting Servs. Employees Local 301 v. Board of Educ.*, 48 Md. App. 339, 427 A.2d 1025 (Md. Ct. Spec. App. 1981).

[12]*Beauboeuf v. Delgado College*, 303 F. Supp. 861, 72 LRRM 2222 (E.D. La. 1969), *aff'd per curiam*, 428 F.2d 470, 74 LRRM 2767 (5th Cir. 1970).

[13]*Beverin v. Board of Police Comm'rs of Kansas City, Mo.*, 722 F.2d 395, 114 LRRM 3525 (8th Cir. 1983). See also *Sikes v. Boone*, 116 LRRM 2192 (11th Cir. 1983), *aff'g* 562 F. Supp. 74, 116 LRRM 2172 (N.D. Fla. 1983), *cert. denied*, _____US _____, 116 LRRM 2192 (1984) (denying bargaining rights to deputy sheriffs while granting them to police and other public employees).

- How much advance notice will be given?[14]
- What will the ballot say and how will it get printed?
- Will the voting be by secret ballot or by mail? (Except in unusual circumstances, in-person voting is preferred to mail ballots.)
- At what location or locations will polling occur?
- What hours will the polls be open?
- What campaigning, if any, can take place near the polls?
- Who will check in eligible voters and pass out ballots?
- Will the parties have observers, and if so, how will they be chosen, what are their duties, and how many will there be?
- How will security of the ballot boxes be assured?
- Who will count the ballots and when?
- How many votes are required to win?
- How will run-off elections be handled?
- How will challenges to the eligibility of voters be handled?
- Will there be a procedure for objections to the conduct of the election?
- Who will bear the cost of the election?

Typically, the answers to most of these questions are contained in election rules or an election agreement. Appendix F contains a sample election agreement.[15]

It is generally best to have an impartial organization conduct the election. It is very important to check reputations and costs of any private organizations that offer this service. In many jurisdictions, a state agency (usually part of the labor department) is available and experienced to conduct the election upon the request of all parties. The American Arbitration Association (AAA), with offices all over the country, also conducts representation elections for a fee upon request in accordance with its published rules.

The Federal Mediation and Conciliation Service (FMCS), an impartial agency of the federal government with offices around the country, on occasion conducts representation elections if all parties consent. FMCS has nothing in writing on its procedures, but tailors them to the needs of the parties on a case-by-case basis.

---

[14]For considerations regarding timing of the election, *See* S.I. Schlossberg & J.A. Scott, *Organizing and the Law*, 188 (3d ed. 1983).

[15]*See* S.I. Schlossberg & J.A. Scott, note 14, above, at 329–332 for samples of election agreement forms under Taft-Hartley.

Part Two

# The Rules of Public Sector Organizing

1

# Know the Rules: State and Local Statutory Structures and Analysis

There are two key points for the organizer to remember when setting out to organize the public workplace: know the local rules; and don't be timid about insisting on employee rights. Take the information gained from experience and the technical rules gathered from this book and be assertive. Use the BNA Digest of State Public Employee Bargaining Statutes, reprinted in Appendix A of this volume, to gain an overview of the statute or statutes in your jurisdiction. Use the State-By-State Overview Chart at the end of Part II to determine whether there is a specific statutory provision in your jurisdiction on a given question which may arise during an organizing drive.

Part II is a discussion of the key categories, concepts, and administrative procedures common to state and local collective bargaining systems. These invariably differ in their use and meaning from one jurisdiction to another. While the discussion is generalized, it refers to specific examples from many jurisdictions. The discussion is presented chronologically, that is, from the point at which no employees are organized through the point at which a union has achieved recognition and is ready to begin negotiating a contract.

What follows presents a method of thinking about any public sector collective bargaining statute in a bargaining context. In whatever jurisdiction an organizing drive takes place, and under whatever system, the organizer should be familiar with seven basic features of the statute or local ordinance involved.

First, is there a statute or ordinance in place; does it give authority to an administrative agency; and what employees does it cover or exclude?

Second, are unions subject to reporting or registration regulation; is the deduction of dues available to support a union during the organizing period which proceeds a contract?

Third, is exclusive recognition available, and if so, are recognition election procedures in place; may an employer recognize an exclusive representative without a recognition election?

Fourth, if formal certification procedures exist, how do they work; what "showing of interest" is required to demand an election or to intervene in one; is there an existing contract or a recent recognition bar to a new certification election; are there procedures for decertification?

Fifth, what collective bargaining unit rules are in place; how are units determined; are supervisors excluded or may they be in the same unit with other employees; once a unit certification has been issued, may it be amended?

Sixth, how does the unfair labor practice procedure work; what are its uses in organizing?

Seventh, what is the law with regard to strikes and picketing?

Each feature of the various systems is discussed separately below. After a general discussion of each feature, which includes references to examples of various key elements of that feature, there is a chart or checklist on the rules applicable to organizing in 75 state and local statutory schemes. The chart is a guide as to whether a specific provision exists in the statute covering your specific situation.

## A Summary of the Law of Organizing

### State and Local Statutes

There are at least 75 separate systems of state and local employee relations. The organizer must first establish whether there is a comprehensive collective bargaining law for the public sector employees that he or she wants to organize and whether the statute covers these specific employees. Many general state employee statutes will exclude local government employees; for example, some systems may exclude police and firefighters. On the other hand, even in states that have no general law, there may be statutes or ordinances governing certain categories of employees. A city ordinance or policy directive may allow bargaining even in the absence of express statutory authority.[1]

---

[1]*See* Chapter 6. *See also Littleton Educ. Ass'n v. Arapahoe County School Dist. No. 6,* 191 Colo. 411, 553 P.2d 793 (1976); *Louisiana Teachers' Ass'n v. New Orleans Parish School Bd.,* 303 So.2d 564 (La. Ct. App. 1974), *cert. denied,* 305 So.2d 541 (La. 1975); *Dayton Classroom Teachers v. Dayton Bd. of Educ.,* 41 Ohio St. 2d 127, 323 N.E.2d 714 (1975). *Contra Virginia v. Arlington County Bd.,* 232 S.E.2d 30, 94 LRRM 2291 (1977); *Fayette County*

If there is no statute or ordinance at all, note it immediately. The organizer in the situation faces the special problems outlined in Chapter 6. Organizing may be possible even in situations where no bargaining authority whatever exists. Such situations generate an extremely difficult organizing climate and should not be entered into without a full understanding of the special problems they may present. However, many well-established labor organizations become established and flourish even in the absence of collective bargaining. Check ordinances and statutes that provide for substitutes for collective bargaining. Civil service systems often provide for employee representation in personnel management decisions including cases of employee discipline.[2] The 1986 Amendments to the Federal Fair Labor Standards Act provide that public employers may not use compensatory time in lieu of overtime without an agreement between the employer and an organization representing employees of that employer where such a representative exists. The statute and related regulations clearly state that the representative need not be an organization formally recognized by the employer. All that is needed is designation by the employees involved.[3]

If there is a collective bargaining law, the organizer should learn its popular name. The most comprehensive, detailed statutes tend to be called "Employment Relations Acts" or "Labor Relations Acts." The organizer should also learn any generally used abbreviation, the official citation for the statute or ordinance, the date it was passed, and the date of its most recent amendment. Most of this information appears in Appendix A. The dates of enactment and amendment provide useful insights on how experienced the agency is likely to be, what degree of organizing has occurred in the past, whether the law is of modern or ancient vintage, and how far back the organizer will have to go to find rulings on particular issues under the statute.

### The Administrative Agency

A good indicator of an effective collective bargaining statute is that an agency has been created to administer the statute. If there is

---

*Educ. Ass'n v. Hardy,* 626 S.W.2d 217, 1979–1980 PBCG 37, 057 (Ky. Ct. App. 1980); Dole, "State and Local Public Employee Collective Bargaining in the Absence of Specific Legislative Authority," 54 *Iowa L. Rev.* 539 (1969).

[2] *See* "Defending Civil Service Employees From Discharge," 24 *Am. Jurisprudence Trials* 421 (1977); 15A *Am. Jr.*2d, "Civil Service" §9 (1976). In 1955 only 23 states had civil service laws covering 65% of full-time state employees. In 1970, 84% of the cities, 83% of the counties, and 96% of the states were covered by a merit system. Perritt, *Employee Dismissal Law and Practice,* at 226 n.54. (1984).

[3] *See* FLSA §7(o)(21), 29 U.S.C. 207; 29 C.F.R. §553.23(b)(1) (*Fed. Reg.,* Vol. 51, No. 75, Apr. 18, 1986, 13407).

no such agency, it is fairly certain that employees do not have many statutory rights to enforce. For example, in Oklahoma, where the Public Employee Relations Board was not funded and was dissolved in 1984, it is not surprising that no comprehensive statute exists.

An organizer should feel free to call on the staff of any local public sector labor agency.[4] The staff of such agencies can supply information on the ground rules, as well as referee on whether the rules have been followed. Further, in many situations, the local staff is the only neutral source of information on the traditions and practices that have led to success in organizing. Thus, the better an organizer knows the staff members of an agency, the more comfortable he or she will be once involved in the organizing process, and the more seriously the agency will regard the organizer.

The rules and regulations of most states contain detailed provisions on how the agency is made up, what its duties are, and how far its powers extend. An effective organizer should be familiar with agency regulations of the jurisdiction in which he or she is working. Most boards will provide the public with copies of their rules, regulations, and hearing procedures upon request. Some do much more. The Massachusetts Labor Relations Commission puts out a booklet on its operations and on public sector labor law in Massachusetts. The booklet includes a very useful discussion of the Commission's decisions interpreting the law. Some boards give seminars or training sessions on their statutes. Such opportunities should not be missed even by those fairly familiar with the statute in question since they provide an ideal opportunity to ask questions and to get to know the people who administer the agency. The state of New Jersey operates a labor studies center at Rutgers University that has been very helpful with this type of training.

Does the agency in a given jurisdiction act like the National Labor Relations Board in investigating, issuing, and prosecuting complaints, and in judging and enforcing them? In many states, the agency does some investigation of complaints, but does not "prosecute" the cases, requiring instead that each party prove its own case.[5]

Other items that should be checked include: how are the members of the agency appointed; are they full-time or part-time; how fully is the agency funded; and does the agency customarily report its deci-

---

[4]The administrative agency (or agencies) is listed under individual states in Appendix A, BNA's Digest of State Public Employee Bargaining Statutes.
[5]See Crestwood Educ. Ass'n, MERC, 276 N.W.2d 592, 101 LRRM 2125 (Mich. Ct. App. 1979).

sions? If the decisions are reported, where are they available, is there a good index to the decisions, and how is it used? Without being a lawyer one can learn a great deal about organizing under a public sector collective bargaining act by reading a series of state labor board cases on representational issues. This is particularly true where the state labor board has a tradition of well-written decisions, as do states like Massachusetts, Connecticut, New York, New Jersey, Michigan, Wisconsin, Hawaii, and others.

## Coverage

What categories of employees fall under the protection of the statute? If this is not absolutely clear, the organizer should check the section of the statute that defines "employees" and "employers." Many statutes cover only a single class of employees. For example, state employees, county and municipal employees, teachers and educational employees, and public safety employees are often covered by separate statutes. Some states have several statutory systems in operation.

In addition, some statutes exclude certain groups of employees even within the covered class. The most common exclusion is of "managerial" and "confidential" employees. In most instances the test of "managerial" and "confidential" will follow the National Labor Relations Act model and require involvement in the labor relations process itself. However, every jurisdiction does not apply the test in the same way, and differences between private and public sector management schemes often make application of the test more problematic than it would be under the National Labor Relations Act.[6]

## Unions

### Regulation of Unions

Approximately 20 states have laws requiring either registration or annual financial reports by employee organizations. Other common requirements on labor organizations include: (a) restrictions on who may serve as officers and reporting requirements, (b) restrictions on union political contributions, (c) no-strike affirmations, (d) prohibitions

---

[6]*See* Steven Schlossberg and Judith Scott, *Organizing and the Law,* at 247ff (1983); hereafter Schlossberg.

against discrimination, including discrimination on the basis of membership, which is commonly identified with the duty of fair representation, (e) standards of conduct for elections and for union officers, and (f) limitations on access to the public employer premises.[7]

Other regulations seem to reflect a general fear of outsiders, particularly those affiliated with unions. These often place restrictions on who may serve as officers. For example, Idaho's Professional Negotiating Act requires that the negotiating representative for teacher unions must be a local school teacher,[8] and Nebraska's Teachers' Professional Negotiations Act has a constitutionally questionable requirement that restricts aliens from holding union office.[9] South Dakota law requires that unions not advocate the overthrow of the constitutional form of government.[10]

Many of the restrictions on unions are in portions of the state code which, at least on their face, apply to all unions, public and private. It goes without saying that some of the restrictions are probably not enforceable under the constitution,[11] while others reflect sensible reporting and disclosure procedures that are less stringent than those under the federal rules that apply to private sector unions. Some of the reporting and disclosure information can be useful during organizing drives, especially those in which two unions are competing against each other. Obviously, the best organizer would have available the basic reporting data on all unions involved in an organizing campaign.

## Dues Deduction

The general rule in most jurisdictions regarding dues checkoff is that voluntary dues may be deducted from public employees' paychecks upon their written request, at least after a union has been certified. Many statutes, however, are silent on the subject. Organizers should presume that employers can grant dues deduction unless a law expressly prohibits it. (Chapter 6 reviews the importance of checkoff.)

---

[7]*See, e.g.,* Alaska Stat., Tit. 14, Ch. 20, §560(a) (1975). Hawaii Rev. Stat., Ch. 89, §§89–2 and 89–15 (1982); Kansas Stat. Ann., Ch. 264, §§44–801, 44–805, and §§75–4323(d), 75–4337, and 75–4337(h) (1982); Massachusetts Gen. Laws. Am., Ch. 150E, §§13, 14 and 55 (1982), plus Rules and Regs. §§14.12(41), 15.04(3), 16.05, and 17.03(4); South Dakota Compiled Laws, Ch. 3-13, §§3–18(1)(3) and 18(17); Wisconsin Stat. Ann., Ch. 111, §111.81(a) (1981).

[8]Code of Idaho, Ch. 20, §§20.1–20.26 and –20.28 (1974).

[9]Nebraska Rev. Stat., Ch. 48, §4–106 (1977, amended 1981).

[10]South Dakota Compiled Laws, Ch. 3–113; and Union Regulation Act, Ch. 86, §§17.1105 to 17.11 (1943, amended 1969).

[11]*See Alkins v. City of Charlotte,* 296 F. Supp. 1068 (W.D.N.C. 1969).

Several states, like Hawaii, require employers to deduct dues after certification.[12] These provisions sometimes include exceptions for employees who object to paying dues on *bona fide* religious grounds. The Oregon statute has such a provision which predates similar language in the National Labor Relations Act.[13]

It is not uncommon for a state to have a separate statute concerning dues deduction. Furthermore, checkoff may be established for only certain public employee groups, most frequently state employees, and not for others. In most situations, litigation challenging such systems on equal protection or first amendment grounds has not been successful.[14]

This is a critical area. A union may not be able to sustain itself over the long pull without dues checkoff of some kind. The assured flow of income that comes with checkoff is both a symbolic and a realistic measure of union strength. An organizer should push hard for it and be creative, if necessary, to get it. In some jurisdictions, where checkoff is not provided for by direct legislative authorization but where a system is in place that permits allotments to credit unions or to savings and loan accounts, organizations have successfully established the practical equivalent of dues checkoff by opening a union account and having each member authorize an allotment of dues to that account. This system has worked well for the police associations in Virginia Beach, Virginia; in Jackson, Mississippi; and for a number of firefighter groups around the country.

## Recognition

### *Exclusive Recognition*

Exclusive recognition means that an employer recognizes an organization as the sole representative of a group of its employees on issues relating to labor relations. Nearly all collective bargaining schemes provide for exclusive recognition. Obviously, a state that does not permit exclusive recognition (Arizona, for instance) is not interested

---

[12]*See AIOU Hamada,* 66 Haw. 41, 664 P.2d 727, 115 LRRM 2135 (1983); Hawaii Rev. Stat., Tit. 7, §89–4 (Supp. 1971).

[13]Oregon Rev. Stat., §292.055 (1971); National Labor Relations Act, §19; see Schlossberg, note 6, above, at 124.

[14]*City of Charlotte v. Firefighters Local 660,* 426 U.S. 283 (1976); *AFF Local 995 v. City of Richmond,* 415 F. Supp. 325 (E.D. Va. 1976); *but see Teamsters Local 728 v. City of Atlanta,* 468 F. Supp. 620 (N.D. Ga. 1979).

in collective bargaining in the conventional sense, although it may encourage or permit input from organizations representing employees.[15]

## Recognition Without a Certification Election

In states that have no general collective bargaining statute, state policy may allow a public employer to bargain collectively with a union.[16] Where there is a collective bargaining law, employee organizations may come to be recognized without a full certification election, either by voluntary recognition or by consent elections.

Statutory authorization of voluntary recognition mechanisms, which makes it easier for the union to become the bargaining agent, is one indication that the statute is encouraging collective bargaining. Generally, voluntary recognition is available only after a satisfactory showing that the union is supported by a majority of employees (this is most commonly achieved by card check or dues deductions), and when no competing union has made a timely challenge.[17] In Florida, unions seeking voluntary recognition need to submit a formal petition, although the more traditional practice has been merely to allege majority support and request recognition.[18]

Nebraska requires actual proof of support rather than a mere allegation.[19] New Hampshire provides for voluntary recognition but withholds certification and the benefits that go with it, such as a certification bar, if no election occurs.[20]

Three statutes, Oklahoma's Police and Fire Law, Washington's SEERA, and Wisconsin's MERA, provide for voluntary recognition only where the employer's commission of unfair labor practices has made it impossible to hold a fair election.[21]

Some states expressly provide for "consent elections." This does not mean that the employer and petitioning union can voluntarily agree to recognition. Rather, a consent election means that the administrative agency does not need to conduct a hearing on the representation questions prior to directing an election.[22]

---

[15]See Comment, "The Privilege of Exclusive Recognition and Minority Rights in Public Employment," 55 Cornell L. Rev. 1004 (1970); Lullo v. Firefighters Local 1066, 55 N.J. 409, 262 A.2d 681 (1970); Minnesota State Bd. for Community Colleges v. Knight, 465 U.S. 271 (1984); Perry Educ. Ass'n v. Perry Local Educators' Ass'n, 460 U.S. 37 (1983).

[16]See Chapter 6.

[17]See Schlossberg, note 6, above, Ch. 8.

[18]See Florida Stat., §447.307(1)(a) (1974).

[19]Nebraska Revised Stat., 48–816, (4); Rule 10 (1981).

[20]New Hampshire Rev. Stat. Ann., Ch. 273-A (1979).

[21]Cf. Wis. Stat. Ann., §111.70(4)(d)(1) (1981).

[22]See Schlossberg, note 6, above, Ch. 8, and 180–181.

When an election is directed, the statutes vary regarding what vote is required for certification. The general rule is that a union which has the majority of votes *cast* wins, but some states make certification more difficult. Illinois and Indiana[23] require a vote by the majority of all unit employees *eligible*. The Vermont MLRA requires a majority of 51 percent of those voting.[24]

A number of statutes, generally the less comprehensive laws, as in Idaho, Rhode Island, and Wyoming, do not specify election procedures but do provide for recognition when a union is "designated or selected" by a majority.[25] It is important to check with the administrative agency to see how these provisions have been interpreted.

An organizer should also know whether time restrictions apply to when elections may be conducted. Beside contract, election, and certification bars discussed below, a few statutes, such as those in Tennessee and Connecticut for teachers, and in Maryland for teachers and school employees, impose additional time constraints.[26]

## Certification Procedures

### *Showing of Interest*

When neither voluntary recognition nor a consent election is possible, a formal certification election must be sought by the union which seeks exclusive representation status. A "showing of interest" is the proof of support required to trigger a certification election. The general rule is a 30 percent showing, but the range among states is considerable, from no required percentage to required proof of majority support.[27] It is common that no showing of interest is required when the public employer rather than the union petitions.[28] However, under at least one statute, Wisconsin's MERA, even a petition by the union alone may need no showing of interest.[29] Generally, the showing of interest is by authorization cards. A sample authorization card is set out in Appendix E.

Once a showing of interest is submitted, the next step in an organizing drive is up to the agency. The agency usually checks the

---

[23]*Cf.* Indiana Code Ann., Art. 7.5, Tit. 20, §20–7.5–1–10(c)(4) (1978).
[24]Vermont Stat. Ann., Ch. 20, §1724(e) (1980).
[25]*Cf.* Rhode Island, Tit. 36, Ch. 11, §§36–11–1 *et seq.* (1984).
[26]*Cf.* Tennessee Code Ann., Tit. 49, §49–5–605 (1971).
[27]*See* Schlossberg, note 6, above, Ch. 9.
[28]Code of Iowa, Ch. 20, §20.14(4) (1979).
[29]*Dodge County Employees Local 1323* (WERC 1968), Case VII, No. 12389 ME-405 (1968).

authorization cards against a list of employees submitted by the employer.[30] Determination by an agency that a showing is sufficient is most often a matter within the agency's discretion and not subject to court review.[31]

## Intervention

At times more than one union will want to represent the same workers. Once a certification procedure is under way, with one union on the ballot, a separate showing for "intervention" is at times required for a competing union to get on the same election ballot. The most common requirement is a 10 percent showing, although some states require up to the same 30 percent showing that the original petitioner must establish. This is the requirement for California teachers.[32] The greater 30 percent showing is particularly common when the "intervenor" seeks an election for an "appropriate unit" which is different from the initially sought unit. Such a provision is expressed under Alaska's PERA.[33]

It is not at all unusual, however, for the laws or regulations to permit incumbent unions to participate with no specified showing of interest, as is the case in Florida, New York, Kansas, and Connecticut for teachers.[34] Finally, many statutes restrict the time frames for intervention, generally within 10 to 20 days of when the notice of election is posted.[35]

## Contract Bar

Under most statutes, the existence of a collective bargaining agreement prevents a rival union from seeking recognition. This "contract bar" doctrine was originally developed by the NLRB.[36] This bar is of limited duration (up to one, two, or three years), and there is almost always a "window" during which the challenging union may petition for a new election. It is common for petitions to be accepted only

---

[30]Many agencies have published rules on the procedures. *See* §95.17 of the Pennsylvania Labor Relations Board's rules.

[31]*See Civil Service Employees Ass'n v. Helsby,* 63 Misc.2d 403, 312 N.Y.2d 386 (N.Y. 1970), *aff'd,* 35 App. Div. 2d 655, 314 N.Y.S.2d 159 (1971); *Union Free School Dist. 21,* 1 PERB §405 (N.Y. PERB 1968); *Commonwealth of Mass.,* 10 MLC 1557 (Mass. LRC 1984); *South Redford School Dist.,* 1965–1966 MERC Lob. op. 160 (Mich.).

[32]*See* California's RODDA Act, Rules and Regulations Act 2, §§33080–33100.

[33]Alaska Stat., Tit. 14, Ch. 20, §1420.550 *et seq.* (1975).

[34]*Cf.* Connecticut Gen. Stat., Tit. 10, Ch. 166, §10–153(d) (1982).

[35]*Id.*

[36]*See Town of Manchester, Dec. No. 813* (Conn. State Bd. of Labor Relations 1968); and Schlossberg, note 6, above, at 266–273, 278–280.

during a designated 30-day period beginning anywhere from 90 to 120 days before the contract expires. As with private sector agreements, the days after the window closes provide an insulated period during which the union and the employer can negotiate a new contract. However, a contract extension usually does not prolong the contract bar.

Because the purpose of the contract bar is to provide for stability in the workplace, some states, such as Oregon and Connecticut (for state and municipal employees), and Indiana also allow a rival union to overcome a contract bar when the public employer has dominated, interfered with, or assisted the incumbent union.[37] Iowa's contract bar is valid only so long as the collective bargaining agreement does not discriminate on the basis of age, race, sex, religion, national origin, or physical disability.[38]

## *Recognition, Certification, Election Bars*

The three concepts of recognition, certification, and election bars are closely related. An election bar means that if employees vote against being represented, another election cannot be held for a period of time, usually 12 months.[39]

The recognition/certification bar (depending upon whether the union is voluntarily recognized or officially certified) gives the new representative an initial period during which it can negotiate a contract free from the pressures of a competing union breathing down its neck. This period lasts for 12 months. In Maryland, however, and in Oklahoma and Tennessee (for teachers) the recognition/certification bar lasts 24 months; and in Vermont (for teachers) the bar extends for 12 months plus the remainder of the fiscal year.[40]

## *Decertification*

Some states expressly provide for decertification procedures based on a showing of support to have a union removed from its exclusive representation status. There may be limitations on when such a challenge can be initiated. Most commonly, the showing of support is the same as that required to petition for an election under the particular statute, and decertification is subject to the contract, election, and recognition/certification bars discussed above.[41]

---

[37]*Cf.* Indiana Certified State Employees Rules and Regulations, §2133.
[38]*See* Iowa Public Employment Relations Rules and Regulations, §5.513.
[39]*See* Alaska Stat. §23.40.100(c) (1983) and Schlossberg, note 6, above, at 265, 272.
[40]Vermont Stat. Ann., Ch. 57, §1992(b) (1986).
[41]*See* Schlossberg, note 6, above, at 125–127.

In a few instances, in California (for municipal employees), Georgia (for public employees), and Idaho (for teachers), recognition can be withdrawn by a simple majority vote of the unit employees.[42] Sometimes a union's unfair labor practices, as in South Dakota, and Wisconsin (for state employees),[43] or failure to comply with agency regulations, as in Nevada and New Hampshire, can form the basis for revocation of recognition.[44] Several jurisdictions, including the District of Columbia, Florida, Iowa, Pennsylvania, and Washington (for higher education employees), have special provisions for inactive unions or those representatives that disclaim interest in continuing to act as the bargaining agent.[45]

In reviewing regulations for decertification, it is important to focus on who may initiate a decertification petition. Is the petitioner limited to another union, or may any employee, or even an employer, begin a move to oust the current representative? Clearly a representative union's bargaining strength is weakened if a hostile employer can attempt or threaten to decertify it.

## Unit Determinations

### Bargaining Units

There are two basic methods for determining an appropriate bargaining unit. First, the administrative agency may make the decision, often after a recommendation from the public employer and the union, and almost always subject to criteria and restrictions written into the law. Alternatively, the law itself may define the composition of appropriate units. Sometimes the statute is a combination of these two methods, with some units specified by statute and some determined by the agency. Where agency unit determinations are made, they are most often made on a case-by-case basis under the NLRA model. However, some agencies have established units by regulation, as in Massachusetts for state employees.[46]

### Supervisors

Supervisors may be covered by a statute. If they are, it is important to know if there are any limitations on the coverage and whether

---

[42]Iowa Public Employment Relations, Rules and Regulations, §4.3(2)(20).
[43]*Cf.* South Dakota, Public Sector Bargaining Rules and Regulations, §47:02:41.
[44]*Cf.* New Hampshire Rev. Stat., Ch. 273-A, §273:10(IV)(b) (1983).
[45]*Cf.* Washington Higher Education Employees Act, Rules and Regulations, WAC 391–25–010 (1977).
[46]*See* Schlossberg, note 6, above, Ch. 10; and Edwards, Clark & Craver, *Labor Relations Law in the Public Sector,* at 174–233 (3d ed. 1985).

supervisors are consigned to separate bargaining units. This information will be useful for organizers making an initial decision on which groups to target in an organizing drive, since it will affect considerations of which employees are properly included in a given unit.[47]

## Modification, Amendment, Merger or Amalgamation

Changes in existing unit certifications are, at times, expressly dealt with in a statute or ordinance. While few statutes include express merger or amalgamation rules for combining two previously existing units, the organizer should be aware of such procedures where they exist. Where the problem arises and no local statute exists, the organizer should refer to National Labor Relations Board policy.[48]

## Unfair Labor Practices

### Filing Unfair Labor Practice Charges

Experience has amply demonstrated that initial organizing efforts are often met with resistance, hostility, and sometimes prohibited activities by public employers. An organizing drive should not be diverted from its primary purpose by minor unfair labor practices (ULPs). However, an organizer should not hesitate to file ULP charges to stop unlawful conduct which, if ignored, may stifle the organizing drive. More than that, the legal consequences of an employer's unfair practices may furnish an important rallying point for a successful organizing drive.[49] The type of activity that constitutes an unfair labor practice varies from place to place, but typically resembles private sector unfair labor practices.[50]

A decision to file ULP charges, however, must always take into account its effect on the recognition process. Will the charges delay recognition? What are the chances of success? Are the possible remedies worth the expenditure of time and resources? Will the mere filing of ULP charges provide progress, or is there more chance of achieving recognition without filing charges?

Some procedures of which an organizer must be aware when contemplating filing a ULP charge include: what is the time frame for

---

[47]Hayford and Sinicropi, "Bargaining Rights Statutes of Public Sector Supervisors," 15 *Indus. Rev.* 44–61 (1976).

[48]*See* Schlossberg, note 6, above, at 207, 273–280.

[49]*See, e.g., Muskego-Norway Consol. Schools v. WERB,* 35 Wis.2d 540, 151 N.W.2d 617 (1967); and *Washington Public Employees Ass'n v. Community College Dist. 9,* 31 Wash. App. 642 P.2d 1248 (1982).

[50]*Id; and see* Schlossberg, note 6, above, at 281–314.

filing a charge after the time the activity occurs or becomes known; must a charge be in writing; must it be on a form supplied by the administrative agency or merely conform to agency requirements as to the contents ("board format")? In some instances, "complaint" is the word used, rather than "charge."

Subsequent processing of the ULP will vary, and an organizer must be aware of how an unfair labor practice charge is processed, from the initial filing, through an investigation and hearing, and through any appeals procedure. The organizer should check the applicable statute and rules and regulations in order to become knowledgeable about the steps of the process.

## Strikes and Picketing

Public sector strikes are generally illegal, although a limited right to strike is recognized under more than 10 statutes (or case law interpretation of those statutes).[51] The conditions that must be met prior to legally striking under these progressive laws are set out in Appendix A.

In a given jurisdiction, there may be restrictions on picketing public employers (often covered under general state statutes that apply to both private and public sector employees), as well as penalties for engaging in a prohibited strike. Penalties may range from the union's forfeiture of checkoff privileges and employees' loss of wages for days on strike to significant fines, discharges with prohibitions against rehire, revocation of the union's certification, or even imprisonment. Certainly any union organizer contemplating the effectiveness of a strike should be well versed in these potential penalties before deciding on such a tactic.

## Finding and Using the Law

This general description of the terms and issues likely to arise in an organizing drive can direct the organizer to the actual rule in the jurisdiction in which the drive is under way and can help the organizer use, understand, and evaluate the rules under which the drive will move forward. Detailed application of the rules and issues discussed above, however, will depend on knowing the specific rules and laws in a given jurisdiction. It is beyond the scope of this book to present

---

[51]*See* discussion of strikes in Part 1, Chapter 1, notes 8 & 10.

all of the rules in each jurisdiction. What it can do is provide a road map to the specific rules. That map is presented in two formats.

The first is an overview of state organizing rules presented in the State-By-State Overview of Public Employee Organizing Rules, set out below. The various states are listed along the left-hand margin of the table followed immediately either by a notation that there is no general collective bargaining law in the jurisdiction or by a specific cite to one or more such laws. The corresponding columns are organized to fit with the discussion outlined above. The columns run from "Administrative Agency" through "Strikes and Picketing" and indicate by use of an x whether a specific statute or collective bargaining structure deals specifically with the topic. In some cases an x may appear where the topic is covered by regulation rather than directly by statute. The organizer should check both the appropriate statute and related regulation.

A reading of the statute involved will be of use to the organizer whether or not the question is ultimately referred to an attorney. In checking a state statute, it is useful to review it as set out in an annotated state code, if one is available. The organizer should look over the annotations as well as the statutory language itself. An annotated state code should be available in a local law library, or even a general public library, and a librarian can help in finding it. It is also useful to try to find out from a librarian whether a detailed lay person's analysis of a state statute is readily available. The Massachusetts Labor Relations Commission has developed a very good overview of their law. James T. O'Reilly's *Ohio Public Employee Collective Bargaining* is a very good detailed review and analysis of law and procedure under the most recent collective bargaining statute.[52]

The State-By-State Overview chart highlights the details of state collective bargaining laws with a focus on the specific provisions that relate to organizing. It fits with the format of this chapter and can be used in conjunction with it to move you toward a specific statute. Appendix A which follows is the Digest of State Public Employee Bargaining Statutes from BNA's *Government Employee Relations Report*. The Digest provides a detailed summary of the complete public employee bargaining statutes in each state. The Digest does not focus solely on organizing questions but rather provides an overview of all provisions of the various statutes from the prerecognition stage through the settlement of contract disputes by arbitration. The organizer needs

---

[52]O'Reilly, *Ohio Public Employee Collective Bargaining: Law Procedure and Analysis* (1984).

to be aware of the complete picture of a jurisdiction's public sector labor law and that is provided in the Digest. Basically, the topics from "Authority" through "Criteria for Unit Determinations," and the sections on "Union Security," "Unfair Labor Practices," and "Strikes" are those which relate most directly to organizing. The other topics focus on achieving and enforcing a contract once an organizing drive is successful. Those sections are necessary knowledge to every organizer for they describe how to achieve the goal of all labor organizing—a legally enforceable role for the working person in the determination of wages, hours, and working conditions.

A review of Appendix A's summary of your state law is indispensable. However, first get an overview of your state's organizing rules by reviewing the Chart set out here:

# A STATE-BY-STATE OVERVIEW OF PUBLIC EMPLOYEE ORGANIZING RULES

| STATE | LAW | % Represented 1982* | UNIONS Agency | UNIONS Regulated Unions | UNIONS Dues Deduction Pre-Contract | RECOGNITION Exclusive Recognition | RECOGNITION Recognition | RECOGNITION Regulated Recognition Election Procedures | CERTIFICATION Showing of Interest | CERTIFICATION Intervention | CERTIFICATION Contract-Bar | CERTIFICATION Recognition/Certification/Election Bars | CERTIFICATION Decertification | UNITS Bargaining Units | UNITS Supervisors | UNITS Modification/Amendment | UNITS Merger/Transfer | ULPS ULP Procedures | ULPS Filing ULP | STRIKES |
|---|---|---|---|---|---|---|---|---|---|---|---|---|---|---|---|---|---|---|---|---|
| **ALABAMA** | No General Law Firefighters Cert. Education | 4.7 | | x | | | | | | | | | | | x | | | | | Prohibited |
| **ALASKA** | General Employees | 75.8 | x | x | x | x | x | x | 30% | 10% | x | x | x | x | x | x | | x | x | Strike on Majority Vote; but no "Essential" Fire & Police |
| | Teachers | | x | x | | x | x | x | 25% | | | | x | x | x | x | | x | x | |
| **ARIZONA** | No General Law | 31.8 | (S.B. 1344, Ch. 149 (1977) Regulates State Officers & Employees/Some Local Ordinances) | | | | | | | | | | | | | | | | | Prohibited |
| **ARKANSAS** | No General Law | 7.1 | | | | | | | | | | | | | | | | | | Prohibited, plus picket rules |
| **CALIFORNIA** | State Civil Service | 83.6 | x | | | x | x | x | x | x | x | | x | x | | x | | x | x | Statute Silent |
| | State Non-Civil Service | | | x | x | | x | | | | | | | | x | | | | x | x | Prohibited by Court |
| | Local Government | | | x | x | x | x | | | x | | | x | x | x | x | | | x | x | Legal by Court |
| | Public School | | x | x | x | x | x | x | 30% | 30% | x | x | x | x | x | x | x | x | x | Statute Silent |
| | Higher Education | | x | x | x | x | x | x | 30% | 10% | x | x | x | x | x | x | x | x | x | Statute Silent |
| **COLORADO** | No General Law Denver Firefighters | 28.6 | | x | | | x | | | | | | | | | | | | | Prohibited, plus picketing rules |
| **CONNECTICUT** | State Employees | 81.7 | x | x | x | x | x | x | 30% | 10% | x | x | x | x | x | x | | x | x | Prohibited |
| | Municipal Employees | | x | x | x | x | x | x | 30% | 30% | x | x | x | x | x | x | x | x | x | |
| | Teachers | | x | x | x | x | x | x | 30% | 10% | x | x | x | x | x | x | | x | x | |
| **DELAWARE** | State, County & Local | 61.7 | x | x | x | x | x | x | 30% | 10% | x | x | x | x | x | x | | x | | Prohibited |
| | Teachers | | x | | | | | | | | | | | | | | | | | |
| | Transit | | x | x | x | x | x | x | 30% | 10% | x | x | x | x | x | | x | | | |
| **DISTRICT OF COLUMBIA** | Public Employees | 95.9 | x | x | x | x | x | x | 30% | 10% | x | x | x | x | x | x | x | x | x | Prohibited, Decertification |
| **FLORIDA** | Public Employees | 59.5 | x | x | x | | x | x | 30% | 10% | x | x | x | x | x | x | | x | x | Prohibited |

# A STATE-BY-STATE OVERVIEW OF PUBLIC EMPLOYEE ORGANIZING RULES—Con't.

| STATE | LAW | % Represented 1982* | Agency | Regulated Unions | Dues Deduction | Pre-Contract | Exclusive Recognition | Recognition | Regulated Election | Procedures | Showing of Interest | Intervention | Contract-Bar | Recognition/Certification/Election Bars | Decertification | Bargaining Units | Supervisors | Modification/Amendment | Merger/Transfer | ULP Procedures | Filing ULP | STRIKES |
|---|---|---|---|---|---|---|---|---|---|---|---|---|---|---|---|---|---|---|---|---|---|---|
| GEORGIA | No General Law | | | | | | | | | | | | | | | | | | | | | |
| | Firefighters | 1.8 | x | x | | x | x | x | | | | | | x | x | x | | | | | | Prohibited |
| HAWAII | Public Employees | 88.9 | x | x | x | x | x | x | | x | 30% | 10% | x | x | x | x | | x | x | x | x | O.K. Exhaustion |
| IDAHO | Firefighters | 25.4 | x | x | x | | x | x | | | | | | x | x | x | x | | | | | Prohibited, plus picket rules |
| | Teachers | | x | x | | | x | x | | | | | | x | x | x | x | | | | | |
| ILLINOIS | Public Employees | 79.9 (1985) | x | x | | x | x | x | x | x | 30% | 10% | x | x | x | x | x | x | x | x | x | Limited Right to Strike |
| | Teachers | | x | x | | | x | x | x | x | 30% | 15% | x | x | x | x | x | | | x | x | |
| INDIANA | No General Law | | | | | | | | | | | | | | | | | | | | | |
| | Teachers | 32.7 | x | x | x | x | x | x | | x | 20% | 20% | x | x | x | x | | x | x | x | x | Prohibited |
| IOWA | Public Employees | 63.6 | x | x | x | x | x | x | x | x | 30% | 10% | x | x | x | x | x | x | x | x | x | Prohibited |
| KANSAS | Public Employees | 35.5 | x | x | x | x | x | x | x | x | 30% | 30% | x | x | x | x | x | x | | x | x | Prohibited |
| | Teachers | | x | x | | x | x | x | x | x | 30% | 30% | x | x | x | x | x | | | x | x | |
| KENTUCKY | Firefighters | 12.2 | x | x | x | x | x | x | | x | 30% | 30% | x | x | x | x | x | | x | x | Prohibited |
| | Police (Pop. 300,000) | | x | x | | x | x | | | | | | | | | | x | | | | | |
| LOUISIANA | No General Law | | | | | | | | | | | | | | | | | | | | | |
| | Public Transit | 12.3 | x | x | x | x | x | x | | | | | | | | | x | x | | | | Prohibited |
| MAINE | City, County, Education, Trans | 66.3 | x | x | | | | x | x | x | 30% | 10% | x | x | x | x | x | x | x | x | Prohibited |
| | State Employees | | x | x | | | | x | x | x | 30% | 10% | x | x | x | x | x | x | x | x | |
| | University Employees | | x | x | | | | x | x | x | 30% | 10% | x | x | x | x | x | x | x | x | |
| MARYLAND | Teachers | 53.0 | x | x | x | | x | x | x | x | x | x | x | x | x | x | x | | x | x | Prohibited |
| | Non-Certified School | | x | x | | | x | x | x | x | 30% | 10% | x | x | x | x | x | | x | x | |
| | Varies: Local Governmental Bodies Have Local C.B., Including Allegany, Baltimore, Montgomery, Annapolis, Howard, & Prince Georges | | | | | | | | | | | | | | | | | | | | | |
| MASSACHU-SETTS | Public Employees | 84.7 | x | x | x | x | x | x | | | 30% | 70% | x | x | x | x | x | x | x | x | Prohibited |
| | Police & Fire | | | | | | | | Impasse Procedures | | | | | | | | | | | | | |

Additional Impasse Procedures

| State | Employees | | Additional | | Impasse Procedures | | | 30% | 10% | | | | | | | | | Strike Rights |
|---|---|---|---|---|---|---|---|---|---|---|---|---|---|---|---|---|---|---|
| MICHIGAN | Public Employees / Firefighters | 66.5 | x | x | x | x | x | 30% | 10% | x | x | x | x | x | x | x | x | Prohibited |
| MINNESOTA | Public Employees | 65 | x | x | x | x | x | 30% | 30% | x | x | x | x | x | x | x | x | Limited Strike Post-Arbitration |
| MISSISSIPPI | No General Law / Local Option to Establish Bargaining | 0.20 | Approved by Court in Case Involving Meridian, Miss. | | | | | | | | | | | | | | | Prohibited |
| MISSOURI | Public Employees | 54.1 | x | x | x | x | | | | x | x | x | | | | x | x | Prohibited |
| MONTANA | Public Employees / Nurses | 46.3 | x | x | x | x | x | 30% x | 10% | x | x | x | x | x | x | x | x | Limited Right to Strike |
| NEBRASKA | Public Employees / Certified Education, Districts III, IV, V | 25.1 | x | x | x | x | x | 30% | 10% | x | x | x | x | x | | x | x | Prohibited |
| NEVADA | Local, Education, Nurses | 41.1 | x | | x | x | | 50% | | x | x | x | x | | | x | x | Prohibited |
| NEW HAMPSHIRE | Public Employees | 55.0 | x | | x | x | x | 30% | 20% | x | x | x | x | x | x | x | x | Prohibited |
| NEW JERSEY | Public Employees / Police & Fire | 83.9 | x Additional | x | x Impasse Procedures | x | x | 30% | 10% | x | x | x | x | x | x | x | x | Prohibited |
| NEW MEXICO | State Certified | 27.8 | x | x | x | x | x | 30% | 10% | x | x | x | x | x | x | x | x | Prohibited |
| NEW YORK | Public Employees / N.Y. City | 98.6 | x x See Appendix A | x | x | x | x | 30% | 10% | x | x | x | | | | x | x | Prohibited |
| N. CAROLINA | No General Law | — | x | x | x | | | | | | | | | | | | | | Prohibited |
| N. DAKOTA | Public Employees / Teachers | 18.1 | x | x | x x | x | x | x | x | x | x | | | | | | | Prohibited |
| OHIO | Public Employees | 51.5 (1986) | x | x | x | x | x | 30% | 10% | x | x | x | x | x | x | x | x | Limited Right |
| OKLAHOMA | No General Law / Police & Fire / School Employees | 18.5 | x x | x | x x | x x | x x | 30% 25% | 10% | x x | x x | x x | | | | | x | |
| OREGON | Public Employees | 72.5 | x | x | x | x | x | 30% | 10% | x | x | x | x | x | x | x | x | Limited Right |
| PENNSYLVANIA | Public Employees / Police & Fire / Transit | 78.3 | x x x | x | x x x | x x x | x x x | 30% 30% | 10% | x x | x x x | x x x | x x | x x | x x | x x | x x | Limited Right Post-Exhaustion |

# A STATE-BY-STATE OVERVIEW OF PUBLIC EMPLOYEE ORGANIZING RULES—Con't.

| STATE | LAW | % Represented 1982* | UNIONS: Agency | Regulated Unions | Dues Deduction Pre-Contract | RECOGNITION: Exclusive Recognition | Recognition | Regulated Recognition | Election Procedures | CERTIFICATION: Showing of Interest | Intervention | Contract-Bar | Recognition/ Certification/ Election Bars | Decertification | UNITS: Bargaining Units | Supervisors | Modification/ Amendment | Merger/ Transfer | ULPS: ULP Procedures | Filing ULP | STRIKES |
|---|---|---|---|---|---|---|---|---|---|---|---|---|---|---|---|---|---|---|---|---|---|
| **RHODE ISLAND** — State Employees | | 86.9 | x | | x | x | | | | 28% | 15% | | | x | x | | | | x | x | Strikes illegal, but no injunctions without showing of irreparable injury |
| Municipal | | | x | x | | x | x | | x | 20% | 15% | x | x | x | x | | | | x | x | |
| Teachers | | | x | x | | x | x | | x | | | x | x | x | x | | | | x | x | |
| Firefighters | | | x | | | x | x | | | | | | | x | x | | | | x | x | |
| Municipal Police | | | x | | | | x | | | | | | | | | | | | x | x | |
| State Police | | | x | | | x | | | | | | | | x | x | | | | x | x | |
| **S. CAROLINA** | No General Law | 0.14 | | | | | | | | | | | | | | | | | | | |
| *State and City Employees Have Civil Service Grievance Procedures* | | | | | | | | | | | | | | | | | | | | | |
| **S. DAKOTA** | Public Employees | 30.1 | x | | | x | | x | x | 30% | | x | x | x | x | x | | | x | x | |
| **TENNESSEE** | No General Law / Teachers | 22 | x | x | x | x | | x | x | 30% | 30% | x | x | x | x | x | | | x | x | |
| **TEXAS** | No General (Legal Ban) Police & Fire (Opt.) | 1.22 | x | x | x | x | | x | | | | | | x | x | x | | | x | x | |
| **UTAH** | No General Law Salt Lake C.B. | 36.1 | x | | x | | x | | | | | | | | x | | | | | | |
| **VERMONT** — State Employees | | 48.9 | x | x | x | x | x | | x | 30% | 10% | | x | x | x | x | | | x | x | Limited post-exhaustion |
| Municipal Employees | | | x | | | x | x | | x | 30% | 10% | | x | x | x | x | | | x | x | |
| Teachers | | | x | | | x | x | | x | 20% | 10% | | x | x | x | x | | | x | x | |
| **VIRGINIA** | No General Law | 0.05 | | | | | | | | | | | | | | | | | | | Prohibited |
| *State and Local Grievance Procedures; Local Opt. C.B. Declared Unconstitutional in State 1977* | | | | | | | | | | | | | | | | | | | | | |
| **WASHINGTON** — Municipal | | 71.4 | x | | | x | x | x | x | 30% | 10% | | x | x | x | x | x | | x | x | Prohibited |
| Teachers | | | x | | | x | x | x | x | 30% | 10% | | x | x | x | x | x | x | x | x | |
| Class. Higher Ed. | | | | | | x | x | x | x | 30% | 10% | | x | x | x | x | x | x | | | |
| Community College | | | x | | | x | x | x | x | 30% | 10% | | x | x | x | x | x | | | | |
| State Civil Service | | | x | | x | x | x | x | x | 30% | 10% | | x | x | x | x | x | | x | x | |
| **W. VIRGINIA** | No General Law | 02.9 | | | x | | x | | | | | | | | | | | | x | x | Limit, Court Decision; no injunctions without showing of injury |
| *Meet and Confer by Attorney General Opinion* | | | | | | | | | | | | | | | | | | | | | |

| State | | | Additional | Impasse Procedures | 30% | 10% | | | Limited Right | Absent clear and Present Danger | Statute Silent |
|---|---|---|---|---|---|---|---|---|---|---|---|
| **WISCONSIN** | Municipal Employees | 63.3 (1985) | x x | x x x | x | x | | x | x x | x x | |
| | Police & Fire | | x x | x x x | | | | x | x x | x x | |
| **WYOMING** | No General Law | 20.7 | | | | | | | | | |
| | Firefighters | | x | x | | | | | x | | x |

*See figures set out in Appendix G, 230–233.

# Appendices

# Appendix A

# Digest of State Public Employee Bargaining Statutes

This Appendix is reprinted from BNA's *Government Employee Relations Report* (GERR) Reference Binder. It provides detailed summaries in outline form of the public bargaining statutes enacted in each of the states listed below:

Alabama
Alaska
California
Connecticut
Delaware
District of Columbia
Florida
Georgia
Hawaii
Idaho
Illinois
Indiana
Iowa
Kansas
Kentucky
Maine
Maryland
Massachusetts
Michigan
Minnesota
Missouri

Montana
Nebraska
Nevada
New Hampshire
New Jersey
New Mexico
New York
North Dakota
Ohio
Oklahoma
Oregon
Pennsylvania
Rhode Island
South Dakota
Tennessee
Texas
Vermont
Washington
Wisconsin
Wyoming

Preceding the summary of the statute or statutes for each state, a boldface headnote highlights the number of statutes for that particular state and the types of employees covered. The headnote is then followed by a summary outlining each statute for every employee group within that particular state.

The summaries are intended to expedite locating the salient features of the bargaining statutes in each state. The complete text of all the statutes is reprinted in BNA's *Labor Relations Reporter, State Laws* Binders 4 and 4A. Readers may also find the statutes directly in their state code.

*Scope of Bargaining*: States with no statutory bargaining rights include Arizona, Arkansas, Colorado, Louisiana, Mississippi, North Carolina, South Carolina, Utah, Virginia, and West Virginia. States that permit some form of negotiations to take place in public include California, Florida, Kansas, Minnesota, and Texas.

Many states define the scope of public employee bargaining as "wages, hours, and other terms and conditions of employment." Topics most often excluded, if they are mentioned at all, are merit pay policies and reitrement benefits. Some states, however, specify each item that may be negotiated. Nevada has one of the most detailed lists of what may be specifically bargained for its local governmnet employees, teachers, and nurses. Other states that also specify several items that may be negotiated instead of providing for a general bargaining clause include Delaware, the District of Columbia, Indiana, Iowa, Maine, Minnesota, Oklahoma, Oregon, Rhode Island, Tennessee, Vermont, and Washington.

*Grievance/Arbitration*: Grievance/arbitration provisions, while generally permitted in many states, are mandatory in others such as Alaska, Florida, Illinois, Minnesota, Oklahoma, and Pennsylvania. Grievance procedures only are required in Delaware (for teachers), New Hampshire, New Jersey, New Mexico, South Dakota, and Vermont (for state employees only in Vermont).

*Union Security*: Some form of union security is permitted by statute in many states with public employee bargaining laws. Mandatory dues deduction is provided for in almost one half of these states. The agency shop, whereby nonunion members pay an amount usually equivalent to union dues, is permitted for some, if not all, employees in 14 states and the District of Columbia. New Jersey and Minnesota limit fees to 85 percent of dues. New York, Minnesota, Massachusetts, New Jersey, Hawaii and a few other jurisdictions cover the subject by regulation.* Hawaii is one of several states that consider religious beliefs in connection with the agency shop by allowing an amount equal to union dues to be paid to a nonreligious, nonunion charity chosen by the employee.

*Strike Penalties and Strike Rights*: Although many statutes prohibit strikes, a few go into detail regarding strike penalties. In Iowa, for example, individuals may be fined up to $500 and unions up to $10,000 for each day of a strike and/or imprisoned up to six months. Individuals also are ineligible for reemployment for one year, and a union may be decertified for a year. Other states that specify penalties for strikes include Florida, Nevada, New York, Pennsylvania, South Dakota, Tennessee, Texas, Wisconsin, and the District of Columbia. Limited strike rights for certain types of employees usually excluding fire fighters and police officers are permitted in several states. In Minnesota, "nonessential" employees and teachers may strike provided certain conditions are met such as completion of the mandatory mediation period after the contract has expired.

*Impasse Procedures*: Fact finding is used as a means to resolve bargaining impasses in more than one half of the states for at least some public employees. Mandatory arbitration is provided for some if not all employees in over one half of the states and usually appears in the form of conventional arbitration, last best offer by package, or last best offer on an issue-by-issue basis. Some states, however, may use more than one type of arbitration. For example, New Jersey's police and fire fighters' bargaining statute provides for the last best offer by package on economic items and the last best offer on an issue-by-issue basis for noneconomic provisions. In Maine, the arbitrator's award is advisory for salaries, pensions, and insurance and binding on all other issues.

The criteria to be used by an arbitrator in making an award are specified in a little over one third of the states. Statutes usually specify that the arbitrator must consider the interest and welfare of the public, ability to pay, cost of living, and "other factors normally considered."

---

*See Hudson v. Chicago Teachers Union Local 1*, ___US ___, 54 USLW 4231 (1986), and its discussion of the need for additional agency fee administration where the union spends dues money for anything not related.

## ALABAMA

**There is one public employee bargaining statute in the State of Alabama. The law permits fire fighters to present proposals on salaries and other conditions of employment.**

### FIRE FIGHTERS

AUTHORITY: Alabama Code, Section 11-43-143 et seq. (1967).

BARGAINING RIGHTS: To present proposals.

SCOPE OF BARGAINING: Salaries and other conditions of employment.

EMPLOYEE RIGHTS: To join unions; refrain from doing so.

STRIKE POLICY: Prohibited; unions may not assert right to strike.

---

## ALASKA

**There are two public employee bargaining statutes in the State of Alaska. One law covers public employees in general and gives them limited strike rights except for policemen, fire fighters, and employees in correctional facilities and hospitals. The other statute requires school boards to negotiate in good faith with teachers.**

### PUBLIC EMPLOYEES IN GENERAL

AUTHORITY: Alaska Statutes Title 23, Chapter 40, Section 23.40.070 et seq. as last amended effective Feb. 24, 1984.

EXCLUSIONS: Teachers and non-certificated employees of school districts; elected or appointed officials.

ADMINISTRATIVE AGENCY: Alaska Labor Relations Agency for state employees; Department of Labor for local employees.

UNIT DETERMINATION: Administrative agency.

CRITERIA FOR UNIT DETERMINATION: Community of interest; wages, hours, and working conditions; history of collective bargaining; desires of employees; and avoidance of over-fragmentation.

RECOGNITION: Exclusive; voluntary or by election.

SCOPE OF BARGAINING: Wages, hours, and other terms and conditions of employment; excludes general policies describing function and purposes of employer.

GRIEVANCE PROCEDURE: Arbitration required.

EMPLOYEE RIGHTS: To organize, form, join or assist a labor organization; engage in concerted activities; bargain collectively.

UNION SECURITY: Dues deduction mandatory; union or agency shop permitted.

UNFAIR LABOR PRACTICES: Employer--Interfere with, restrain, or coerce employees; dominate labor organizations; discriminate on account of labor organization membership or testimony; refusal to bargain in good faith. Labor organization--Restrain or coerce employees or employer's representative; refusal to bargain in good faith.

IMPASSE PROCEDURE: MEDIATION--Either party may request or administrative agency may initiate mediation; mediator may be appointed by parties or administrative agency. ARBITRATION--Mandatory for law enforcement and fire protection employees; jail, prison, and other correctional institution employees; and hospital employees; voluntary in other cases.

STRIKE POLICY: Strikes prohibited for law enforcement and fire protection employees; jail, prison, and correctional institution employees. Strikes may be enjoined. Public utility, snow removal, sanitation, public school and other educational institution employees may strike until there is a threat to public safety, health, or welfare. At that time superior court may enjoin strike, and parties shall submit to arbitration. All other employees may strike after majority vote.

NOTE: Contract duration may not exceed three years; up to three student representatives shall be allowed to attend and observe negotiation sessions involving public postsecondary institutions.

## TEACHERS

AUTHORITY: Alaska Statutes Title 14, Chapter 20, Section 14.20.550 et seq. (1970) as last amended 1975.

EXCLUSIONS: Superintendents of schools.

UNIT DETERMINATION: Statute. All teachers in school district; administrative personnel including principals and assistant principals may choose to be in a separate unit.

RECOGNITION: Exclusive; voluntary requires showing of interest from majority in unit; election requires 25 percent to petition.

BARGAINING RIGHTS: Duty to bargain.

SCOPE OF BARGAINING: Matters pertaining to employment and fulfillment of professional duties.

GRIEVANCE PROCEDURE: Arbitration required.

IMPASSE PROCEDURE: Parties may appoint own mediator or request mediator from FMCS; mediator issues report on unresolved issues; parties have 10 days to accept or reject report; if rejected, mediator has five days to review objections and prepare final report. If final report is rejected, governor may appoint advisory arbitrator to reveiw issues and recommend solution.

NOTE: Negotiations may be held in executive session by mutual agreement; final agreements made at public meeting. Each party may select not more than five representatives to negotiate for them.

## CALIFORNIA

There are five public employee bargaining statutes in the State of California. State civil service employees and teachers employed by the state Department of Education or the Superintendent of Public Instruction are covered by one law. State noncivil service workers, local government employees, public school workers, and employees of higher education are covered by the other four statutes.

## *STATE CIVIL SERVICE EMPLOYEES*

AUTHORITY: Government Code Annotated, Title 1, Division 4, Section 3512 et seq. (1977) as last amended effective Jan. 1, 1987. *Note: Statute covers state civil service employees and teachers employed by the Department of Education or the Superintendent of Public Instruction; supervisors have limited coverage under the statute.*

EXCLUSIONS: Managerial and confidential employees; employees of the Department of Personnel Administration; professional employees of the Department of Finance engaged in technical or analytical state budget preparation other than the auditing staff; employees of the Legislative Counsel Bureau; employees of the Public Employment Relations Board (PERB); conciliators of the State Conciliation Service within the Department of Industrial Relations; intermittent athletic inspectors of the State Athletic Commission.

ADMINISTRATIVE AGENCY: Public Employment Relations Board (PERB).

UNIT DETERMINATION: PERB.

CRITERIA FOR UNIT DETERMINATION: Community of interest; effect on meet and confer relationship; effect on efficient operations; number of employees and classifications; impact on meet and confer created by fragmentation; craft employees have right to a separate unit; presumption that professionals should not be in same unit as nonprofessionals may be rebutted; supervisors may not be in nonsupervisory units.

RECOGNITION: Exclusive; by election.

BARGAINING RIGHTS: Meet and confer.

SCOPE OF BARGAINING: Wages, hours, and other terms and conditions of employment; excluding merits, necessity, or organization of any service provided by law or Executive Order; amount of rental rates for state owned housing charged to state employees.

EMPLOYEE RIGHTS: To form, join, and participate in unions; refrain from doing so; employees may represent themselves in employer-employee matters.

UNION SECURITY: Dues deduction mandatory.

UNFAIR LABOR PRACTICES BY EMPLOYER: Interfere with, intimidate, restrain, coerce, or discriminate against employees; deny union rights guaranteed under the statute; refusal or failure to meet and confer in good faith; dominate unions; refusal to participate in mediation procedure.

UNFAIR LABOR PRACTICES BY UNION: Cause or attempt to cause employer to commit a ULP; interfere with, intimidate, restrain, coerce, or discriminate against employees; refusal or failure to meet and confer in good faith; refusal to participate in mediation procedure.

IMPASSE PROCEDURE: Mediation–Either party may request PERB to appoint a mediator or the parties may mutually appoint a mediator; costs shared equally by the parties if they appoint their own mediator; if PERB appoints mediator, costs borne by PERB.

NOTE: All initial meet and confer proposals shall be presented at public meetings. No meeting and conferring for at least seven days so that the public can become informed and express opinions in a public meeting. New proposals arising in negotiations shall be made public within 48 hours. In cases where specified provisions of the law relating to state civil service are in conflict with provisions of a memorandum of understanding entered into pursuant to the act, memorandum is controlling, except where expenditures of funds are required.

## STATE NONCIVIL SERVICE EMPLOYEES

AUTHORITY: Government Code Annotated, Title 1, Division 4, Section 3525 et seq. (1971) as last amended effective Jan. 1, 1983. *Note: Statute covers state noncivil service employees; employees of the Department of Personnel Administration and of the Legislative Counsel Bureau; employees of the Public Employment Relations Board; nonclerical employees of the State Personnel Board engaged in personnel functions; conciliators of the State Conciliation Service within the Department of Industrial Relations.*

EXCLUSIONS: Elected or appointed officials; state civil service employees; employees of the University of California, Hastings College of the Law, and the California State University and Colleges; employees of the California Maritime Academy; managerial and confidential employees.

CRITERIA FOR UNIT DETERMINATION: Professionals may be represented separately from nonprofessionals; state may not prohibit peace officers from joining unions composed solely of such employees.

BARGAINING RIGHTS: Meet and confer.

SCOPE OF BARGAINING: Matters relating to employment conditions and employer-employee relations, including but not limited to wages, hours, and other terms and conditions of employment.

EMPLOYEE RIGHTS: To form, join, and participate in unions; refrain from doing so; employees may represent themselves in employer-employee matters.

UNFAIR LABOR PRACTICES: Interfere with, intimidate, restrain, coerce, or discriminate against employees.

## LOCAL GOVERNMENT EMPLOYEES

AUTHORITY: Government Code Annotated, Title 1, Division 4, Section 3500 et seq. (1961) as last amended effective Oct. 16, 1981.

EXCLUSIONS: Elected or appointed officials; school district employees.

UNIT DETERMINATION: Absent local procedures, disputes submitted to the Department of Industrial Relations (DIR).

CRITERIA FOR UNIT DETERMINATION: Professionals may be in their own units; governing body may not prohibit peace officers from joining unions composed solely of such employees.

RECOGNITION: Exclusive; by election.

BARGAINING RIGHTS: Meet and confer.

SCOPE OF BARGAINING: Matters relating to employment conditions and employer-employee relations including but not limited to wages, hours, and other terms and conditions of employment; excluding merits, necessity, or organization of any service or activity provided by law or Executive Order.

EMPLOYEE RIGHTS: To form, join, and participate in unions; refrain from doing so; may represent themselves in employer-employee matters.

UNION SECURITY: Dues deduction permitted. Agency shop permitted. Employees with religious objections may pay agency fees to nonreligious, nonlabor, tax-exempt charity from list of at least three funds designated by the parties or chosen by employee if parties fail to designate. Agency shop may be rescinded by majority vote if request for vote is supported by petition of 30 percent of bargaining unit; vote is by secret ballot and only allowed once during contract term; parties may decide alternative procedure for vote.

UNFAIR LABOR PRACTICES: Interfere with, intimidate, restrain, coerce, or discriminate against employees on account of union membership.

IMPASSE PROCEDURE: Mediation—Parties may mutually agree to mediation; costs shared equally by the parties.

NOTE: Local collective bargaining ordinances cover a majority of city and county employees in California.

## PUBLIC SCHOOL EMPLOYEES

AUTHORITY: Government Code Annotated, Title 1, Division 4, Section 3540 et seq. (1975) as last amended effective Jan. 1, 1986. *Note: Statute covers any person employed by any public school employer, employees of school and community college districts.*

EXCLUSIONS: Elected or appointed officials; managerial and confidential employees.

ADMINISTRATIVE AGENCY: Public Employment Relations Board (PERB).

UNIT DETERMINATION: PERB in cases of dispute.

CRITERIA FOR UNIT DETERMINATION: Community of interest; extent of organization; effect on efficient operations of employer; unit of classroom teachers must include all teachers except managerial, confidential, and supervisory employees; unit of supervisors must include all supervisors and must be represented by a different union than nonsupervisory unit; classified and certificated employees shall not be included in same unit. *Note: If a district employs 20 or more supervisory peace officers, unit of supervisory employees is appropriate if it includes (1) all supervisory nonpeace officers employed by the district and supervisory peace officers employed by the district or (2) all supervisory nonpeace officers employed by the district, exclusively or (3) all supervisory peace officers employed by the district, exclusively. Unit of supervisors shall not be represented by same union representing supervisors' employees.*

RECOGNITION: Exclusive; by voluntary designation or by election.

BARGAINING RIGHTS: Meet and negotiate.

SCOPE OF BARGAINING: Wages, hours, and other terms and conditions of employment; consultation on policy.

GRIEVANCE PROCEDURE: Arbitration permitted.

EMPLOYEE RIGHTS: To form, join, and participate in unions; refrain from doing so; present grievances; file unfair labor practice charges.

EMPLOYER RIGHTS: Formulate district policies; administer district programs; hire, transfer, suspend, lay off, recall, promote, discharge, assign, reward, or discipline employees; assign work; direct employees; adjust grievances.

UNION SECURITY: Dues deduction mandatory. Agency shop or maintenance of membership permitted. Employer may require separate ratification of union security provision. If religious beliefs prohibit employee's payment of dues, equivalent amount may be paid to nonreligious charity; union may charge such employees reasonable costs of processing grievances.

UNFAIR LABOR PRACTICES BY EMPLOYER: Threaten, discriminate against, interfere with, restrain, or coerce employees; deny union rights guaranteed under statute; refusal to meet and negotiate in good faith; dominate unions; refusal to participate in impasse procedure in good faith.

UNFAIR LABOR PRACTICES BY UNION: Cause or attempt to cause employer to commit unfair labor practice; threaten, discriminate against, interfere with, restrain, or coerce employees; refusal to meet and negotiate in good faith; refusal to participate in impasse procedure in good faith.

IMPASSE PROCEDURE: Mediation–Either party may request PERB to appoint a mediator or parties may mutually appoint a mediator; costs shared equally by the parties if they appoint their own mediator; if PERB appoints mediator, costs are borne by PERB. Fact Finding–Either parety may request after 15 days of mediation; tripartite panel; advisory report issued within 30 days, made public after 10 days; mutually incurred costs shared equally by the parties; chairperson paid by PERB.

CRITERIA FOR FACT FINDING REPORT: Applicable state and federal laws; stipulations of the parties; interest and welfare of the public; ability to pay; comparison with employees performing similar services and other employees generally in comparable communities; cost of living; overall compensation; other factors normally considered.

NOTE: Initial proposals must be made in public; agreement may not exceed three years.

## HIGHER EDUCATION EMPLOYEES

AUTHORITY: Government Code Annotated, Title 1, Division 4, Section 3560 et seq. (1978) as last amended effective July 1, 1983. *Note: Statute covers employees of the University of California, Hastings College of the Law, and California State University.*

EXCLUSIONS: Managerial and confidential employees; students if work is related to education.

ADMINISTRATIVE AGENCY: Public Employment Relations Board (PERB).

UNIT DETERMINATION: PERB in cases of dispute.

CRITERIA FOR UNIT DETERMINATION: Community of interest; effect on meet and confer relationship; effect on efficient operations of employer; number of employees and classifications; impact on meet and confer relationship created by fragmentation; presumption that professionals and nonprofessionals shall be in separate units; presumption that all employees with occupational group(s) shall be in separate units; members of academic senate of University of California are in separate statewide or divisional units; peace officers shall not be in units with other employees; supervisors must be in separate units; skilled craft employees have right to be in separate units.

RECOGNITION: Exclusive; by voluntary designation or by election.

BARGAINING RIGHTS: Meet and confer.

SCOPE OF BARGAINING: Wages, hours, and other terms and conditions of employment.

GRIEVANCE PROCEDURE: Arbitration permitted.

EMPLOYEE RIGHTS: To form, join, and participate in unions; refrain from doing so; present grievances.

EMPLOYER RIGHTS: Merits, necessity, or organization of service, activity or program established by law; fees that are not a condition of employment; admission and degree requirements of students, content and supervision of courses and research programs; appointment, tenure, promotion of members of academic senate, grievance procedure for senate (consultation rights on this category); housing rental rates for California State University employees.

UNION SECURITY: Dues deduction mandatory; maintenance of membership permitted.

UNFAIR LABOR PRACTICES BY EMPLOYER: Threaten, discriminate, interfere with, restrain, or coerce employees; deny unions rights guaranteed under statute; refusal to meet and confer; dominate unions; refusal to participate in impasse procedure; consult with groups other than exclusive representative.

UNFAIR LABOR PRACTICES BY UNION: Interfere with, restrain, or coerce employees; cause or attempt to cause employer to commit ULP; refusal to meet and confer; refusal to participate in impasse procedure; failure to represent all employees fairly; charge excessive service fees; cause or attempt to cause employer to pay for services not rendered.

IMPASSE PROCEDURE: Mediation–Either party may request PERB to appoint mediator; costs borne by PERB; parties may establish their own procedure in which case costs are shared equally by the parties. Fact Finding–Either party may request after 15 days of mediation; tripartite panel; report issued within 30 days, made public within 10 days; mutually incurred costs shared equally by the parties, chairperson paid by PERB.

NOTE: Initial proposals must be made at a public meeting; a student representative shall be allowed to attend meet and confer sessions involving student service or academic personnel.

---

## CONNECTICUT

**There are three public employee bargaining statutes in the State of Connecticut. The laws cover state employees, municipal employees, and teachers. The statutes for state and municipal workers provide for bargaining over wages, hours, and other employment conditions, excluding merit systems. Teachers may bargain over salaries and other conditions of employment. All three statutes prohibit strikes.**

### STATE EMPLOYEES

AUTHORITY: Connecticut General Statutes, Title 5, Section 5-270 et seq. (1975) as last amended effective July 1, 1986.

EXCLUSIONS: Elected or appointed officials; board and commission members; part-time and confidential employees.

ADMINISTRATIVE AGENCY: State Board of Labor Relations (SBLR).

UNIT DETERMINATION: SBLR.

CRITERIA FOR UNIT DETERMINATION: Community of interest; effects of over-fragmentation; professionals must vote for inclusion in nonprofessional units; statewide bargaining; separate units for public institutions of higher education and non-faculty professional staff unless both agree to be included in one unit.

RECOGNITION: Exclusive; by voluntary designation or by election.

BARGAINING RIGHTS: Duty to bargain.

SCOPE OF BARGAINING: Wages, hours, and other conditions of employment excluding merit system.

GRIEVANCE PROCEDURE: Arbitration permitted.

EMPLOYEE RIGHTS: To organize, form, join, or assist unions; bargain collectively; engage in other concerted activities; present grievances.

UNION SECURITY: Agency shop mandatory.

UNFAIR LABOR PRACTICES BY EMPLOYER: Interfere with, restrain, or coerce employees, including a lockout; dominate unions; discriminate on account of union membership or testimony; refusal to bargain in good faith; refusal to reduce agreement to writing and to sign it; violation of SBLR rules regarding conduct of representation elections.

UNFAIR LABOR PRACTICES BY UNION: Restrain or coerce employees or employer's representative; refusal to bargain in good faith; violation of SBLR rules regarding conduct of representation elections; refusal to reduce agreement to writing and to sign it.

IMPASSE PROCEDURES: Mediation—May be jointly requested by both parties from the State Board of Mediation and Arbitration (SBMA). Arbitration—By either or both parties' request from SBMA; single arbitrator selected jointly by the parties or by rules of American Arbitration Association if parties are unable to agree; last best offer on issue-by-issue basis on mandatory subjects for bargaining; arbiter selected within 10 days after filing for arbitration; hearings begin 20 days after selection; after 30-day period of hearings, arbiter issues award; fees and expenses shared equally by the parties; legislature may return matter within 30 days if there are insufficient funds for full implementaion of award.
CRITERIA FOR ARBITRATION AWARD: History of bargaining; existing employment conditions of similar employee groups; prevailing wages, fringes, and working conditions in labor market; overall compensation; ability to pay; cost of living; interests and welfare of employees.

STRIKE POLICY: Prohibited.

NOTE: No union shall be eligible to participate in a recognition election until it has been in existence in state employment for at least six months.

## MUNICIPAL EMPLOYEES

AUTHORITY: Connecticut General Statutes, Title 7, Section 7-467 et seq. (1965) as last amended effective Oct. 1, 1985.

EXCLUSIONS: Elected and administrative officials; board and commission members; certified teachers; some part-time employees; department heads; some supervisors.

ADMINISTRATIVE AGENCY: State Board of Labor Relations (SBLR).

UNIT DETERMINATION: SBLR.

CRITERIA FOR UNIT DETERMINATION: Single unit for each fire and police department of uniformed and investigatory employees; professionals must vote for inclusion in nonprofessional units; community of interest; no unit shall include both supervisory and nonsupervisory employees except police and fire fighters units.

RECOGNITION: Exclusive; by voluntary designation or by election.

BARGAINING RIGHTS: Duty to bargain.

SCOPE OF BARGAINING: Wages, hours, and other conditions of employment excluding merit system.

GRIEVANCE PROCEDURE: Arbitration permitted.

EMPLOYEE RIGHTS: To organize, form, join, or assist unions; bargain collectively; engage in other concerted activities; present grievances.

UNFAIR LABOR PRACTICES BY EMPLOYER: Interfere with, restrain, or coerce employees; dominate unions; discriminate on account of testimony; refusal to bargain in good faith; refusal to discuss grievances; refusal to comply with an arbitration award.

UNFAIR LABOR PRACTICES BY UNION: Restrain or coerce employees or employer's representative; refusal to bargain in good faith; refusal to comply with an arbitration award.

IMPASSE PROCEDURE: Mediation--If there is no agreement within 50 days after negotiations begin or either party has not requested mediation, State Board of Mediation and Arbitration (SBMA) will appoint a mediator. Fact Finding--Either party may request fact finding from SBMA; parties may select a fact finder or SBMA will appoint one; report issued within 60 days; costs shared equally except when a party has been found not to have bargained in good faith and may be required to pay entire cost; fact finder may mediate. If parties do not request fact finding within 75 days after negotiations begin, SBMA will initiate; fact finding report due 14 days before expiration of contract. Arbitration--Mandatory; if either party rejects fact finder's report, party may request arbitration from SBMA; tripartite panel; final offer or on an issue-by-issue basis; costs of chairperson shared equally by the parties. If neither party requests arbitration within 90 days after expiration of current contract, SBMA will impose final offer arbitration on issue-by-issue basis; tripartite panel; parties must supply cost data for all provisions of their proposed agreement; costs of chairperson shared equally by the parties.

CRITERIA FOR ARBITRATION AWARD: Negotiations prior to arbitration; public interest; ability to pay; interests and welfare of the employees; cost of living; existing employment conditions of employees and those of similar groups; prevailing wages, salaries, fringe benefits, and other conditions of employment in labor market.

STRIKE POLICY: Prohibited.

NOTE: No union shall be eligible to petition for exclusive recognition or to participate in recognition elections unless it has been in existence for at least six months.

---

## TEACHERS

AUTHORITY: Connecticut General Statutes, Title 10, Section 10-153a et seq. (1958) as last amended effective July 1, 1984.

EXCLUSIONS: Superintendent and assistant superintendent; employer's negotiators; personnel or budget employees; temporary substitutes; non-certified employees.

ADMINISTRATIVE AGENCY: For representation and impasses--State Board of Education (SBE). For prohibited practices--State Board of Labor Relations (SBLR).

UNIT DETERMINATION: Statute; two units established--administrators, teachers.

RECOGNITION: Exclusive; voluntary requires showing of interest from majority in unit; election requires 20 percent to petition.

BARGAINING RIGHTS: Duty to bargain.

SCOPE OF BARGAINING: Salaries and other conditions of employment.

EMPLOYEE RIGHTS: To form, join, or assist unions; refrain from doing so; present grievances.

UNFAIR LABOR PRACTICES BY EMPLOYER: Interfere with, restrain, or coerce employees; dominate unions; discriminate on account of testimony; refusal to bargain in good faith; refusal to participate in mediation or arbitration in good faith.

UNFAIR LABOR PRACTICES BY UNION: Interfere with, restrain, or coerce employees or employer's representative; discriminate on account of testimony; refusal to bargain in good faith; refusal to participate in mediation or arbitration in good faith; solicit or advocate support of students.

UNION SECURITY: Agency shop permitted.

IMPASSE PROCEDURE: Mediation--Either party may request mediation from the Commissioner of the State Board of Education; if no agreement 110 days prior to budget submission and mediation has not been initiated, Commissioner will initiate mediation; costs shared equally by the parties. Arbitration--If mediation fails by fourth day or 85 days prior to budget submission date, Commissioner will initiate arbitration; parties may mutually agree to a single arbitrator, otherwise tripartite panel; final offer on issue-by-issue basis; award due within 20 days; costs shared equally by the parties.

CRITERIA FOR ARBITRATION AWARD: Negotiations prior to arbitration; public interest; ability to pay; interests and welfare of the employees; existing conditions of employment of employees and those of similar groups; prevailing salaries, benefits, and other working conditions in state labor market.

STRIKE POLICY: Prohibited; may be enjoined by courts.

NOTE: Arbitration awards are not subject to legislative approval.

## DELAWARE

**There are four public employee bargaining laws in the State of Delaware. One statute covers state and county employees together with employees of local governments that elect coverage. Two other two statutes cover teachers and transit workers, while a fourth law grants bargaining rights to police officers and fire fighters.**

### *STATE, COUNTY, AND LOCAL EMPLOYEES*

AUTHORITY: Delaware Code Title 19, Section 1301 et seq. (1965) as last amended July 9, 1986.

EXCLUSIONS: Teachers, elected or appointed officials; inmates; police officers; fire fighters.

ADMINISTRATIVE AGENCY: Department of Labor.

UNIT DETERMINATION: Department of Labor.

CRITERIA FOR UNIT DETERMINATION: Duties, skills, and working conditions; history of bargaining; extent of organization; desire of employees.

RECOGNITION: Exclusive; by election.

BARGAINING RIGHTS: Duty to bargain.

SCOPE OF BARGAINING: Wages, salaries, hours, vacations, sick leave, grievance procedures, and other terms and conditions of employment.

EMPLOYEES RIGHTS: To organize and select bargaining representatives; present grievances.

UNION SECURITY: Dues deduction mandatory.

IMPASSE PROCEDURE: Any issue in dispute, except wages and salaries, may be submitted to Department of Labor or, if agreed to by the parties, to an arbitrator.

STRIKE POLICY: Prohibited.

---

## TEACHERS

AUTHORITY: Delaware Code Title 14, Chapter 40, Section 4001 et seq. (1969) as last amended effective Aug. 29, 1983.

EXCLUSIONS: Administrators.

ADMINISTRATIVE AGENCY: Public Employment Relations Board (PERB).

UNIT DETERMINATION: PERB.

CRITERIA FOR UNIT DETERMINATION: Similarity of duties, skills, and working conditions; history and extent of organization; recommendations of party involved; over-fragmentation; other factors PERB deems appropriate.

RECOGNITION: Exclusive; by election.

BARGAINING RIGHTS: Duty to bargain.

SCOPE OF BARGAINING: Wages, salaries, hours, grievance procedures, and working conditions.

GRIEVANCE PROCEDURE: Required.

EMPLOYEE RIGHTS: Organize, form, join, or assist employee organization; negotiate collectively or grieve through representatives of own choosing; other concerted activities; be represented without discrimination.

EMPLOYER RIGHTS: Matters of inherent policy, including functions and programs, standards of service, budget, technology, organizational structure, curriculum, discipline, and selection and direction of personnel.

UNION SECURITY: Dues deduction mandatory.

UNFAIR LABOR PRACTICES BY EMPLOYER: Interfere with, restrain, or coerce employees; dominate unions; encourage or discourage union membership; discriminate on account of testimony; refusal to bargain in good faith; refusal to comply with statute; refusal to reduce agreement to writing and to sign it; refusal to disclose public records.

UNFAIR LABOR PRACTICES BY UNION: Interfere with, restrain, or coerce employees; refusal to bargain in good faith; refusal to comply with statute; refusal to reduce agreement to writing and to sign it; soliciting employees during work hours; hindering or preventing pursuit of work; solicit or advocate support of students on school property.

IMPASSE PROCEDURE: Mediation — Voluntary or PERB appoints mediator at request of either party; costs paid by PERB. Fact finding — Parties may jointly or individually petition PERB to initiate fact finding or mediator may recommend fact finding. If PERB initiates fact finding, party may mutually select fact finder or PERB appoints one from list of five if parties do not designate fact finder from list; recommendations due 30 days after hearings end but not later than 45 days from day of appointment. PERB may publicize recommendations if dispute continues; costs shared equally by the parties.

CRITERIA FOR FACT FINDING REPORT: interests and welfare of public; comparison of wages and benefits of employees involved with those of other employees performing similar work and with other public and private employees generally in same and comparable communities; overall compensation; increases in wages in private sector of the state; stipulations of the parties; lawful authority of employer; ability to pay; other factors normally considered.

STRIKE POLICY: Prohibited.

NOTE: Contract duration must be for minimum of two years; hearings conducted by fact finders shall be open to the public.

---

## TRANSIT EMPLOYEES

AUTHORITY: Delaware Code Title 2, Chapter 16, Sec. 1613 et seq. effective May 1, 1968.

SCOPE OF BARGAINING: Wages, salaries, hours, working conditions, health benefits, pensions, and retirement allowances.

IMPASSE PROCEDURE: Final and binding arbitration at request of either party.

STRIKE POLICY: Prohibited.

---

## POLICE OFFICERS AND FIRE FIGHTERS

AUTHORITY: Delaware Code Title 19, Section 1601 et seq. effective Sept. 6, 1986.

EXCLUSIONS: Those determined by public employment relations board to be inappropriate; state employees covered under state merit system.

ADMINISTRATIVE AGENCY: Public Employment Relations Board (PERB).

UNIT DETERMINATION: PERB.

CRITERIA FOR UNIT DETERMINATION: Similarity of duties, skills, and working conditions of employees; history and extent of organization; recommendations of the parties; overfragmentation of unit on efficient administration of government; other factors PERB deems appropriate.

RECOGNITION: Exclusive; by designation or by election.

BARGAINING RIGHTS: Duty to bargain.

SCOPE OF BARGAINING: Wages, salaries, hours, grievance procedures, working conditions.

GRIEVANCE PROCEDURE: Required.

EMPLOYEE RIGHTS: To organize, form, join, or assist unions; bargain collectively, grieve through representatives of own choosing; engage in other concerted activity; be represented without discrimination; present grievances.

EMPLOYER RIGHTS: Functions and programs; standards of services; budget; use of technology; organizational structure and staffing levels; selection and direction of personnel.

UNION SECURITY: Dues deduction mandatory.

UNFAIR LABOR PRACTICES BY EMPLOYER: Interfere with, restrain, or coerce employees; dominate unions; discriminate on account of union membership or testimony; refusal to bargain in good faith; refusal to comply with statute; refusal to reduce agreement to writing and to sign it; refusal to disclose public records.

UNFAIR LABOR PRACTICES BY UNION: Interfere with, restrain, or coerce employees; refusal to bargain in good faith; refusal to comply with statute; refusal to reduce agreement to writing and to sign it; distribute union literature or solicit employees during work hours; hinder or prevent pursuit of work.

IMPASSE PROCEDURE: Mediation — If parties do not voluntarily submit to mediation and fewer than 30 days remain before contract expiration or more than 90 days have elapsed since bargaining began in case of newly certified agent, PERB appoints mediator at either party's request; costs of mediator paid by PERB. Fact finding — Either party may petition PERB for fact finding; mediator may recommend fact finding; parties may mutually initiate at any time; parties may mutually select fact finder, parties may select from PERB list, or PERB appoints fact finder; recommendation limited to determination of last-best final offer.

CRITERIA FOR FACT FINDING REPORT: Interest and welfare of public; comparison with wages and benefits of other employees performing similar work and with other employees generally in same community and in comparable communities and in private employment in same community and in comparable communities; overall compensation; increases in private sector weekly wages within state; stipulations of the parties; lawful authority of employer; ability to pay; other factors not normally considered.

STRIKE POLICY: Prohibited; employee loses pay and benefits for strike days.

NOTE: Minimum two-year contract duration unless otherwise agreed to; election bar of one year.

---

## DISTRICT OF COLUMBIA

**There is one public employee bargaining statute in the District of Columbia. Covering all employees of the city government, the law includes provisions for bargaining over compensation and terms and conditions of employment. The statute permits negotiation of union security in the form of an agency shop.**

## *ALL PUBLIC EMPLOYEES*

AUTHORITY: D.C. Law 2-139, Section 103 et seq. (1978) as last amended effective April 8, 1980.

EXCLUSIONS: Chief judges, associate judges, and non-judicial personnel of the Superior Court and Court of Appeals; supervisors, management officials, or employees whose participation in a union would result in conflict of interest.

ADMINISTRATIVE AGENCY: Public Employee Relations Board (PERB).

UNIT DETERMINATION: PERB.

CRITERIA FOR UNIT DETERMINATION: Community of interest; promotion of effective labor relations; efficiency of agency operations; skills, working conditions, common supervision, physical location, organizational structure, distinctiveness of functions performed, and existence of integrated work process; extent of organization; supervisors must be in separate units except with respect to fire fighters; no unit shall include confidential employees, employees engaged in personnel work other than in a clerical capacity, employees engaged in administering statute, and employees of the city council; professionals must vote for inclusion in nonprofessional unit; two or more units for which union holds exclusive recognition within agency may be consolidated into one larger unit.

RECOGNITION: Exclusive; by voluntary designation or by election.

BARGAINING RIGHTS: Duty to bargain.

SCOPE OF BARGAINING: Compensation, union security, and terms and conditions of employment. Compensation includes salary, wages, health benefits, within-grade increases, overtime, education pay, shift differentials, premium pay, hours, and other compensation matters.

GRIEVANCE PROCEDURE: Arbitration permitted.

EMPLOYEE RIGHTS: To organize, join, or assist unions; bargain collectively; refrain from doing so; present grievances.

EMPLOYER RIGHTS: Direct employees; hire, promote, transfer, assign, and retain employees; suspend, demote, discharge, or take other disciplinary action against employees for just cause; relieve employees from duties because of lack of work; maintain efficiency; determine mission of agency, budget, number of employees, types and grades of positions of employees assigned to organizational unit; determine technology of work and internal security practices; take whatever actions may be necessary to carry out mission in emergencies.

UNION SECURITY: Dues deduction mandatory; agency shop permitted.

UNFAIR LABOR PRACTICES BY EMPLOYER: Interfere with, restrain, or coerce employees; dominate unions; discriminate on account of union membership or testimony; refusal to bargain in good faith.

UNFAIR LABOR PRACTICES BY UNION: Interfere with, restrain, or coerce employees; cause or attempt to cause management to coerce employees; refusal to bargain in good faith; participate in a strike or work stoppage; recognitional strikes or secondary boycott.

IMPASSE PROCEDURE (COMPENSATION): Mediation--Any party may request and PERB may impose anytime if at impasse, after 180 days of bargaining, or 90 days before expiration of contract. Costs borne by moving party or shared by mutual request. Fact Finding--Permitted by statute; costs borne by moving party or shared by mutual request. Arbitration--Any party may request after 30 days or less of mediation; final offer by package; award due within 20 days; costs shared equally by the parties.

IMPASSE PROCEDURE (TERMS AND CONDITIONS): May be invoked by either party or on application of PERB; PERB may impose procedures of its choice.

CRITERIA FOR PROCEDURE: Existing laws, rules, and regulations; ability of city to comply with award; public safety, health and welfare; need to maintain fair, reasonable, and consistent personnel policies.

STRIKE POLICY: Prohibited; union may be decertified.

NOTE: Impasse resolution machinery includes, but is not limited to, (1) mediation, (2) fact finding, (3) advisory arbitration, (4) request for injunction, (5) binding arbitration, (6) final best offer binding arbitration, and (7) final best offer binding arbitration item by item on noncompensation matters. Bargaining sessions shall not be open to the public; fact finding proceedings shall be open to the public; no compensation agreement can be negotiated for fewer than three years.

## FLORIDA

**There is one collective bargaining statute covering all public employees in the State of Florida. In addition to granting employees the right to negotiate wages, hours, and terms and conditions of employment, the statute also carries strong sanctions against strikes and extends the state's "sunshine law" to negotiations by requiring that meetings with public officials must be open to the public.**

## *ALL PUBLIC EMPLOYEES*

AUTHORITY: Florida Statutes, Chapter 447, Section 447.201 et seq. (1974) as last amended effective June 18, 1984.

EXCLUSIONS: Appointed or elected officials; heads of agencies; members of boards and commissions; militia; employer's negotiators; managerial, confidential, and legislative employees; inmates.

ADMINISTRATIVE AGENCY: Public Employees Relations Commission (PERC).

UNIT DETERMINATION: PERC.

CRITERIA FOR UNIT DETERMINATION: Principles of efficient administration of government; number of organizations with which employer might negotiate; compatibility of unit with parties' responsibilities to represent the public; power of employer to agree or recommend action; employer's organizational structure; statutory authority of employer to administer a job classification and pay plan; other policies PERC finds appropriate; exclusion of professionals and nonprofessionals from same unit unless both groups vote for inclusion; community of interest of unit employees. *Note: Employees' community of interest includes manner in which wages and other terms of employment are determined; manner in which jobs and salary classifications are determined; interdependence of jobs and interchange of employees; desires of employees; history of bargaining.*

RECOGNITION: Exclusive; by voluntary designation or by election.

BARGAINING RIGHTS: Duty to bargain.

SCOPE OF BARGAINING: Wages, hours, and terms and conditions of employment.

GRIEVANCE PROCEDURE: Arbitration required; certified union not required to process grievances for nonmembers; career service employees may use civil service appeal procedure as an alternative.

EMPLOYEE RIGHTS: To form, join, and participate in unions; refrain from doing so; be represented by a union in negotiations and grievances; present grievances; engage in concerted activities; refrain from doing so.

EMPLOYER RIGHTS: Determine purpose, set standards of service, and exercise discretion and control over organization and operation; direct employees; discipline for proper cause; relieve employees from duty for legitimate reasons.

UNION SECURITY: Dues deduction mandatory.

UNFAIR LABOR PRACTICES BY EMPLOYER: Interfere with, restrain, or coerce employees; discriminate on account of union membership or testimony; refusal to bargain in good faith or refusal to sign final agreement; dominate unions; refusal to discuss grievances in good faith.

UNFAIR LABOR PRACTICES BY UNION: Interfere with, restrain, or coerce employees; cause or attempt to cause employees to commit ULP; refusal to bargain in good faith; discriminate on account of testimony; participate in a strike; solicit support from students.

IMPASSE PROCEDURE: Mediation--Either or both parties may appoint or request a mediator; costs shared equally by the parties. Fact finding--If mediator has not been appoint or if either party requests, PERC will appoint a fact finder; report issued within 15 days after final hearing; report deemed acceptable unless specifically rejected by either party; costs shared equally by the parties. *Note: Criteria for fact finding report include comparison of annual income with other employees in the locality and in the state; public interest and welfare; peculiarities of employment; availability of funds.*

OTHER ACTIONS UNDER IMPASSE PROCEDURE: If either party rejects fact finder's report, impasse is submitted to legislature for resolution; if agreement is not ratified, legislatively imposed items are effective only for remainder of fiscal year; legislature cannot impose contract provisions such as preambles or recognition or duration clauses.

STRIKE POLICY: Prohibited and may be enjoined by courts; unions may be fined by courts up to maximum of $5,000 for contempt; officers, $50 to $100 per day; PERC may fine union up to $20,000 per day; employer may be awarded damages; employee may be dismissed or placed on probation for six months; certification and dues deduction may be revoked.

NOTE: Contract duration may not exceed three years; negotiations shall be open to the public; two student representatives will be allowed to attend and observe bargaining sessions involving public postsecondary institutions.

---

## GEORGIA

**The one public employee bargaining law in the State of Georgia covers fire fighters. The statute applies only to municipalities of 20,000 or more provided that a city's governing authority passes an ordinance for coverage under the statute.**

### *FIRE FIGHTERS*

AUTHORITY: Code of Georgia Title 54, Section 54-1301 et seq. (1971) as last amended effective July 1, 1976.

EXCLUSIONS: Municipalities under 20,000 population.

RECOGNITION: Exclusive; by election.

BARGAINING RIGHTS: Meet and confer.

SCOPE OF BARGAINING: Wages, rates of pay, hours, working conditions, and all other terms and conditions of employment.

IMPASSE PROCEDURE: Mediation Board--Mandatory 30 days from first bargaining session; tripartite panel; advisory report issued within 10 days of hearing; costs of chairperson shared equally by the parties.

CRITERIA FOR MEDIATION BOARD DECISION: Comparison with comparable fire departments; interest and welfare of the public; comparison of skills, qualifications, and hazards in other trades or professions.

STRIKE POLICY: Prohibited.

NOTE: Contract duration may not exceed one year.

---

## HAWAII

There is one public employee bargaining statute covering all employees in the State of Hawaii. The statute provides for bargaining on wages, hours, contributions to the Hawaii public employees' health fund, and other terms and conditions of employment. The law also calls for final offer arbitration of fire fighters' disputes and grants a limited right to strike provided certain conditions are met.

## *ALL PUBLIC EMPLOYEES*

AUTHORITY: Hawaii Revised Statutes, Chapter 89, Section 89-1 et seq. (1970) as last amended effective May 14, 1986.

EXCLUSIONS: Elected or appointed officials; members of boards or commissions; employer's representatives who are top-level managerial and administrative personnel; confidential employees; part-time and temporary employees; employees in the Governor's office, Lt. Governor's office, and mayor's office; household employees in the Governor's residence; legislative employees; legislative branch employees of the city and county of Honolulu and counties of Hawaii, Maui, and Kauai, except for clerk's office employees; inmates, patients, wards, or students of a state institution; student help; National Guard.

ADMINISTRATIVE AGENCY: Hawaii Labor Relations Board (HLRB).

UNIT DETERMINATION: The following consolidated statewide units are designated by statute: nonsupervisory blue-collar employees; supervisory blue-collar employees; nonsupervisory white-collar employees; supervisory white-collar employees; teachers; educational officers; University of Hawaii and community college faculty; non-faculty personnel of the University of Hawaii and community colleges; registered nurses; nonprofessional hospital and institutional employees; fire fighters; police officers; professional and scientific employees. The last five groups may vote to be included in the general white- or blue-collar units. Supervisors may vote to be included in nonsupervisory units.

RECOGNITION: Exclusive; by election.

BARGAINING RIGHTS: Duty to bargain.

SCOPE OF BARGAINING: Wages, hours, number of incremental and longevity steps and movement between steps within the salary range; amounts of contributions by the state and counties to the Hawaii public employees health fund, and other terms and conditions of employment; excluded are classifications and reclassifications, benefits of—but not contributions to—the Hawaii public employees health fund, retirement, salary ranges provided by law, matters inconsistent with merit principles and equal pay for equal work principle, managerial discipline and control; consultation on all other matters affecting employee relations.

GRIEVANCE PROCEDURE: Arbitration permitted; absent such procedure, disputes may be submitted to HLRB for final decision.

EMPLOYEE RIGHTS: To organize, form, join, or assist unions; engage in lawful concerted activity; refrain from doing so; present grievances.

EMPLOYER RIGHTS: Direct employees; determine qualifications and standards of work; nature and contents of examinations; hire, promote, transfer, assign, and retain employees; discipline employees for proper cause; relieve employees because of lack of work or other legitimate reason; maintain efficiency of operations; determine methods, means, and personnel to implement operations; take actions as might be necessary to carry out mission of agency in cases of emergency.

UNION SECURITY: Dues deduction and agency shop mandatory; employees whose religious beliefs prohibit payment of dues may pay an equivalent amount to a non-religious, non-union charity chosen by the employee from list designated in contract or to any fund chosen by employee if contract does not designate fund; procedure for rebate on demand of any employee for pro rata share of expenditures for activities of political or ideological nature unrelated to terms of employment.

UNFAIR LABOR PRACTICES BY EMPLOYER: Interfere with, restrain, or coerce employees; dominate unions; discriminate on account of union membership or testimony; refusal to bargain in good faith; refusal to participate in impasse procedures in good faith; refusal to comply with statute; violation of contract terms.

UNFAIR LABOR PRACTICES BY UNION: Interfere with, restrain, or coerce employees; refusal to bargain in good faith; refusal to participate in impasse procedures in good faith; refusal to comply with statute; violation of contract terms.

IMPASSE PROCEDURE: Parties may establish their own procedure with arbitration as the final step; absent such procedure, parties may request assistance or HLRB may initiate. Mediation--Mediator(s) appointed by HLRB within three days after date of impasse; costs paid by HLRB. Fact Finding--Excluding fire fighters; HLRB appoints panel of not more than three members 15 days after date of impasse; report issued within 10 days; made public within five days if not referred to arbitration; costs paid by HLRB. Arbitration--Voluntary, excluding fire fighters; procedure begins 30 days after date of impasse; tripartite panel; award due within 20 days; costs of arbitration hearing and neutral arbitrator shared equally by the parties. *Note: If parties do not submit to arbitration, employer will submit recommendations on all cost items together with those of fact finding board to appropriate legislative bodies. Union may submit recommendations.* Mandatory arbitration, fire fighters; begins 15 days after date of impasse; parties may agree on their own procedure and arbitrator(s); if not agreed on after 18 days, dispute is submitted to tripartite panel; award on final package offer due within 30 days of conclusion of hearing; costs of neutral arbitrator shared equally by the parties.

CRITERIA FOR FIRE FIGHTERS' AWARD: Lawful authority of employer; stipulations of the parties; interest and welfare of the public; ability to pay; present and future economic conditions; comparability with persons performing similar services and with other state and county employees; cost of living; overall compensation; changes in circumstances; other factors normally considered.

STRIKE POLICY: Prohibited unless impasse procedures have been complied with, impasse is not submitted to arbitration, 60 days have elapsed since fact finding report, 10-day notice of intent to strike is given, employees are part of the bargaining unit, and employees have been designated by HLRB as being nonessential; HLRB may set requirements to avoid or remove danger to public health or safety; strikes in violation of these procedures may be enjoined; prohibited on issue of contributions to public employees health fund.

---

## IDAHO

**The two public employee bargaining laws in the State of Idaho cover fire fighters and teachers. Fire fighters are allowed to bargain over wage rates, working conditions, and all other terms and conditions of employment. For teachers, matters subject to negotiations are by agreement between the parties.**

## *FIRE FIGHTERS*

AUTHORITY: Idaho Code Chapter 138, Section 44-1801 et seq. (1970) as last amended effective July 1, 1977.

EXCLUSIONS: Supervisors.

ADMINISTRATIVE AGENCY: Department of Labor and Industrial Services.

RECOGNITION: Exclusive; selected by majority.

BARGAINING RIGHTS: Duty to bargain.

SCOPE OF BARGAINING: Wages, rates of pay, working conditions, and all other terms and conditions of employment.

EMPLOYEE RIGHTS: To bargain collectively; be represented by bargaining agent.

IMPASSE PROCEDURE: Fact Finding--Begins 30 days after negotiations commence; tripartite panel; costs incurred by panel shared equally by the parties.

STRIKE POLICY: Prohibited.

---

## TEACHERS

AUTHORITY: Idaho Code Chapter 103, Section 33-1271 et seq. (1971) as last amended effective July 1, 1977.

EXCLUSIONS: Superintendents, supervisors, and principals may be excluded by collective bargaining agreement.

ADMINISTRATIVE AGENCY: State Superintendent of Public Instruction.

RECOGNITION: Exclusive; by voluntary designation or by election.

BARGAINING RIGHTS: Duty to bargain.

SCOPE OF BARGAINING: Matters and conditions subject to negotiations by agreement of the parties.

EMPLOYER RIGHTS: To take necessary actions in cases of emergency.

IMPASSE PROCEDURE: Mediation--Either party may request mediation; procedures and compensation determined by the parties. Fact Finding--Either party may request fact finding if mediation fails; one or more fact finders appointed by mutual agreement of parties; if no agreement within 30 days, appointment made by Superintendent of Public Instruction; report issued within 30 days.

NOTE: Accurate records of negotiation proceedings shall be kept and made available for public inspection; joint ratification of all final settlements shall be made in open meetings.

---

## ILLINOIS

There are two public employee bargaining statutes in the State of Illinois. One law covers public employees in general, including police officers and fire fighters. The second statute covers educational employees. Both statutes provide for union security in the form of an agency shop whereby "fair share" fees may be paid instead of union dues.

## PUBLIC EMPLOYEES IN GENERAL

AUTHORITY: Illinois Public Act 1012, Section 1 et seq. (1984) as last amended effective Sept. 9, 1986.

EXCLUSIONS: Elected officials; executive department heads; members of boards and commissions; employees of any agency, board, or commission created by public employee bargaining statute; temporary or emergency employees; educational, managerial, and confidential employees; independent contractors and supervisors. *Note: Employer may choose to bargain with supervisors; statute not applicable to local government units of fewer than 35 employees unless unit existed before statute took effect.*

ADMINISTRATIVE AGENCY: Illinois State Labor Relations Board (ILRB) for state employees, local government units of less than one million population, and the Regional Transportation Authority; Illinois Local Labor Relations Board (ILLRB) for local government units of more than one million excluding the Regional Transportation Authority.

UNIT DETERMINATION: ILRB or ILLRB.

CRITERIA FOR UNIT DETERMINATION: Historical pattern of recognition; community of interest; degree of functional integration; interchangeability and contact among employees; fragmentation of employee groups; common supervision, wages, hours, and other working conditions; desires of employees; professionals and nonprofessionals must be in separate units unless both groups vote for inclusion in same unit. Majority of employees of a craft may form own unit.

RECOGNITION: Exclusive; by voluntary designation or by election.

BARGAINING RIGHTS: Duty to bargain.

SCOPE OF BARGAINING: Wages, hours, and other conditions of employment.

GRIEVANCE PROCEDURE: Arbitration required.

EMPLOYEE RIGHTS: To organize, form, join, or assist unions; bargain collectively; present grievances; engage in lawful concerted activities; refrain from doing so; present grievances.

EMPLOYER RIGHTS: Functions of employer; standards of services; budget; organizational structure; selection of new employees; examination techniques; direct employees.

UNION SECURITY: Agency shop fair share fee permitted; dues and fair share fees deduction mandatory; board may establish list of charities for fair share payments if employee and union cannot agree on employee's proportionate share to be paid to a non-religious charity because of employee's religious beliefs.

UNFAIR LABOR PRACTICES BY EMPLOYER: Interfere with, restrain, or coerce employees; discriminate on account of union membership or testimony; dominate unions; refusal to bargain in good faith; violation of board's rules and regulations.

UNFAIR LABOR PRACTICES BY UNION: Restrain or coerce employees or employer's representative; cause or attempt to cause employer to discriminate against an employee on account of union membership or testimony; refusal to bargain in good faith; violation of board's rules and regulations; picketing to force employer to bargain.

IMPASSE PROCEDURE: (Excluding security employees, peace officers, fire fighters, and paramedics) Mediation—Upon request of the parties from mediation roster established by governing boards; costs shared equally by the parties; other mediators may be selected by the parties. Fact Finding—By mutual consent of the parties; parties designate fact finder from list submitted by board; fact finder may mediate; report issued within 45 days of appointment; advisory findings made public; if fact finder does not make recommendations and publicize such findings within 45 days of date of appointment, party may resume negotiations. Arbitration—Voluntary. (Security employees, peace officers, fire fighters, and paramedics) Mediation—Mandatory 30 days before contract expiration. Arbitration—Mandatory 14 days before contract expiration at request of either party; tripartite panel; costs of arbitration hearing and neutral arbitrator shared equally by the parties; award on last best offer on each economic item within 30 days after hearing. *All terms of arbiter's decision subject to review by employer's governing body who may reject any term by three fifths vote in which case parties return to arbitration panel for supplemental decision of rejected term(s). Unresolved disputes may be submitted to alternative form of impasse resolution.*

Note: For peace officers, fire fighters, and paramedics, arbitration decision is limited to wages, hours, and conditions of employment. Excludes residency requirements; type of equipment other than uniforms and turnout gear; manning; total number of employees in department; mutual aid and assistance agreements to other governmental units; and criterion pursuant to which force, including deadly force, can be used. Exception: Decisions are allowed regarding equipment or manning levels if there is finding of serious risk to safety in specific work assignment beyond normal duties.

CRITERIA FOR ARBITRATION AWARD: Lawful authority of employer and stipulations of the parties; interest and welfare of the public; ability to pay; comparison of wages, hours, and working conditions with other employees performing similar services and with other employees generally in public and private employment in comparable communities; average consumer prices; overall compensation; changes in circumstances during arbitration proceedings; other factors normally considered.

STRIKE POLICY: Permitted—except for security employees, peace officers, fire fighters, and paramedics—but only if employees are represented, contract has expired and does not prohibit strike, disputed issues are not submitted to binding arbitration, mediation has been unsuccessful, five days have elapsed after notice to strike; may be enjoined if there is danger to public health and safety.

## *EDUCATIONAL EMPLOYEES*

AUTHORITY: Illinois Public Act 1014, Section 1 et seq. effective Jan. 1, 1984.

EXCLUSIONS: Supervisors; managerial, confidential, and short-term employees; students and part-time employees of community colleges.

ADMINISTRATIVE AGENCY: Illinois Educational Labor Relations Board (IELRB).

UNIT DETERMINATION: IELRB.

CRITERIA FOR UNIT DETERMINATION: Historical pattern of recognition; community of interest; desires of employees; multi-unit bargaining permitted; majority of craft employees have right to decide on own unit.

RECOGNITION: Exclusive; by voluntary designation or by election; certification requires majority of employees in unit.

BARGAINING RIGHTS: Duty to bargain.

SCOPE OF BARGAINING: Wages, hours, and other terms and conditions of employment.

GRIEVANCE PROCEDURE: Arbitration required.

EMPLOYEE RIGHTS: To organize, form, join, or assist unions; engage in lawful concerted activities; bargain collectively; right to refrain from any and all activities; present grievances.

EMPLOYER RIGHTS: Determine functions; standards of services; budget; organizational structure; selection of new employees; direct employees.

UNION SECURITY: Agency shop fair share fee permitted; dues and fair share fees deduction mandatory; IELRB may establish list of charities for fair share payments if employee and union cannot agree on employee's proportionate share to be paid to a non-religious charity because of employee's religious beliefs.

UNFAIR LABOR PRACTICES BY EMPLOYER: Interfere with, restrain, or coerce employees; dominate unions; discriminate in hiring, tenure; discriminate on account of union membership or testimony; refusal to bargain in good faith or to sign agreement; violation of rules and regulations of IELRB; refusal to comply with binding arbitration award.

UNFAIR LABOR PRACTICES BY UNION: Restrain or coerce employees or employer; refusal to bargain in good faith or to sign agreement; violation of rules and regulations of IELRB; refusal to comply with binding arbitration award.

IMPASSE PROCEDURE: Either party may petition or IELRB may initiate mediation 45 days from start of school year; mediator may perform fact finding if requested by the parties; IELRB invokes mediation 15 days before start of school year; costs shared equally by the parties. Arbitration--Voluntary.

STRIKE POLICY: Prohibited unless employees are represented, mediation has been unsuccessful, five days have elapsed after notice to strike, contract has expired, disputed issues are not submitted to binding arbitration. May be enjoined if danger to public health and safety.

NOTE: Contract may not exceed three years.

---

## INDIANA

**The one public employee bargaining statute in the State of Indiana covers teachers. The law provides for teachers to bargain over pay, hours, and wage-related fringes, allows "discussion" on other employment matters, and prohibits strikes.**

### *TEACHERS*

AUTHORITY: Indiana Code Title 20, Article 7.5, Section 20-7.5-1-1 et seq. (1973) as last amended May 1, 1978.

EXCLUSIONS: Supervisors, confidential, and part-time employees; employees performing security work; non-certificated employees.

ADMINISTRATIVE AGENCY: Educational Employment Relations Board (EERB).

UNIT DETERMINATION: EERB in cases of dispute.

CRITERIA FOR UNIT DETERMINATION: Efficient administration of school operations; community of interest; avoidance of over-fragmentation; recommendations of the parties.

RECOGNITION: Exclusive; by voluntary designation requires showing of interest from majority in unit; by election requires majority of employees in unit.

BARGAINING RIGHTS: Duty to bargain.

SCOPE OF BARGAINING: Salaries, wages, hours, and salary- and wage-related fringe benefits. Duty to discuss curriculum development and revision; textbook selection; teaching methods; selection, assignment, or promotion of personnel; student discipline, expulsion, or supervision of students; pupil-teacher ratio; class size; budget appropriations.

GRIEVANCE PROCEDURE: Arbitration permitted.

EMPLOYEE RIGHTS: To form, join, or assist unions; participate in bargaining; engage in other activities; present grievances.

EMPLOYER RIGHTS: Direct work; establish policy; hire, promote, demote, transfer, assign, or retain employees; suspend or discharge employees; maintain efficiency of school operations; relieve employees because of lack of work; take actions necessary to carry out mission.

UNION SECURITY: Dues deduction mandatory.

UNFAIR LABOR PRACTICES BY EMPLOYER: Interefere with, restrain, or coerce employees; dominate unions; discriminate on account of union membership or testimony; refusal to bargain or discuss; failure or refusal to comply with statute.

UNFAIR LABOR PRACTICES BY UNION: Interfere with, restrain, or coerce employees or employer's representative; cause or attempt to cause employer to commit unfair labor practice; refusal to bargain; failure or refusal to comply with statute.

IMPASSE PROCEDURE: Mediation--Either party may request EERB to appoint mediator or EERB shall appoint mediator if no agreement 75 days prior to budget submission date; costs paid by EERB. Fact Finding--Either party may request fact finding after five days of mediation or EERB shall appoint a fact finder if no agreement 45 days prior to budget submission date; report issued, made public within 10 days; upon petition of both parties, EERB may bypass mediation; fact finder may mediate; costs paid by EERB. *Criteria for fact finding report: Past agreements; comparison with public and private sector employees doing comparable work, giving consideration to factors peculiar to schools; public interest; financial impact.* Arbitration--Voluntary; arbitrator appointed by EERB; costs shared equally by the parties.

STRIKE POLICY: Prohibited; union loses dues deduction for one year; employees may not be paid for strike days.

NOTE: Election bar of two years.

---

## IOWA

**There are three public employee bargaining statutes in the State of Iowa. One law covers public employees in general, including state, county, municipal, school, and special purpose district personnel. Another statute permits arbitration of disputes of municipal fire fighters, while a third law allows bargaining for judicial employees.**

### *PUBLIC EMPLOYEES IN GENERAL*

AUTHORITY: Code of Iowa, Chapter 20, Sec. 20.1 et seq. (1974) as last amended effective July 1, 1986.

EXCLUSIONS: Elected or appointed officials; members of boards and commissions; employer's representatives; chief executive officers and deputies; supervisors; confidential employees; students working part time; temporary employees; National Guard; judges and their employees; patients; inmates; Department of Justice employees; Commission of the Blind employees.

ADMINISTRATIVE AGENCY: Public Employment Relations Board (PERB).

UNIT DETERMINATION: PERB.

CRITERIA FOR UNIT DETERMINATION: Efficient administration; community of interest; history and extent of organization; geographic location; recommendations of the parties; separate units for professionals and nonprofessionals unless both groups vote for inclusion.

RECOGNITION: Exclusive; by election.

BARGAINING RIGHTS: Duty to bargain.

SCOPE OF BARGAINING: Wages, hours, vacations, insurance, holidays, leave, shift differential, overtime, supplemental pay, seniority, transfer procedures, job classifications, health and safety, evaluation, staff reduction, in-service training, and other mutually agreed upon matters; excluding merit system and retirement.

GRIEVANCE PROCEDURE: Arbitration permitted.

EMPLOYEE RIGHTS: To organize, form, join, or assist unions; negotiate; engage in other concerted activities; refrain from doing so; meet and adjust individual complaints with employer.

EMPLOYER RIGHTS: Direct work of employees; hire, promote, demote, transfer, assign, and retain; discipline employees; maintain efficiency of operations; relieve employees from duty because of lack of work; determine means to implement operations; prepare budget; take actions necessary to carry out mission; exercise all powers granted by law.

UNION SECURITY: Dues deduction permitted.

UNFAIR LABOR PRACTICES BY EMPLOYER: Refusal to bargain in good faith; interfere with, restrain, or coerce employees; dominate unions; discriminate on account of union membership or testimony; deny union its rights; refusal to participate in impasse procedure in good faith; lockout.

UNFAIR LABOR PRACTICES BY UNION: Refusal to bargain in good faith; interfere with, restrain, or coerce employees or employer's representative; refusal to participate in impasse procedure in good faith; strike; picket.

IMPASSE PROCEDURE: Parties must attempt to agree upon impasse procedure; if no agreement is reached, the following procedure is used: Mediation—Begins 120 days prior to budget submission date; mediator appointed by PERB at request of either party. Fact Finding— Fact Finder appointed by PERB 10 days after mediator's appointment; report due within 15 days and made public 10 days later if no agreement is reached. Arbitration—Either party may request arbitration; tripartite or single arbitrator; arbitrator may select final offer of either party or fact finder's recommendations on an issue-by-issue basis; arbitrator(s) may not mediate; award due in 15 days; costs of chairperson and all other costs shared equally by the parties; hearings open to the public.

CRITERIA FOR ARBITRATION AWARD: Past agreements; comparison with comparable public employees, considering factors peculiar to area or job; interest and welfare of the public; ability to pay; effect of award on standard of services; employer's taxing or appropriating power.

STRIKE POLICY: Prohibited; may be enjoined by court with violation punishable for each day of strike by up to $500 for an individual and up to $10,000 for a union or employer for each day of violation and/or up to six months of imprisonment; individuals ineligible for reemployment for one year and union decertified for one year.

NOTE: All agreements and/or arbitration awards must be completed no later than March 15; initial proposals must be made in a session open to the public—all other sessions are closed; unions shall not negotiate or attempt to negotiate with employer's governing board if the employer has designated a bargaining representative.

## *FIRE FIGHTERS*

AUTHORITY: Iowa Code, Section 90.15 et seq.

IMPASSE PROCEDURE: Either or both parties may request a county district court judge to appoint tripartite board of arbitration and conciliation; neutral member of board may be recommended by parties to the dispute; expenses of board's third member shared equally by the parties; board completes investigation within 20 days from date of appointment and makes findings five days afterwards. Hearings and advisory decision made public.

## *JUDICIAL EMPLOYEES*

AUTHORITY: Iowa Code, Section 602.1401(3) as amended by S.F. 547, effective July 1, 1985.

ADMINISTRATIVE AGENCY: Public Employment Relations Board (PERB).

CRITERIA FOR UNIT DETERMINATION: Units are organized by judicial districts.

NOTE: Bargaining is conducted on a statewide basis.

## KANSAS

**There are two public employee bargaining statutes in the State of Kansas. One statute covers all public employees except teachers, provides for the parties to meet and confer, and prohibits strikes. The law covering teachers requires school boards to negotiate in good faith to reach agreement with recognized employee organizations and also prohibits strikes.**

## *PUBLIC EMPLOYEES IN GENERAL*

AUTHORITY: Kansas Statutes Annotated, Chapter 264, Section 75-4321 et seq. (1971) as last amended effective July 1, 1981.

EXCLUSIONS: Supervisors (at employer's discretion); professional employees of school districts; elected and management officials; confidential employees.

ADMINISTRATIVE AGENCY: Public Employee Relations Board (PERB).

UNIT DETERMINATION: PERB in cases of dispute.

CRITERIA FOR UNIT DETERMINATION: Efficient administration of government; community of interest; history and extent of organization; geographical location; effects of over-fragmentation of units; recommendations of the parties; separate units for uniformed police, security guards, and fire fighters.

RECOGNITION: Exclusive; by voluntary designation or by election.

BARGAINING RIGHTS: Meet and confer.

SCOPE OF BARGAINING: Wages, salaries, hours, and other conditions of employment; specifically excluded are subjects pre-empted by federal, state, or municipal law, employer and employee rights, and state merit system.

GRIEVANCE PROCEDURE: Arbitration permitted.

EMPLOYEE RIGHTS: To form, join, and participate in unions; refrain from doing so.

EMPLOYER RIGHTS: To direct work of employees; hire, promote, demote, transfer, assign, and retrain; discipline for proper cause; maintain efficiency; relieve employees because of lack of work; carry out mission of agency in emergencies; determine methods and means for carrying out operations.

UNFAIR LABOR PRACTICES BY EMPLOYER: Interfere with, restrain, or coerce employees; dominate unions; discrimination on account of union membership or testimony; refusal to meet and confer in good faith; deny union its rights; avoid participation in impasse procedure; lockout.

UNFAIR LABOR PRACTICES BY UNION: Interfere with, restrain, or coerce employees; interfere with employer's rights and representatives; refusal to meet and confer in good faith; avoid participation in impasse procedure; strike; endorse political candidates or make contributions to same.

IMPASSE PROCEDURE: Parties may agree on impasse procedure prior to negotiations; if no agreement, the following procedure applies: Mediation--Either party or PERB may request appointment of mediators from state Secretary of Human Resources; costs paid by Secretary. Fact finding--If impasse exists seven days after appointment of mediator, PERB requests appointment of fact finding board from Secretary of Human Resources; report due within 21 days and made public 14 days after submission; costs paid by Secretary.

OTHER ACTIONS UNDER IMPASSE PROCEDURE: If impasse continues for 40 days or 14 days prior to submission of budget, local governing body determines what action to take with consideration given to fact finder's recommendations and positions of the parties. *Note: Not applicable to the state and its agencies and employees.*

STRIKE POLICY: Prohibited.

NOTE: Contract duration may not exceed three years.

------

## *TEACHERS*

AUTHORITY: Kansas Statutes Annotated 72, Section 72-5411 et seq. (1970) as last amended effective May 15, 1986, and upon publication in statute book.

EXCLUSIONS: Supervisors, principals, superintendents, or employees in an administrative capacity in any area vocational-technical school or community junior college.

ADMINISTRATIVE AGENCY: Secretary of Human Resources.

UNIT DETERMINATION: Secretary of Human Resources.

CRITERIA FOR UNIT DETERMINATION: Community of interest; desires of employees and/or established practice, including extent of organization; unit of classroom teachers must include all teachers in the district.

RECOGNITION: Exclusive; by voluntary designation or by election; majority of employees must vote in order for election to be valid.

BARGAINING RIGHTS: Duty to bargain.

SCOPE OF BARGAINING: Salaries, wages, hours, and terms and conditions of professional service, excluding matters fixed by statute or state constitution.

GRIEVANCE PROCEDURE: Arbitration permitted.

EMPLOYEE RIGHTS: To form, join, or assist unions; participate in negotiations; refrain from doing so.

UNFAIR LABOR PRACTICES BY EMPLOYER: Interfere with, restrain, or coerce employees; dominate unions; discriminate on account of union membership or testimony; refusal to bargain in good faith; deny union its rights; refusal to participate in impasse procedure in good faith; lockout.

UNFAIR LABOR PRACTICES BY UNION: Interfere with, restrain, or coerce employees; interfere with employer's rights and representatives; refusal to bargain in good faith; refusal to participate in impasse procedure in good faith; strikes or picketing.

IMPASSE PROCEDURE: Secretary of Human Resources must establish that impasse exists before impasse procedure can be used. Mediation--Mediator appointed by Secretary of Human Resources; costs shared equally by the parties. Fact finding--After determination that mediation has failed, either party may request fact finding; each party shall submit to the Secretary its final position on each issue; Secretary appoints fact finding board of not more than three members; report issued within 10 days and made public 10 days later; if no resolution, Board of Education shall take any action it deems in the public interest; costs shared equally by the parties.

STRIKE POLICY: Prohibited.

NOTE: All meetings, conferences, consultation, and discussions during negotiations are subject to state's open meeting law, along with all hearings held by Secretary of Human Resources; contract duration may not exceed three years.

---

## KENTUCKY

**There are two public employee bargaining statutes in the State of Kentucky. One law covers fire fighters in cities with populations over 300,000 (Louisville) or any city petitioning for inclusion. The other statute covers policemen in any county with a population of over 300,000 that has adopted the merit system for its police force.**

### FIRE FIGHTERS

AUTHORITY: Kentucky Revised Statutes Chapter 345, Section 345.010 et seq. (1972) as last amended effective July 15, 1984.

ADMINISTRATIVE AGENCY: State Labor Relations Board (SLRB).

UNIT DETERMINATION: SLRB.

CRITERIA FOR UNIT DETERMINATION: Community of interest; wages, hours, and working conditions of employees involved; history of collective bargaining; desires of employees.

RECOGNITION: Exclusive; by voluntary designation or by election.

BARGAINING RIGHTS: Duty to bargain.

SCOPE OF BARGAINING: Rates of pay, wages, hours, and other conditions of employment.

EMPLOYEE RIGHTS: To organize, form, join, or assist unions; bargain collectively.

UNION SECURITY: Dues deduction mandatory; union shop permitted.

UNFAIR LABOR PRACTICES BY EMPLOYER: Interfere with, restrain, or coerce employees; dominate unions; discriminate on account of union membership or testimony; refusal to bargain in good faith.

UNFAIR LABOR PRACTICES BY UNION: Restrain or coerce employees or employer's representative; refusal to bargain in good faith.

IMPASSE PROCEDURE: Mediation--Commissioner of Labor may mediate upon request of either party for fact finding after 30 days of bargaining. Fact Finding--Either party may request; tripartite panel; report issued within 120 days of first request for fact finding; costs shared equally by the parties.

STRIKE POLICY: Prohibited.

## POLICE OFFICERS

AUTHORITY: Kentucky Revised Statutes Chapter 78, Section 78.400 et seq. effective June 16, 1972.

BARGAINING RIGHTS: Duty to bargain.

SCOPE OF BARGAINING: Wages, hours, and terms and conditions of employment; excluding managerial policy.

EMPLOYEE RIGHTS: To organize, form, join, or participate in unions; bargain; refrain from doing so.

STRIKE POLICY: Prohibited.

## MAINE

There are four public employee bargaining statutes in the State of Maine. The laws cover state employees; municipal and county workers, including school employees and employees of the Maine Turnpike Authority; university workers; and judicial employees. All four statutes prohibit strikes and provide for final and binding arbitration of items disputed in negotiations except for salaries, pensions, and insurance benefits, which are subject to advisory arbitration.

## STATE EMPLOYEES

AUTHORITY: Maine Revised Statutes Title 26, Chapter 9-B, Section 979 et seq. (1974) as last amended effective Sept. 19, 1985.

EXCLUSIONS: Elected or appointed officials, confidential employees whose duties relate to collective bargaining matters; department or division heads; persons employed less than six months; temporary, seasonal, or on-call employees; militia and National Guard; staff attorney, assistant and deputy attorneys general; persons appointed to major positions influencing policy; department or agency policy makers; employees having a major role in administering a collective bargaining agreement in a department or agency.

ADMINISTRATIVE AGENCY: Maine Labor Relations Board (MLRB).

UNIT DETERMINATION: Executive Director of MLRB in cases of dispute.

CRITERIA FOR UNIT DETERMINATION: Insuring employees fullest freedom; supervisors excluded from units that include nonsupervisory employees; community of interest; avoidance of over-fragmentation.

RECOGNITION: Exclusive; by voluntary designation or by election.

BARGAINING RIGHTS: Duty to bargain.

SCOPE OF BARGAINING: Wages, hours, working conditions, and grievance arbitration, including wage and salary schedules, work schedules, use of vacation or sick leave; general working conditions; overtime; rules and regulations for personnel administration; compensation system for state employees; procedures governing appeals of allocation or reallocation of job classifications to pay grades. Excluded are matters proscribed by law; regulations governing application for state service; merit system principles and personnel laws.

GRIEVANCE PROCEDURE: Arbitration permitted; if no provision, grievances are submitted to State Employees Appeal Board.

EMPLOYEE RIGHTS: To join, form, and participate in unions; present grievances.

UNFAIR LABOR PRACTICES BY EMPLOYER: Interfere with, restrain, or coerce employees; discriminate on account of union membership or testimony; dominate unions; refusal to bargain; blacklist.

UNFAIR LABOR PRACTICES BY UNION: Interfere with, restrain, or coerce employees or employer's representative; refusal to bargain; engage in work stoppages, slowdowns, strikes, or blacklist.

IMPASSE PROCEDURE: Mediation--Either party may request or MLRB or Executive Director may initiate; MLRB may appoint more than one mediator; services of state's panel of mediators, up to maximum of three mediation days per case, available at no cost; thereafter costs shared equally by the parties. Fact Finding--If parties jointly do not call MLRB, either may request Executive Director to appoint tripartite panel; report may be made public after 30 days; mediator may not be fact finder; costs shared equally by the parties. Arbitration--If no resolution within 45 days of fact finding report, either party may request arbitration; single or tripartite arbitration; award is due within 30 days; award is advisory as to salaries, pensions, and insurance, binding on all other issues; costs of hearing and neutral arbitrator shared equally by the parties; services of State Board of Arbitration and Conciliation are available to the parties without cost.

CRITERIA FOR ARBITRATION AWARD: Interest and welfare of the public; ability to pay; comparison with other private or public sector employees doing similar work; overall compensation; other factors normally considered including Consumer Price Index; need for qualified employees; conditions of employment for similar positions outside the state government; relationships between groups of employees; need for fair and reasonable conditions in relation to job qualifications and responsibilities.

STRIKE POLICY: Prohibited.

NOTE: Contract duration may not exceed three years; either party may publicize parties' written initial proposals 10 days after both parties have made their initial proposals.

---

## MUNICIPAL, COUNTY, SCHOOL, AND TURNPIKE EMPLOYEES

AUTHORITY: Maine Revised Statutes Annotated Title 26, Section 961 et seq. (1969) as last amended effective 1985, 90 days after adjournment of legislature.

EXCLUSIONS: Elected or appointed officials; deputies, administrative assistants, or secretaries whose duties imply confidential relationship with employers; department or division heads; superintendents or assistant superintendents of schools; persons employed for less than six months; temporary, seasonal, or on-call employees. *Note: Statute includes employees of any school, water, sewer, or other district.*

ADMINISTRATIVE AGENCY: Maine Labor Relations Board (MLRB).

UNIT DETERMINATION: Executive Director in cases of dispute.

CRITERIA FOR UNIT DETERMINATION: Insuring employees fullest freedom; supervisors excluded from units that include nonsupervisory employees; community of interest; professionals must vote for inclusion in nonprofessional units.

RECOGNITION: Exclusive; by voluntary designation or by election.

BARGAINING RIGHTS: Duty to bargain.

SCOPE OF BARGAINING: Wages, hours, working conditions, and grievance arbitration; teachers may meet and confer on educational policy; excluding merit system for appointments and promotions.

GRIEVANCE PROCEDURE: Arbitration permitted.

EMPLOYEE RIGHTS: To form, join, and participate in unions; present grievances.

UNFAIR LABOR PRACTICES BY EMPLOYER: Interfere with, restrain, or coerce employees; discriminate on account of union membership or testimony; dominate unions; refusal to bargain; blacklist.

UNFAIR LABOR PRACTICES BY UNION: Interfere with, restrain, or coerce employees or employer's representative; refusal to bargain; engage in work stoppages, slowdowns, strikes, or blacklist.

IMPASSE PROCEDURE: Mediation--Either party may request or MLRB or Executive Director may initiate; MLRB may appoint more than one mediator; services of state's panel of mediators, up to a maximum of three mediation days per case, available at no cost; thereafter costs shared equally by the parties. Fact Finding-- If parties do not jointly call MLRB, either may request Executive Director to appoint tripartite panel; report may be made public after 30 days; mediator may not be fact finder; fact finding may be waived upon joint request; costs shared equally by the parties. Arbitration--If no resolution within 45 days of fact finding report, parties may mutually agree to an arbitration process; failing that, either party may petition MLRB for arbitration; tripartite panel; mediators and fact finders may serve on the panel only with consent of both parties; award is advisory as to salaries, pensions, and insurance, binding on all other issues; cost shared equally by the parties; services of State Board of Arbitration and Conciliation are available to the parties without cost.

STRIKE POLICY: Prohibited.

NOTE: Contract duration may not exceed three years; either party may publicize parties' written initial proposals 10 days after both parties have made their initial proposals.

---

## *UNIVERSITY EMPLOYEES*

AUTHORITY: Maine Revised Statutes Annotated Title 26, Chapter 12, Section 1021 et seq. (1975) as last amended effective Sept. 19, 1985.

EXCLUSIONS: Appointed officials; vice president, dean, director, or member of chancellor's or superintendent's immediate staff; confidential employees whose duties relate to collective bargaining matters; persons employed less than six months. *Note: Statute includes regular employees of the University of Maine; Maine Maritime Academy employees; vocational-technical institute employees; employees of state schools for practical nursing.*

ADMINISTRATIVE AGENCY: Maine Labor Relations Board (MLRB).

UNIT DETERMINATION: Statute. The following units are structured on a University system-wide basis: faculty; professional and administrative staff; clerical, office, laboratory, and technical; service and maintenance; supervisory classified; police. Units for Maine Maritime Academy: faculty; administrative staff; classified employees. Units for vocational-technical institute and schools for practical nursing employees: faculty and instructors; administrative staff.

CRITERIA FOR UNIT DETERMINATION: In case of dispute over placement in a unit, community of interest and work tasks are considered; additional units may be created by MLRB using criteria of community of interest, legislative desire to avoid over-fragmentation, and intent to give employees their full rights under the law.

RECOGNITION: Exclusive; by voluntary designation or by election.

BARGAINING RIGHTS: Duty to bargain.

SCOPE OF BARGAINING: Wages, hours, working conditions, and grievance arbitration.

GRIEVANCE PROCEDURE: Arbitration permitted.

EMPLOYEE RIGHTS: To join, form, and participate in unions.

UNION SECURITY: Closed shop prohibited.

UNFAIR LABOR PRACTICES BY EMPLOYER: Interfere with, restrain, or coerce employees; discriminate on account of union membership or testimony; dominate unions; refusal to bargain; blacklist.

UNFAIR LABOR PRACTICES BY UNION: Interfere with, restrain, or coerce employees or employer's representative; refusal to bargain; engage in work stoppages, slowdowns, strikes, or blacklist.

IMPASSE PROCEDURE: Mediation--Either party may request or MLRB may initiate; MLRB may appoint more than one mediator; services of state's panel of mediators, up to a maximum of three mediation days, available at no cost; thereafter costs shared equally by the parties. Fact Finding--If parties do not jointly call MLRB, either may request Executive Director to appoint tripartite panel; report may be made public after 30 days; mediator may not be fact finder; costs shared equally by the parties. Arbitration--Either or both parties may request MLRB for arbitration; single arbitrator or tripartite panel; award due within 60 days; award is advisory as to salaries, pensions, and insurance, binding on all other issues; costs shared equally by the parties; services of State Board of Arbitration and Conciliation are available to the parties without cost.

CRITERIA FOR ARBITRATION AWARD: Interest and welfare of students and the public; ability to pay; comparison with other private or public sector employees doing similar work; overall compensation; other factors normally considered; need for qualified employees; conditions of employment in similar positions; need to maintain appropriate relationships between different occupations; need to establish fair and reasonable conditions in relation to job qualifications and responsibilities.

STRIKE POLICY: Prohibited.

NOTE: Contract duration may not exceed three years; panel of three students shall be allowed to meet and confer with parties prior to bargaining and at reasonable times with university bargaining team during course of negotiations; either party may publicize the parties' written initial proposals 10 days after both parties have made their initial proposals.

## JUDICIAL EMPLOYEES

AUTHORITY: Maine Revised Statutes Annotated Title 26, Chapter 14, Section 1281 et seq. effective July 24, 1984.

EXCLUSIONS: Governor; state court administrators; confidential employees whose duties relate to collective bargaining matters; department or division heads; law clerks to judges or justices; temporary, seasonal, on-call employees, including interns; persons employed less than six months.

ADMINISTRATIVE AGENCY: Maine Labor Relations Board (MLRB).

UNIT DETERMINATION: Executive Director in cases of dispute.

CRITERIA FOR UNIT DETERMINATION: Insuring employees fullest freedom; supervisors excluded from units that include nonsupervisory employees; community of interest; avoidance of over-fragmentation.

RECOGNITION: Exclusive; by voluntary designation or by election.

BARGAINING RIGHTS: Duty to bargain.

SCOPE OF BARGAINING: Wages, hours, working conditions, and grievance arbitration. Excluded are matters proscribed by law; rules relating to application for employment.

GRIEVANCE PROCEDURE: Arbitration permitted.

EMPLOYEE RIGHTS: To join, form, and participate in unions; present grievances.

UNFAIR LABOR PRACTICES BY EMPLOYER: Interfere with, restrain, or coerce employees; discriminate on account of union membership or testimony; dominate unions; refusal to bargain; blacklist.

UNFAIR LABOR PRACTICES BY UNION: Interfere with, restrain, or coerce employees or employer's representative; refusal to bargain; engage in work stoppages, slowdowns, strikes, or blacklist.

IMPASSE PROCEDURE: Mediation--Either party may request or MLRB or Executive Director may initiate; MLRB may appoint more than one mediator; services of state's panel of mediators, up to a maximum of three mediation days, available at no cost; thereafter costs shared equally by the parties. Fact Finding--Either party may request from MLRB; Executive Director appoints tripartite panel; mediator may not be fact finder; report may be made public after 30 days; costs shared equally by the parties. Arbitration--If no resolution within 45 days of fact finding report, either party may request arbitration; single or tripartite arbitration; award due within 30 days; award is advisory as to salaries, pensions, and insurance, binding on all other issues; costs of neutral arbitrator shared equally by the parties; services of State Board of Arbitration and Conciliation are available to parties at no cost.

CRITERIA FOR ARBITRATION AWARD: Interest and welfare of the public; ability to pay; comparison with other private or public sector employees doing similar work; overall compensation; other factors normally considered including Consumer Price Index; need for qualified employees; conditions of employment for similar positions outside state government; relationships between groups of employees; need for fair and reasonable conditions in relation to job qualifications and responsibilities.

STRIKE POLICY: Prohibited.

NOTE: Mediation-Arbitration procedure may be agreed to by parties. Parties may select or either may request Executive Director to select mediator-arbitrator; mediator at earlier stage of proceedings not acceptable; report submitted 30 days after hearing; mediator-arbitrator may initiate arbitration after reasonable period of mediation; recommendations on salaries, pensions, and insurance are advisory, binding on all other issues; costs shared equally by the parties; services of state's panel of mediators, up to a maximum of three mediation days per case, available at no costs; services of State Board of Arbitration and Conciliation are available to parties at no cost. Criteria for recommendations are same as criteria for arbitration award for state employees.

---

## MARYLAND

**There are two major public employee bargaining statutes in the State of Maryland. Covering teachers and non-certified public school employees, both laws provide for bargaining over wages, hours, and other working conditions. Both statutes also prohibit strikes, and strike penalties include revocation of union recognition for two years and deduction of dues for one year. Other bargaining statutes include coverage of Allegany County public employees, Baltimore County classified employees, and Montgomery County Community College employees. In addition, a bargaining law covers police officers up through the rank of sergeant employed by the Maryland-National Capital Park and Planning Commission.**

## *TEACHERS*

AUTHORITY: Article 77, Section 160 (1969), as last amended effective July 1, 1978.

EXCLUSIONS: Superintendent of schools; employer's negotiators.

ADMINISTRATIVE AGENCY: State Board of Education.

UNIT DETERMINATION: Jointly by parties.

CRITERIA FOR UNIT DETERMINATION: No more than two units in any county or Baltimore City; all teachers must be in one unit.

RECOGNITION: Exclusive for minimum of two years; by voluntary designation or by election.

BARGAINING RIGHTS: Duty to bargain.

SCOPE OF BARGAINING: Wages, salaries, hours, and other working conditions.

GRIEVANCE PROCEDURE: Arbitration permitted.

EMPLOYEE RIGHTS: To form, join, and participate in unions; refrain from doing so.

UNION SECURITY: Permitted in Montgomery County and Baltimore City under authority of Section 6-407, Article--Education (1983) as last amended effective July 1, 1985.

UNFAIR LABOR PRACTICES: Interfere with, intimidate, restrain, coerce, or discriminate against employees.

IMPASSE PROCEDURE: Mediation--On consent of both parties, mediation by State Board of Education; absent consent, at request of either party; mediation by tripartite panel; costs shared equally by the parties. Fact Finding: By mediation panel; report issued within 30 days; costs shared equally by the parties.

STRIKE POLICY: Prohibited; recognition revoked for two years, dues deduction for one year.

## NON-CERTIFIED PUBLIC SCHOOL EMPLOYEES

AUTHORITY: Article 77, Section 160A (1974) as last amended effective July 1, 1975.

EXCLUSIONS: Counties of Caroline, Carroll, Cecil, Dorchester, Frederick, Howard, Kent, Queen Anne, Somerset, Talbot, Wicomico, and Worcester; employees of Baltimore City, Mayor and Baltimore City Council; employees covered by a collective bargaining contract prior to July 1, 1974; management personnel; confidential employees; employer's negotiators.

UNIT DETERMINATION: Jointly by the parties.

CRITERIA FOR UNIT DETERMINATION: No more than three units per county; no supervisors in nonsupervisory units.

RECOGNITION: Exclusive for minimum of two years; by voluntary designation or by election.

BARGAINING RIGHTS: Duty to bargain.

SCOPE OF BARGAINING: Salaries, wages, hours, and other working conditions.

GRIEVANCE PROCEDURE: Arbitration permitted.

EMPLOYEE RIGHTS: To form, join, or participate in unions; refrain from doing so.

UNION SECURITY: Agency shop mandatory in Prince George's County under authority cited above; agency shop permitted in Montgomery County and Baltimore City under authority of Section 6-407, Article--Education (1983) as last amended effective July 1, 1985.

UNFAIR LABOR PRACTICES: Interfere with, intimidate, restrain, coerce, or discriminate against employees.

IMPASSE PROCEDURE: Mediation--On consent of both parties, mediation by State Board of Education; absent consent, at request of either party; mediation by tripartite panel; costs shared equally by the parties. Fact Finding: By mediation panel; report issued within 30 days; costs shared equally by the parties.

STRIKE POLICY: Prohibited; recognition revoked for two years; dues deduction for one year.

## ALLEGANY COUNTY PUBLIC EMPLOYEES

AUTHORITY: Article 1, Section 64B, Code of Public Local Laws effective July 1, 1974.

ADMINISTRATIVE AGENCY: County Commission.

RECOGNITION: Exclusive.

BARGAINING RIGHTS: Duty to bargain.

SCOPE OF BARGAINING: Wages, hours, and working conditions.

IMPASSE PROCEDURE: Tripartite panel named if Commission determines impasse exists or at union's request; panel issues final and binding report within 30 days from date of determination or request if impasse is not resolved otherwise; costs shared by employer and union.

STRIKE POLICY: Prohibited.

---

## BALTIMORE COUNTY CLASSIFIED EMPLOYEES

AUTHORITY: Article 77A, Section 1(n) effective July 1, 1977. *Note: Statute covers classified employees of Baltimore County community colleges.*

ADMINISTRATIVE AGENCY: Board of Trustees of Baltimore County community colleges.

RECOGNITION: Exclusive.

SCOPE OF BARGAINING: Wages, hours, working conditions, and manner for resolving impasses.

GRIEVANCE PROCEDURE: Arbitration permitted.

EMPLOYEE RIGHTS: To organize and bargain through representatives of own choosing.

UNION SECURITY: Dues deduction permitted.

STRIKE POLICY: Prohibited.

---

## MONTGOMERY COUNTY COMMUNITY COLLEGE EMPLOYEES

AUTHORITY: Montgomery County Public Employment Relations Act, Section 16-510.1(A) to (K) effective Oct. 1, 1978.

EXCLUSIONS: Employees who determine policy; supervisory or confidential employees; student assistants.

ADMINISTRATIVE AGENCY: State commissioner of labor and industry.

UNIT DETERMINATION: Montgomery Community College board of trustees; may be appealed to state commissioner.

CRITERIA FOR UNIT DETERMINATION: Efficiency of operations; over-fragmentation of unit; community of interest of employees; employer's administrative structure. *Note: No more than two professional units allowed; unit may not include both professionals and nonprofessionals unless majority of each group votes for inclusion.*

RECOGNITION: Exclusive; by election.

BARGAINING RIGHTS: Negotiate in good faith.

SCOPE OF BARGAINING: Wages, hours, and other terms and conditions of employment.

GRIEVANCE PROCEDURE: Arbitration permitted.

EMPLOYEE RIGHTS: To organize, form, join, or assist unions; bargain through representatives of own choice; engage in lawful concerted activities; refrain from doing so; present grievances.

**EMPLOYER RIGHTS:** To determine mandates and goals, including functions and programs; budget; organizational structure; direct personnel.

**IMPASSE PROCEDURE:** Mediation--Either party may request if it deems impasse exists. Fact Finding--By mutual agreement between the parties or at request of either party after reasonable period of mediation; initiated by commissioner; if parties do not select fact finder, commissioner submits list for selection; fact finder's report no later than 30 days after appointment; if impasse continues 10 days after fact finder's report, report made available to public; costs of fact finding borne equally by the parties.

**STRIKE POLICY:** Prohibited; court may enjoin strike, employee may lose pay for period engaged in a strike, union loses certification and representation rights for one year following end of strike.

---

## PARK AND PLANNING COMMISSION POLICE OFFICERS

**AUTHORITY:** Article 28, Section 5-114.1(a) et seq. effective July 1, 1986.

**EXCLUSIONS:** Confidential employees; employees above rank of sergeant.

**ADMINISTRATIVE AGENCY:** State commissioner of labor and industry.

**RECOGNITION:** Exclusive; by election.

**BARGAINING RIGHTS:** Duty to bargain.

**SCOPE OF BARGAINING:** Wages, hours, other terms and conditions of employment, and retirement systems; excluded are hiring practices.

**GRIEVANCE PROCEDURE:** Arbitration permitted.

**EMPLOYEE RIGHTS:** To form, join, or assist unions; bargain collectively; engage in concerted activities; refrain from doing so; present grievances.

**EMPLOYER RIGHTS:** To carry out statutory mandate and goals, functions and programs, overall budget and organizational structure; direct personnel.

**UNION SECURITY:** Dues deduction, maintenance of membership, and agency shop permitted.

**UNFAIR LABOR PRACTICES BY EMPLOYER:** Interfere with, restrain, coerce, or discriminate against employees.

**UNFAIR LABOR PRACTICES BY UNION:** Interfere with, restrain, coerce, or discriminate against employees.

**IMPASSE PROCEDURE:** Mediation — Either party may request. Fact Finding — Either party may request; fact finder makes report no later than 30 days after appointment; if impasse continues 10 days after fact finder's recommendations, report is made public; costs shared equally by the parties.

**STRIKE POLICY:** Prohibited; employee may not receive pay for any period while on strike; revocation of union certification for one year.

**NOTE:** Election bar for two years; dispute over employee eligibility in bargaining unit is submitted for binding arbitration to party mutually agreed on from list provided by the American Arbitration Association or the Federal Mediation and Conciliation Service.

## MASSACHUSETTS

The comprehensive bargaining statute in the State of Massachusetts covers state, county, and municipal employees, including teachers. The law broadens the scope of negotiations to include "standards of productivity and performance" and stipulates that contract terms prevail over local ordinances. Separate statutes cover arbitration for municipal police and fire fighters and impasses of uniformed state police and metropolitan district commission police subordinate to captains.

### PUBLIC EMPLOYEES IN GENERAL

AUTHORITY: Massachusetts General Laws Annotated Chapter 150E, Section 1 et seq. (1973) as last amended effective Jan. 14, 1987.

EXCLUSIONS: Elected or appointed officials; members of boards and commissions; employer's representatives; managerial and confidential employees; militia and National Guard; employees of the Labor Relations Commission; officers and employees of departments of state secretary, state treasurer, state auditor, and attorney general.

ADMINISTRATIVE AGENCIES: Labor Relations Commission (LRC) and Board of Conciliation and Arbitration (BCA).

UNIT DETERMINATION: LRC.

CRITERIA FOR UNIT DETERMINATION: Community of interest; efficiency of operations and effective dealings; right of employees for effective representation; professionals must vote for inclusion in nonprofessional units; no uniformed members of the fire department below the rank of chief may be classified as managerial, professional, or confidential; for state police, appropriate unit is all ranks up to and including sergeant—others may be in own unit; for judicial employees, probation and court officers in one unit, nonmanagerial or nonconfidential staff and clerical personnel in another unit; for metropolitan district commission police, appropriate unit is all ranks subordinate to captain; for state lottery commission, appropriate unit is all employees below rank of assistant director.

RECOGNITION: Exclusive; by voluntary designation or by election.

BARGAINING RIGHTS: Duty to bargain.

SCOPE OF BARGAINING: Wages, hours, standards of productivity and performance, and other terms and conditions of employment, including, for teaching personnel employed by a school committee, class size and workload.

GRIEVANCE PROCEDURE: Arbitration permitted; if not in contract, may be ordered by LRC upon request of either party.

EMPLOYEE RIGHTS: To organize, form, join, or assist unions; engage in lawful concerted activities; refrain from doing so; present grievances.

UNION SECURITY: Agency shop permitted by election; service fee equal to membership dues; union must establish procedure to rebate portion of service fee not germaine to services as bargaining agent if requested by employee.

UNFAIR LABOR PRACTICES BY EMPLOYER: Interfere with, restrain, or coerce employees; dominate unions; discriminate on account of union membership or testimony; refusal to bargain in good faith; refusal to participate in impasse procedure in good faith.

UNFAIR LABOR PRACTICES BY UNION: Interfere with, restrain, or coerce employer; refusal to bargain in good faith; refusal to participate in impasse procedure in good faith.

IMPASSE PROCEDURE: Mediation—Either party may request mediation from BCA or name own mediator. Fact Finding—After 20 days of mediation, either party may request fact finding from BCA or name own fact finder; fact finder may mediate; report due within 30 days; made public 10 days after being issued; parties may jointly agree to waive fact finding and petition BCA for arbitration.

STRIKE POLICY: Prohibited; enforceable by court; employees subject to discipline and discharge by employer.

NOTE: Contract duration may not exceed three years; arbitration awards are binding on the parties and on appropriate legislative body.

## POLICE AND FIRE FIGHTERS

AUTHORITY: Chapter 1078, Section 4A (1973) as last amended effective July 1, 1981, and Chapter 594, Section 4B (1979).

ADMINISTRATIVE AGENCIES: Board of Conciliation and Arbitration (BCA) and Joint Labor-Management Committee.

ARBITRATION—Non-binding for municipal police and fire fighters; joint labor-management committee has jurisdiction over any police or fire fighter negotiation dispute; either party may petition the committee to take jurisdiction of a dispute. If committee declines jurisdiction or fails to act within 30 days, petition is referred to BCA. Committee may meet with the parties, conduct conferences, and take other action, including mediation, to encourage agreement. Committee may remove at any time from BCA jurisdiction any dispute in which BCA has exercised jurisdiction.

*Note: If committee determines impasse exists, it shall: specify issue(s) to be arbitrated; nominate panel of neutral arbitrators—if parties cannot agree, committee appoints arbitrator(s); determine form of arbitration; determine procedures to be followed. In dispute resolution conducted by other than the committee or staff, parties share equally all costs.*

ARBITRATION—State police and metropolitan district commission police officers below rank of captain; if impasse continues for 30 days after fact finder's report or if both parties waive fact finding, union petitions BCA for investigation; single arbitrator or tripartite panel; hearings begin within 10 days, must conclude within 40 days; at conclusion of hearings, each party submits last best offer on each issue; panel or single arbitrator selects one of the offers or the fact finder's recommendations; costs of arbitration hearing and neutral arbiter shared equally by the parties.

SCOPE OF ARBITRATION AWARD: For police, limited to wages, hours, and conditions of employment; does not include right to appoint, promote, assign, and transfer.

CRITERIA FOR ARBITRATION AWARD: Ability of district or commonwealth to pay; interest and welfare of the public; hazards of employment and skills involved; comparison with other private or public sector employees doing similar work; fact finder's recommendations; cost of living; overall compensation; changes in circumstances; stipulation of the parties; other factors normally considered. *Note: Ability to pay is based on district's state reimbursements and assessments; long- and short-term indebtedness; district's estimated share in metropolitan district commission deficit; district's estimated share in Massachusetts Bay Transportation Authority's deficit.*

STRIKE POLICY: Prohibited; enforceable by court; fines determined by court.

## MICHIGAN

The comprehensive public employee bargaining statute in the State of Michigan covers all public employees except, as dictated by the state constitution, those in the

**state classified service. In addition, separate statutes provide for arbitration for municipal police and firemen and for state police troopers and sergeants.**

## PUBLIC EMPLOYEES IN GENERAL

AUTHORITY: Michigan Compiled Laws Annotated, Section 423.201 et seq. (1947) as last amended effective Oct. 8, 1978.

EXCLUSIONS: Employees in the state classified civil service.

ADMINISTRATIVE AGENCY: Michigan Employment Relations Commission (MERC).

UNIT DETERMINATION: MERC.

CRITERIA FOR UNIT DETERMINATION: In fire fighter units, employees below rank of commissioner are considered nonsupervisory and are included in the unit.

RECOGNITION: Exclusive; by voluntary designation or by election.

BARGAINING RIGHTS: Duty to bargain.

SCOPE OF BARGAINING: Wages, hours, and other terms and conditions of employment.

EMPLOYEE RIGHTS: To organize, form, join, or assist unions; engage in lawful concerted activities; present grievances; bargain collectively.

UNION SECURITY: Agency shop permitted.

UNFAIR LABOR PRACTICES BY EMPLOYER: Interfere with, restrain, or coerce employees; dominate unions; discriminate on account of union membership or testimony; refusal to bargain.

UNFAIR LABOR PRACTICES BY UNION: Restrain or coerce employees or employer's representative; cause or attempt to cause employer to commit a ULP; refusal to bargain.

IMPASSE PROCEDURE: Mediation--Either party may request or MERC appoints a mediator if no resolution 30 days prior to expiration of current contract.

STRIKE POLICY: Prohibited.

----

## POLICE AND FIRE FIGHTERS

AUTHORITY: Michigan Compiled Laws Annotated, Section 423.271 et seq. (1980) applies to state police troopers and sergeants; Section 423.231 et seq. (1969) as last amended effective Jan. 3, 1978, applies to municipal police and fire fighters.

ADMINISTRATIVE AGENCY: Michigan Employment Relations Commission (MERC).

IMPASSE PROCEDURE: Arbitration--Either party may petition MERC for arbitration after 30 days of mediation; tripartite panel; hearings within 15 days; final offer arbitration on an issue-by-issue basis for economic issues, conventional for noneconomic issues; award due within 30 days; either party may be fined $250 per day for failing to comply with arbitration award; costs of arbitration hearing and neutral arbitrator shared equally by the parties and the state.

CRITERIA FOR ARBITRATION AWARD: Lawful authority of employer; stipulation of the parties; interest and welfare of public; ability to pay; for municipal police and fire fighters--comparison with public and private sector employees performing similar work in comparable communities; for state police--comparison with state police troopers and sergeants in comparable states; cost of living; overall compensation; changes in circumstances; other factors normally considered.

STRIKE POLICY: Prohibited; parties may be fined no more than $250 per day for violation.

---

## MINNESOTA

**There is one comprehensive public employee bargaining law in the State of Minnesota. The statute covers state employees, including employees of the University of Minnesota, state and junior colleges, and school districts, but excluding employees of charitable hospitals. The law allows nonessential employees to strike after certain conditions are met. However, unions that engage in illegal strikes lose representation status and are ineligible for certification and deduction of dues for two years.**

### *ALL PUBLIC EMPLOYEES*

AUTHORITY: Minnesota Statutes Annotated, Chapter 179A, Section 179A.01 et seq. (1984) as last amended effective May 21, 1985.

EXCLUSIONS: Elected officials; election officers; National Guard; emergency, part-time, temporary, or seasonal employees; employees of charitable hospitals; students; confidential employees of the state and University of Minnesota.

ADMINISTRATIVE AGENCIES: Bureau of Mediation Services (BMS); Appeals, Minnesota Public Employment Relations Board (MPERB).

UNIT DETERMINATION: BMS; may be appealed to MPERB.

CRITERIA FOR UNIT DETERMINATION: Essential and other-than-essential employees may not be in same unit; all employees under same appointing authority in one unit except when factors require otherwise, such as: employees' classification, compensation, profession, or craft; relevant administrative supervisory levels of authority; geographical location; history and extent of organization; wishes of the parties. State and University of Minnesota units are established by statute. Supervisory employees, confidential employees, school prinicipals, and assistant principals may form own organizations.

RECOGNITION: Exclusive; by election or by verified majority on joint petition.

BARGAINING RIGHTS: Duty to bargain; meet and confer with professional employees on policy.

SCOPE OF BARGAINING: Grievance procedure, hours, fringe benefits, and terms and conditions of employment; excluding retirement contributions or benefits, employer's personnel policies, educational policies of school district.

GRIEVANCE PROCEDURE: Arbitration mandatory.

EMPLOYEE RIGHTS: To form or join unions; refrain from doing so; present grievances; designate exclusive representative by secret ballot.

EMPLOYER RIGHTS: Policy, budget, technology, organizational structure, and selection of personnel; direction and number of personnel.

UNION SECURITY: Dues deduction mandatory; agency shop permitted; fair share fee limited to no more than 85 percent of dues.

UNFAIR LABOR PRACTICES BY EMPLOYER: Interfere with, restrain, or coerce employees; dominate unions; discriminate on account of union membership or testimony; refusal to bargain in good faith; blacklist; refusal to comply with grievance procedure; violate rules and regulations of BMS; refusal to comply with arbitration award; violate or refuse to comply with orders of director of BMS or MPERB; refusal to provide budget information to union.

UNFAIR LABOR PRACTICES BY UNION: Restrain or coerce employees or employer's representative; refusal to bargain in good faith; violate rules and regulations of BMS; refusal to comply with arbitration award; call a jurisdictional strike; damage property or endanger safety of persons while on strike; force or require employer to assign work to certain employees in a particular union; cause or attempt to cause employer to pay for services not performed; engage in unlawful strike; picketing that has unlawful purpose; picketing that unreasonably interferes with access to employer's facilities; seize, occupy, or destroy employer's property; violate or refuse to comply with orders of director of BMS or MPERB; restrain or coerce any person. *Note: Restraining or coercing any person includes forcing or requiring employer to cease dealing with any other person; forcing or requiring employer to recognize a noncertified union; refusing to handle goods or to perform services; preventing employee from providing services to employer.*

IMPASSE PROCEDURE: Mediation--Either party may petition BMS for mediation or director of BMS may initiate. Arbitration--Mandatory for essential employees in the event the parties are determined to be at impasse by the director of BMS; tripartite panel unless parties agree to single arbitrator; for principals and assistant principals, panel selects final offer on each impasse item; for others, if parties agree, panel selects final offer on each impasse item or final offer of one party by package; award issued within 10 days of conclusion of hearing; costs shared equally by the parties.

CRITERIA FOR ARBITRATION AWARD: Statutory rights of employer to efficiently manage operations.

STRIKE POLICY: Prohibited for confidential, essential, and managerial employees; nonessential employees may strike provided contract has expired, mandatory mediation period has been completed, or, if there is no agreement, impasse has occurred; teachers generally may strike if contract has expired or if there is no contract and impasse has occurred, mandatory mediation period has been completed, neither party requests interest arbitration or arbitration has been rejected, employer refuses to comply with arbitration award; unions that violate strike ban lose representative status and are ineligible for certification and dues deduction for two years.

NOTE: All negotiations, mediation sessions, and hearings between employer and union shall be in public except as provided by director of BMS. Contract duration may not exceed three years except for duration of teachers' contracts, which may not exceed two years. Teacher contracts shall not contain wage reopeners or any other provision for renegotiation of compensation.

---

## MISSOURI

**There is one public employee bargaining statute in the State of Missouri. The law provides for the parties to meet and confer on salaries and other conditions of employment and prohibits strikes.**

### PUBLIC EMPLOYEES IN GENERAL

AUTHORITY: Section 105.500 et seq. (1967) as last amended effective Oct. 13, 1969.

EXCLUSIONS: Police; deputy sheriffs; highway patrol; National Guard; teachers at schools, colleges, and universities.

ADMINISTRATIVE AGENCY: State Board of Mediation (SBM).

UNIT DETERMINATION: SBM; may be appealed to court.

CRITERIA FOR UNIT DETERMINATION: Community of interest.

RECOGNITION: Exclusive; designated or selected by majority of employees in unit.

BARGAINING RIGHTS: Meet and confer.

SCOPE OF BARGAINING: Salaries and other conditions of employment.

EMPLOYEE RIGHTS: To form and join unions; present proposals through representatives.

STRIKE POLICY: Prohibited.

## MONTANA

**There are two public employee bargaining laws in the State of Montana. One statute covers state, county, municipal employees, including teachers, and professional educational employees of the university and community colleges. The other law covers registered and practical nurses employed by public as well as private health care facilities and allows employees to strike on 30 days' written notice if there is no other strike at another facility within a 150-mile radius.**

### *PUBLIC EMPLOYEES IN GENERAL*

AUTHORITY: Montana Compiled Laws Chapter 31, Title 39, Section 39-31-101 (1973) as last amended effective March 29, 1985.

EXCLUSIONS: Elected or appointed officials; supervisors; managerial employees; members of boards and commissions; clerks and administrators of school districts; registered professional nurses; professional engineers or engineers-in-training.

ADMINISTRATIVE AGENCY: Board of Personnel Appeals (BPA).

UNIT DETERMINATION: BPA.

CRITERIA FOR UNIT DETERMINATION: Community of interest; wages, hours, fringe benefits, and other working conditions; history of bargaining; common supervision and personnel policies; extent of integration and interchange of work functions; desires of employees; board employees may not be represented by a union affiliated with any group representing non-board employees.

RECOGNITION: Exclusive; by voluntary designation or by election.

BARGAINING RIGHTS: Duty to bargain.

SCOPE OF BARGAINING: Wages, hours, fringe benefits, and other conditions of employment.

GRIEVANCE PROCEDURE: Arbitration permitted.

EMPLOYEE RIGHTS: To organize, form, join, or assist unions; bargain collectively through chosen representatives; engage in concerted activities.

EMPLOYER RIGHTS: Direct employees; hire, promote, transfer, assign, and retain employees; relieve employees because of lack of work or funds or when continuation of work would be inefficient; maintain efficiency of government operations; determine methods, means, job classifications, and personnel; take necessary actions in cases of emergency; establish methods and processes by which work is performed.

UNION SECURITY: Dues deduction mandatory; agency shop permitted; persons whose religious beliefs prohibit payment of dues may pay an equivalent amount to a non-religious, non-union charity designated by the union.

UNFAIR LABOR PRACTICES BY EMPLOYER: Interfere with, restrain, or coerce employees; dominate unions; discriminate on account of union membership or testimony; refusal to bargain in good faith.

UNFAIR LABOR PRACTICES BY UNION: Restrain or coerce employees or employer's representative; refusal to bargain in good faith; use of agency shop fees for political purposes.

IMPASSE PROCEDURE: Mediation--Parties must request mediation after reasonable period of time or upon expiration of the agreement. Fact Finding--Either party may request or BPA may initiate fact finding upon expiration of the contract or 30 days after certification of union; single fact finder; report issued within 20 days of appointment; report made public if no resolution within 15 days; fact finder may mediate; costs shared equally by BPA and the parties. Arbitration--Voluntary, except for fire fighters. For fire fighters (Section 39-34-101 et seq. effective July 1, 1979): Either party may request from BPA; final offer on issue-by-issue basis; arbitrator may remand back to parties for further negotiations; costs shared equally by the parties.

CRITERIA FOR FIRE FIGHTER ARBITRATION AWARD: Comparison with other employees performing similar services and other services generally; interest and welfare of the public; ability to pay; cost of living; other factors normally considered.

STRIKE POLICY: For fire fighters only--prohibited.

NOTE: Fire fighter arbitration awards are not subject to approval of any governing body; persons wishing to serve as arbitrators and fact finders must complete a special education course established by BPA or complete an equivalent program; at negotiations involving institutions of higher education, a student observer may be designated to meet and confer with the parties prior to bargaining, attend negotiation sessions, and meet and confer with the board of regents regarding terms of agreement prior to execution of the contract.

---

## *NURSES*

AUTHORITY: Montana Compiled Laws Chapter 32, Title 39, Section 39-32-101 et seq. (1969) as last amended effective Oct. 1, 1983.

EXCLUSIONS: Members of religious orders assigned to health care facilities.

ADMINISTRATIVE AGENCY: Board of Personnel Appeals (BPA).

UNIT DETERMINATION: By mutual consent between the health care facility and employees; if no determination, either may appeal to BPA.

CRITERIA FOR UNIT DETERMINATION: Majority of professionals must vote for inclusion in nonprofessional unit; similarities of duties, licensure, and conditions of employment; other relevant factors.

SCOPE OF BARGAINING: Establishment and maintenance of desirable employment practices.

UNFAIR LABOR PRACTICES BY EMPLOYER: Interfere with, restrain, or coerce employees; dominate unions; discriminate on account of union membership or testimony; refusal to bargain in good faith; prevent employees from working in order to interfere with, restrain, or coerce employees in exercise of rights under bargaining law.

UNFAIR LABOR PRACTICES BY UNION: Restrain or coerce employees in right to form, join, or assist unions, to bargain through employees representative; to engage in other concerted activities; restrain or coerce employer's representative; refusal to bargain in good faith; use of agency shop fees for political purposes.

STRIKE POLICY: Permitted upon 30 days' notice provided there is no other strike at a health care facility within a 150-mile radius.

## NEBRASKA

**There are two public employee bargaining statutes in the State of Nebraska. One law covering all public employees, except teachers, provides for the parties to meet and confer and prohibits strikes. The other statute, which covers teachers, requires school boards to negotiate in good faith to reach agreement with recognized employee organizations and also prohibits strikes.**

### *PUBLIC EMPLOYEES IN GENERAL, INCLUDING PUBLIC UTILITIES*

AUTHORITY: Revised Statutes Nebraska Chapter 48, Section 48-801 et seq. (1947) as last amended effective July 16, 1986.

EXCLUSIONS: National Guard or state militia.

ADMINISTRATIVE AGENCY: Commission of Industrial Relations (CIR).

UNIT DETERMINATION: CIR.

CRITERIA FOR UNIT DETERMINATION: Police or fire fighters in all ranks subordinate to the chief may be included in one unit; established bargaining units and employer policies; presumption that units less than departmental in size are inappropriate; supervisory employees may not be in nonsupervisory units.

RECOGNITION: Exclusive; by voluntary designation or by election.

BARGAINING RIGHTS: Duty to bargain.

SCOPE OF BARGAINING: Wages, hours, and other conditions of employment.

EMPLOYEE RIGHTS: To form, join, and participate in unions; refrain from doing so; present grievances.

EMPLOYER RIGHTS: To hire, transfer, suspend, lay off, recall, promote, discharge, assign, reward, or discipline employees.

UNFAIR LABOR PRACTICES: Strike or lockout; induce or coerce employees to strike; aid or assist a strike or lockout; interfere with, restrain, or coerce employees.

IMPASSE PROCEDURE: Mediation--CIR has authority to establish panels of qualified mediators; CIR may order mediation. Fact Finding--CIR has authority to establish panel of qualified members for fact finding boards; CIR may order fact finding. Arbitration--CIR holds hearings to determine wages, hours, and conditions of employment.

CRITERIA FOR ARBITRATION AWARD: Comparison with employees having similar skills and working conditions; overall compensation; prevailing economic conditions.

STRIKE POLICY: Strikes and lockouts prohibited; violators guilty of Class I misdemeanor.

## TEACHERS IN CLASS III, IV, AND V SCHOOL DISTRICTS

AUTHORITY: Revised Statutes Nebraska Chapter 518, Section 79-1287 et seq. effective Oct. 23, 1967.

RECOGNITION: Exclusive; recognition is for one year; if there is more than one union requesting certification, Board of Education may recognize union that has enrolled a majority of employees in two preceding years.

BARGAINING RIGHTS: Meet and confer if majority of school board members agree to recognize the teacher organization.

SCOPE OF BARGAINING: Terms of employment and labor-management relations.

EMPLOYEE RIGHTS: To form, join, and participate in unions; refrain from doing so; present grievances.

IMPASSE PROCEDURE: Fact Finding—Tripartite panel; report issued in 30 days.

NOTE: If no resolution of dispute, procedures in general public employee statute apply.

---

### NEVADA

**The single public employee bargaining statute in the State of Nevada covers local government employees, including teachers and nurses. The statute carries strong penalties for strikes. Unions may be fined $50,000 per day; union leaders, $1,000 per day, or they may be imprisoned. Employers may dismiss, suspend, or demote striking employees, cancel a collective bargaining agreement, or withhold wages for the period of a strike.**

## LOCAL GOVERNMENT EMPLOYEES, TEACHERS, AND NURSES

AUTHORITY: Nevada Revised Statutes, Section 288.010 et seq. (1969) as last amended effective July 1, 1985.

EXCLUSIONS: Confidential employees.

ADMINISTRATIVE AGENCY: Local Government Employee-Management Relations Board (EMRB).

UNIT DETERMINATION: Local government employer; EMRB in cases of dispute.

CRITERIA FOR UNIT DETERMINATION: Community of interest; department heads, administrative employees, and supervisors shall not be in same unit as employees they supervise-- may form own unit; police officers may only join unions composed of law enforcement personnel. *Note: Principals, assistant principals, or other school administrators below rank of superintendent, associate superintendent, or assistant superintendent shall not be members of same unit with teachers, unless school district employs fewer than five principals, but may join others of same rank in separate unit.*

RECOGNITION: Exclusive; by voluntary designation or by election.

BARGAINING RIGHTS: Duty to bargain.

SCOPE OF BARGAINING: Salary, wage rates, or other forms of direct monetary compensation; sick leave, vacation leave, holidays, and other paid or nonpaid leaves of absence; insurance benefits; total hours of work required of an employee on each work day or work week; total number of days of work required in a work year; discharge and disciplinary procedures; recognition clause; method used to classify employees in the bargaining unit; deduction of dues for the recognized union; protection of employees in the bargaining unit from discrimination because of participation in recognized unions; no strike provisions; grievance and arbitration procedures for resolution of disputes relating to interpretation or application of collective bargaining agreements; general saving clauses; duration of collective bargaining agreement; safety; teacher preparation time; procedures for reduction in workforce.

EMPLOYEE RIGHTS: To join or refrain from joining any union; present grievances.

EMPLOYER RIGHTS: Manage operations in most efficient manner consistent with public interest; take necessary actions in cases of emergency; hire, direct, assign, or transfer an employee, but excluding right to assign or transfer as a form of discipline; layoff of any employee because of lack of work or funds, subject to established procedures; determine appropriate staffing levels and work performance standards except for safety considerations; determine content of work day, including, without limit, workload factors, except for safety considerations; determine quality and quantity of services to be offered to public; determine means and methods of offering services; safety of the public.

UNFAIR LABOR PRACTICES BY EMPLOYER: Interfere with, restrain, or coerce employees; dominate unions; discriminate on account of union membership or testimony; refusal to bargain in good faith, including impasse procedure; discriminate on account of race, color, religion, sex, age, physical or visual handicap, national origin, political or personal reasons or affiliations; failure to provide information requested by union concerning matters to be negotiated.

UNFAIR LABOR PRACTICES BY UNION: Interfere with, restrain, or coerce employees; refusal to bargain in good faith, including impasse procedure; discriminate on account of race, color, religion, sex, age, physical or visual handicap, national origin, political or personal reasons or affiliations; failure to provide information requested by employer concerning matters to be negotiated.

IMPASSE PROCEDURE: As first step in negotiations, parties shall discuss procedures to be followed in case of impasse. Mediation--Either party may request mediator after July 1; before July 1, dispute may be submitted to mediator if both parties agree; labor commissioner submits list of mediators if parties cannot agree; mediator tries to help settle disputes by July 10; if dispute goes to fact finding, mediator must report to commissioner by July 15 on efforts to settle dispute; costs shared equally by the parties. Fact Finding--If agreement is not reached in mediation by Aug. 1 or if the unit has fewer than 30 employees, either party may request fact finding up to Sept. 20; single fact finder; mediator may also be fact finder; if parties cannot agree on fact finder, either may request seven-name list from AAA or FMCS; FMCS used if parties cannot agree on service to use; non-binding report due within 30 days after end of hearing; costs shared equally by the parties. Arbitration--Parties may agree in advance to be bound by any or all parts of fact finding report; if they do not agree, either party may request three-member panel to determine if any or all of fact finder's recommendations are binding; panel makes determination based on public interest, fiscal effect, and public safety. For fire fighters only--if parties have not agreed in advance to be bound by fact finder's report, dispute is submitted to arbitration; hearing within 10 days of selection of arbitrator; last best offer by package; award due within 10 days of submission of last best offer; costs shared equally by the parties.

CRITERIA FOR ARBITRATION AWARD: Ability to pay must be established first, then normal standards used in interest disputes are applied.

STRIKE POLICY: Prohibited; strikes may be enjoined; union may be fined $50,000 per day, its leaders may be fined $1,000 per day or jailed; employer may dismiss, suspend, or demote strikers, cancel collective bargaining agreement, or withhold wages for period of strike.

NOTE: An employee-management advisory committee has been created consisting of three designees of unions and three designees of local government employers. Duties include: interviewing applicants and submitting an agreed-upon list of applicants to the governor for positions on EMRB; advising EMRB; filing a report with legislature regarding procedures in statute and recommending desirable legislation.

---

## NEW HAMPSHIRE

**The single statewide public employee bargaining law in the State of New Hampshire permits organizing and bargaining over wages, hours, and working conditions except managerial policy. If the parties are at impasse in negotiations, arbitration is voluntary on non-cost items only, and in the case of a strike, the employer may be awarded costs and legal fees at the court's discretion.**

## *ALL PUBLIC EMPLOYEES*

AUTHORITY: Revised Statutes Annotated, Chapter 273-A (1975) as last amended effective Aug. 6, 1985.

EXCLUSIONS: Elected or appointed officials; confidential employees; probationary, temporary, seasonal, irregular, on-call employees.

ADMINISTRATIVE AGENCY: Public Employee Labor Relations Board (PELRB).

UNIT DETERMINATION: PELRB or its designee.

CRITERIA FOR UNIT DETERMINATION: Community of interest; minimum size of unit is 10 employees; professionals and nonprofessionals must vote for inclusion in same unit; supervisors may not be in unit of employees whom they supervise. *Note: Criteria for community of interest include employees with same conditions of employment, history of bargaining, same craft or profession, and employees functioning within the same organizational unit.*

RECOGNITION: Exclusive; by election requires 30 percent of employees to petition.

BARGAINING RIGHTS: Duty to bargain.

SCOPE OF BARGAINING: Wages, hours, and other conditions of employment; excluding merit system.

GRIEVANCE PROCEDURE: Mandatory in all collective bargaining agreements.

EMPLOYEE RIGHTS: To organize and be represented by a union; present grievances.

EMPLOYER RIGHTS: Functions, programs, and methods of employer, including use of technology, employer's organizational structure and selection, and direction and number of employees.

UNFAIR LABOR PRACTICES BY EMPLOYER: Restrain, coerce, or interfere with employees; dominate unions; discriminate on account of union membership or testimony; refusal to bargain in good faith; lockout; failure to comply with statute; adopt any law or regulation that would invalidate any part of agreement; breach a collective bargaining agreement.

UNFAIR LABOR PRACTICES BY UNION: Restrain, coerce, or interfere with employees or employer's representative; cause or attempt to cause employer to discriminate on account of membership ; refusal to bargain in good faith; strike; breach a collective bargaining agreement.

IMPASSE PROCEDURE: Mediation--Parties may request mediation at impasse or PELRB will initiate 60 days prior to budget submission date (90 days for state employees); costs shared equally by the parties. Fact Finding--Parties may request or may be initiated by PELRB 45 days prior to budget submission date (75 days for state employees); parties select neutral or PELRB appoints; report made public after 10 days; if report is rejected by either party, it is submitted to employer's board and union membership; if rejected by either, report is then submitted to legislature, which votes to accept or reject any part of the report; if still no resolution, negotiations may be reopened; costs shared equally by the parties. Arbitration--Voluntary on non-cost items.

STRIKE POLICY: Prohibited; may be enjoined by court; employer may be awarded costs and legal fees at discretion of the court.

NOTE: Statewide bargaining for state employees; unique terms and conditions to be bargained with individual units; state negotiating committee includes representatives of attorney general's office, department of administration and control, department of personnel, and other members of executive branch as governor designates.

## NEW JERSEY

**One employee bargaining statute in the State of New Jersey extends collective bargaining rights to public as well as private employees. The law permits bargaining over grievance procedures and terms and conditions of employment but excludes standards of employee performance. A separate law provides for arbitration of contract disputes for police and fire fighters.**

### *ALL PUBLIC AND PRIVATE EMPLOYEES*

AUTHORITY: New Jersey Statutes Annotated, Title 34, Section 34:13A-1 et seq. (1968) as last amended July 30, 1982.

EXCLUSIONS: Elected officials; members of boards and commissions; managerial executives; confidential employees.

ADMINISTRATIVE AGENCY: Public Employment Relations Commission (PERC).

UNIT DETERMINATION: PERC in cases of dispute.

CRITERIA FOR UNIT DETERMINATION: (Except where established practice, prior agreement, or special circumstances dictate to the contrary)--supervisors may not be in nonsupervisory units; police may not join nonpolice organizations; community of interest; professionals may not be in same unit as nonprofessionals unless majority of professionals vote for inclusion; craft employees may not be in same unit as noncraft employees unless majority of craft employees vote for inclusion.

RECOGNITION: Exclusive; by voluntary designation or by election.

BARGAINING RIGHTS: Duty to bargain.

SCOPE OF BARGAINING: Grievances, disciplinary disputes, and terms and conditions of employment; excluded are standards of employee performance.

GRIEVANCE PROCEDURE: Mandatory in all agreements; arbitration permitted.

EMPLOYEE RIGHTS: To form, join, and assist unions; refrain from doing so; present grievances.

UNION SECURITY: Dues deduction mandatory; agency shop permitted; fair share fee limited to no more than 85 percent of dues; must provide for a procedure for rebate upon demand of any employee of pro rata share for activities or causes only incidentally related to terms and conditions of employment.

UNFAIR LABOR PRACTICES BY EMPLOYER: Interfere with, restrain, or coerce employees; dominate unions; discriminate on account of union membership or testimony; refusal to bargain or to process grievances in good faith; refusal to reduce agreement to writing and to sign it; violate PERC rules and regulations.

UNFAIR LABOR PRACTICES BY UNION: Interfere with, restrain, or coerce employees or employer's representatives; refusal to bargain in good faith; refusal to reduce agreement to writing and to sign it; violate PERC rules and regulations; discriminate on account of union membership or testimony.

IMPASSE PROCEDURE: Mediation--Either party may request; costs paid by PERC. Fact Finding--PERC may initiate or recommend fact finding; statute provides costs to be paid by PERC. Arbitration--Voluntary; tripartite panel.

NOTE: Statute also covers private sector employees; PERC, in conjunction with Rutgers, The State University, shall develop and maintain an employee-management program for the guidance, assistance, and training of public employees and employers.

## POLICE AND FIRE FIGHTERS

AUTHORITY: Chapter 85, Section 34:13A-14 et seq. (1977).

ADMINISTRATIVE AGENCY: Public Employment Relations Commission (PERC).

IMPASSE PROCEDURE: Mediation--Either party may request or PERC may initiate; costs borne by PERC. Fact Finding--Either partry may request; cost borne by PERC. Arbitration--Mandatory; 60 days prior to budget submission, parties must submit arbitration procedure mutually agreed upon to PERC for approval or must use prescribed procedure.

TYPES OF ARBITRATION: Include, but not limited to, conventional; last offer by package; last offer by issue; last offer or fact finder's recommendations by package; last offer or fact finder's recommendations by issue; last offer on economic items as a package and last offer on noneconomic items by issue.

ARBITRATION THAT MAY BE IMPOSED: If parties do not agree on an arbitration procedure 50 days prior to budget submission, parties submit disputed issues to PERC with reasons for lack of agreement on arbitration procedure. Single or tripartite panel; last best offer on economic items as a single package and on noneconomic issues on an issue-by-issue basis; arbitrator(s) may mediate; parties pay costs subject to fee schedule approved by PERC.

CRITERIA FOR ARBITRATION AWARD: Interest and welfare of public; comparison of wages, hours, and conditions of employment of employees performing same or similar work in public employment in same or comparable jurisdiction, in comparable private employment, and in public and private employment in general; overall compensation presently received; stipulations of the parties; lawful authority of the employer; financial impact on governing unit and its residents and taxpayers; cost of living; continuity and stability of employment; other factors normally considered.

## NEW MEXICO

**State employees in the classified service are covered for collective bargaining purposes by rules and regulations adopted by the State Personnel Board.**

## STATE EMPLOYEES IN THE CLASSIFIED SERVICE

AUTHORITY: State Personnel Board rules and regulations for labor-management relations in the classified service of state employees as last reissued effective Sept. 30, 1983.

EXCLUSIONS: Managerial, supervisory, or confidential employees; temporary or emergency employees.

ADMINISTRATIVE AGENCY: State Personnel Board (SPB).

UNIT DETERMINATION: SPB.

CRITERIA FOR UNIT DETERMINATION: Community of interest; desires of employees and agency; effect on efficient operations; unit may not cross agency lines; supervisory, managerial, or confidential employees must be excluded from unit; temporary or emergency employees must be excluded from unit.

RECOGNITION: Exclusive; by election.

BARGAINING RIGHTS: Duty to bargain.

SCOPE OF BARGAINING: Terms and conditions of employment; excludes matters of classification, reclassification, retirement benefits, salaries.

GRIEVANCE PROCEDURE: Required in all agreements; arbitration permitted; arbitration may not cover suspensions, demotions, dismissals, SPB rules and regulations, or conflict with law; either party may file exceptions to arbitrator's award to SPB. SPB may set aside award in whole or in part if arbitrator exceeded his authority; award was procured by corruption, fraud, or other undue means; if there was evident partiality or misconduct by arbitrator; if hearing was conducted so as to prejudice rights of a party; because award is contrary to law, rule, or regulation of any appropriate authority; costs borne by parties as provided by agreement or equally if agreement does not provide for costs.

EMPLOYEE RIGHTS: To form, join, or assist unions; refrain from doing so; present grievances.

EMPLOYER RIGHTS: Determine work standards; direct employees; hire, promote, transfer, assign, and retain employees; suspend, demote, or dismiss employees; relieve employees because of lack of work; maintain efficient operations; determine methods, means, and personnel to perform operations; take necessary actions in cases of emergency.

UNION SECURITY: Dues or service fee deductions permitted; union shop, agency shop prohibited.

UNFAIR LABOR PRACTICES BY EMPLOYER: Interfere with, restrain, or coerce employees; discriminate on account of union membership or testimony; refusal to bargain in good faith; dominate unions.

UNFAIR LABOR PRACTICES BY UNION: Interfere with, restrain, or coerce employees; refusal to bargain in good faith; coerce or discipline an employee in an effort to hinder job performance.

IMPASSE PROCEDURE: Mediation--Voluntary. Fact Finding--Either party may request fact finding from SPB if mediation fails; if SPB determines that impasse exists, fact finder will be appointed; report made public; costs shared equally by the parties. *Note: Upon declaration by SPB of an impasse, SPB shall direct that terms of an existing collective bargaining contract remain in effect until impasse has been resolved.*

CRITERIA FOR FACT FINDING REPORT: Lawful authority of agency; interest and welfare of the public; ability to pay; comparison of employment conditions with other private or public sector employees performing similar work; continuity and stability of employment; other facts deemed relevant by fact finder.

STRIKE POLICY: Prohibited; striking is cause for disciplinary action, and union may lose dues deduction privileges and certification.

NOTE: Contract duration may not exceed three years.

---

## NEW YORK

**One public employee bargaining statute covers public employees in general in the State of New York. The statute permits bargaining over wages, hours, grievance procedures, and other terms and conditions of employment. The statute also provides for strike penalties for employees of two days' pay for each day that they strike. In addition, unions may lose dues deduction privileges and agency shop fee deductions.**

### PUBLIC EMPLOYEES IN GENERAL

AUTHORITY: Civil Service Law, Section 200 et seq. (1967) as last amended June 30, 1985.

EXCLUSIONS: Appointed officials; state militia; confidential and managerial employees; court system judges.

ADMINISTRATIVE AGENCY: Public Employment Relations Board (PERB).

UNIT DETERMINATION: PERB.

CRITERIA FOR UNIT DETERMINATION: Community of interest; employer's recommendations concerning terms of employment upon which employees desire to negotiate; unit must not interfere with joint responsibility of employer and employees to serve the public.

RECOGNITION: Exclusive; by voluntary designation or by election.

BARGAINING RIGHTS: Duty to bargain.

SCOPE OF BARGAINING: Wages, hours, grievance procedure, and other terms and conditions of employment.

EMPLOYEE RIGHTS: To form, join, and participate in unions; refrain from doing so; be represented in negotiations or grievance administration.

UNION SECURITY: Dues deduction mandatory. Agency shop mandatory for state bargaining units and permitted at local level; must provide for procedure for rebate on demand of any employee of the pro rata share of expenditures for activities or causes only incidentally related to terms and conditions of employment.

UNFAIR LABOR PRACTICES BY EMPLOYER: Interfere with, restrain, or coerce employees; dominate unions; discriminate on account of union membership or testimony; refusal to bargain in good faith; refusal to continue terms of expired contract until new contract is negotiated.

UNFAIR LABOR PRACTICES BY UNION: Interfere with, restrain, or coerce employees; cause or attempt to cause an employer to interfere with, restrain, or coerce employees; refusal to bargain in good faith.

IMPASSE PROCEDURE: Parties may establish own impasse procedure that may include arbitration; absent such agreement, the following will be used. Mediation--Either party may request or PERB may initiate. Fact Finding--Neutral panel of up to three members appointed by PERB; police and fire fighters disputes go from mediation directly to arbitration. Arbitration--Mandatory for police and fire fighters, voluntary for all other employees; tripartite panel; panel specifies basis for award; each party pays for its member, parties share costs of neutral chairperson; award as to duration of agreement shall not exceed two years.

CRITERIA FOR POLICE AND FIRE FIGHTER ARBITRATION AWARD: Comparison with other employees in public and private sectors in comparable communities; comparison of wages, hours, and conditions of employment with other employees performing similar work under similar conditions; comparison with other trades and professions, including hazards of employment, physical qualifications, educational and mental qualifications, and job training and skills; interest and welfare of the public; ability to pay; peculiar hazards, qualifications, training, and skills; past negotiated terms of collective bargaining agreements.

STRIKE POLICY: Prohibited; loss of two days' pay for each day or part thereof of the strike; union loses dues deduction privileges and agency shop fee deductions; employer may seek to enjoin strike.

NOTE: Police and fire fighter arbitration awards are not subject to legislative approval; some counties and other jurisdictions have local ordinances providing for collective bargaining for their public employees.

---

## NORTH DAKOTA

**There are two public employee bargaining statutes in the State of North Dakota. The law for all public employees except teachers provides for mediation of grievances and bargaining impasses, while the statute for teachers allows fact finding if mediation does not resolve negotiations disputes.**

### *PUBLIC EMPLOYEES EXCEPT TEACHERS*

AUTHORITY: Century Code Chapter 34-11, Section 34-11-01 et seq. (1951).

IMPASSE PROCEDURE: Either party may request the appointment of a mediation board by the chief executive officer of the governmental unit; tripartite board; mediation board issues recommendations within 30 days; upon rejection of recommendations by either party, mediation board holds new hearings; members serve without compensation, actual expenses being borne by the employer.

GRIEVANCE PROCEDURE: Same as impasse procedure.

---

### *TEACHERS AND SCHOOL ADMINISTRATORS*

AUTHORITY: Century Code Chapter 15-38.1, Section 15-38.1-01 et seq. (1969) as last amended May 4, 1983.

ADMINISTRATIVE AGENCY: Education Fact Finding Commission.

UNIT DETERMINATION: School board.

CRITERIA FOR UNIT DETERMINATION: Common interest; common problems; common employer; history of common representation; administrators and teachers must be in separate units.

RECOGNITION: Exclusive; by voluntary designation requires showing of interest from majority in unit; by election requires 25 percent to petition.

BARGAINING RIGHTS: Duty to bargain.

SCOPE OF BARGAINING: Salary, hours, and other terms and conditions of employment; employer-employee relations.

GRIEVANCE PROCEDURE: Arbitration permitted.

EMPLOYEE RIGHTS: To form, join, and participate in unions; refrain from doing so.

UNION SECURITY: Dues deduction mandatory if a teacher petitions.

IMPASSE PROCEDURE: Mediation--After a reasonable period of negotiations, parties may mutually agree to mediation and to distribution of the cost of mediation. Fact Finding--If mediation fails or is not used, either party may ask the commission for assistance; commission shall act as fact finding commission or appoint fact finder; report issued within 20 days of request for assistance; report made public 10 days thereafter if impasse continues; costs shared equally by the parties.

STRIKE POLICY: Prohibited; employee may be denied pay for period of the strike.

---

## OHIO

**There is one public employee bargaining statute in the State of Ohio. The law covers state workers, except safety personnel, county workers, and municipal employees. Villages and townships with fewer than 2,000 residents are exempt from the statute. Nonsafety personnel may strike if a bargaining impasse cannot be resolved, while safety personnel in bargaining stalemates go to binding arbitration where differences are settled on an issue-by-issue basis by the arbitrator choosing the last best offer of either the employer or the union.**

### *PUBLIC EMPLOYEES IN GENERAL*

AUTHORITY: Ohio Revised Code Chapter 4117, Section 4117.01 et seq. effective April 1, 1984.

EXCLUSIONS: Elected officials; legislative employees; employees on governor's staff or chief executive of public employer; state militia; state employment relations board; confidential and managerial employees, judicial employees, and supervisors; students; employees of county election boards; seasonal and casual employees; part-time faculty in higher education.

ADMINISTRATIVE AGENCY: State Employment Relations Board (SERB).

UNIT DETERMINATION: SERB; may not be appealed.

CRITERIA FOR UNIT DETERMINATION: Desires of employees; community of interest; wages, hours, and other working conditions; fragmentation of unit; efficiency of operations; administrative structure of employer; history of bargaining; professionals and nonprofessionals must be in separate units unless both groups vote for inclusion; exclusion of guards, corrections officers, and special police in units with other employees; separate units for police, fire fighters, state highway patrol; separate units for each institution of higher education; separate units for employees in each jurisdiction of more than one elected county office holder unless otherwise agreed to; separate unit for police at sergeant rank or above.

RECOGNITION: Exclusive; by voluntary designation or by election.

BARGAINING RIGHTS: Duty to bargain.

SCOPE OF BARGAINING: Wages, hours, terms and other conditions of employment; continuation, modification, or deletion of existing contract provisions; excluding civil service exams.

GRIEVANCE PROCEDURE: Arbitration permitted; may not be appealed to state personnel board of review or civil service commissions.

EMPLOYEE RIGHTS: Present grievances; form, join, assist, participate in any employee organization; refrain from doing so; engage in other concerned activities for bargaining purposes; representation by employee organization; bargain collectively.

EMPLOYER RIGHTS: Functions and programs of employer; standards of services, budget, technology, organizational structure; direct employees; efficiency of operations; methods of conducting operations; discipline for cause; adequacy and management of workforce; mission of employer; layoff, transfer, assign, schedule, promote, or retain employees.

UNION SECURITY: Dues deduction mandatory; agency shop permitted; for persons whose religious beliefs prohibit fair share payment equivalent amount is paid to non-religious charity agreed to by employee and union; must provide rebate procedure on demand of non-union employee for activities and causes incidentally related to bargaining.

UNFAIR LABOR PRACTICES BY EMPLOYER: Interfere with, restrain, or coerce employees; dominate unions; discriminate on account of union membership or testimony; refusal to bargain collectively; refusal to process grievances and requests for arbitration; lockout; cause or attempt to cause union employee organization to coerce employees.

UNFAIR LABOR PRACTICES BY UNION: Restrain or coerce employees; cause or attempt to cause employer to coerce employees; refusal to bargain collectively; boycott; refusal to handle goods or perform services; failure to represent fairly all employees; picketing; strikes.

IMPASSE PROCEDURE: Mediation--SERB appoints mediator 45 days before contract expires. Fact Finding--SERB appoints tripartite panel not later than 31 days before contract expires; panel may mediate; recommendations due 14 days after appointment; costs shared equally by the state and the parties. If legislature or union rejects by three fifths vote recommendations after seven days, SERB shall publicize findings. Final Offer Procedure-- Police, fire fighters, and highway patrol submit to procedure with conciliator selected by the parties; conciliator may mediate; parties may submit issues to alternative procedure such as arbitration; final offer settlement; conciliator's resolution on final offer on issue-by-issue basis.

CRITERIA FOR CONCILIATOR'S CONSIDERATION: Bargaining history; comparison of final offers to other employees in comparable work in area; interest and welfare of the public; ability to pay; lawful authority of employer; stipulations of the parties; other factors normally considered; costs shared equally by the parties.

STRIKE POLICY: Prohibited by police, fire fighters, and state highway patrol (other employees have right to strike after 10 days' notice); strikes may be enjoined; no compensation while on strike and two days' pay charged for each day on strike; if court enjoins strike for health-safety reasons, parties shall bargain for 60 days with assistance of mediator appointed by SLRB; may be required to bargain in public and report made public 45 days after bargaining.

NOTE: Seven-member Public Employment Advisory and Counseling Effort Commission appointed by employers, unions, and general public to explain purpose of bargaining statute, advise and assist concerning implementation of statute, and obtain comments.

---

## OKLAHOMA

There are two public employee bargaining laws in the State of Oklahoma. One statute covers police and fire fighters, while the second law covers public school employees. Both statutes prohibit strikes and call for strike penalties. Police and fire fighters can be fined from $10 to $100 per day and dismissed if convicted of striking. School employees may not be paid for the duration of a strike, and the union loses recognition.

## POLICE AND FIRE FIGHTERS

AUTHORITY: Oklahoma Statutes Title 11, Section 51-101 et seq. (1971) as last amended effective Oct. 18, 1985.

EXCLUSIONS: Chief of police and an administrative assistant; chief of fire department and an administrative assistant; legislative, judicial, and supervisory employees; elected and appointed officials; confidential employees.

ADMINISTRATIVE AGENCY: Public Employees Relations Board (PERB).

UNIT DETERMINATION: PERB.

CRITERIA FOR UNIT DETERMINATION: Community of interest; wages, hours, and other working conditions; history of bargaining; desires of employees; supervisory and professional municipal employees may not join unit including nonsupervisory employees; supervisory, professional, or confidential municipal employees are not extended formal recognition by corporate authority for meet and confer purposes with respect to grievances and conditions of employment, but may be consulted by authority on appropriate matters.

RECOGNITION: Exclusive; by election.

BARGAINING RIGHTS: Meet and confer.

SCOPE OF BARGAINING: Wages, salaries, hours, rates of pay, grievances, working conditions, and all other terms and conditions of employment.

GRIEVANCE PROCEDURE: Arbitration required.

EMPLOYEE RIGHTS: Organize, be represented by a union, and bargain collectively; refrain from doing so.

UNFAIR LABOR PRACTICES BY EMPLOYER: Interfere with, restrain, intimidate, or coerce employees; dominate unions; discriminate on account of union membership or testimony; refusal to bargain in good faith; refusal to process grievances in good faith; attempt to institute a lockout.

UNFAIR LABOR PRACTICES BY UNION: Interfere with, restrain, intimidate, or coerce employees or employer's representative; refusal to bargain in good faith; refusal to process grievances in good faith.

IMPASSE PROCEDURE: Arbitration — May be advisory; either party may request after 30 days of bargaining; tripartite panel; hearings within 10 days and concluded within 20 days from commencement; report due 10 days after hearings; costs of neutral shared equally by the parties. Bargaining shall be required to resume if majority opinion is not adopted.

CRITERIA FOR ARBITRATION REPORT: Comparison with skilled employees in building trades in the locality; comparison with other employees doing similar work in the locality; comparison with other departments of similar size and economic status; interest and welfare of the public; ability to pay; peculiar qualifications, skills, or hazards.

STRIKE POLICY: Prohibited; employees may be fined $10-100 per day and dismissed upon conviction.

NOTE: Contract duration may not exceed one year.

## PUBLIC SCHOOL EMPLOYEES

AUTHORITY: Oklahoma Statutes Annotated, Title 70, Chapter 7, Section 509.1 et seq. (1971) as last amended effective Sept. 11, 1986.

EXCLUSIONS: Employees may individually petition local school board for exclusion from unit.

UNIT DETERMINATION: Principals and assistant principals are appropriate unit; licensed or certified teachers or entry-year teachers without supervisory authority are appropriate unit; all other employees without formal responsibility for making recommendations concerning employment of other employees are appropriate unit. *Exceptions: Employees in teachers unit and those in "other employees" unit who were bargaining as single unit when statute took effect or who are employed at any time in a district with fewer than 75 employees in both units constitute appropriate unit as long as majority in each category votes by secret ballot that it shares community of interest; state supreme court may decide against parties' community of interest, however.*

RECOGNITION: Exclusive; at least 35 percent of employees eligible to be in bargaining unit must sign petition for election.

BARGAINING RIGHTS: Duty to bargain.

SCOPE OF BARGAINING: Wages, hours, fringe benefits, and other terms and conditions of employment.

UNFAIR LABOR PRACTICES: Discrimination by employer or union to impede, restrain, or coerce employer or employees.

IMPASSE PROCEDURE: If negotiations are not concluded by first day of school, impasse exists; either party may declare impasse at earlier time. Fact Finding—Tripartite panel formed 20 days after impasse; panel makes recommendations to parties 20 days after panel chairman is selected; parties may reject one or more recommendations within seven days; parties then resume effort to resolve remaining differences, but may discontinue efforts after 14 days.

STRIKE POLICY: Prohibited; employees may not be paid for duration of strike; union loses recognition.

NOTE: Election bar of two years.

---

## OREGON

**There is one public employee bargaining law in the State of Oregon. The statute covers employees of all state agencies, cities, counties, community colleges, school districts, special districts, public and quasi-public corporations, and state government institutions of higher education. The law permits "fair share" agency shop contracts and compulsory arbitration of disputes involving emergency telephone workers, police, fire fighters, and guards.**

## *PUBLIC EMPLOYEES IN GENERAL*

AUTHORITY: Oregon Revised Statutes, Section 243.650 et seq. (1963) as last amended effective Jan. 1, 1986.

EXCLUSIONS: Elected officials; members of boards and commissions; confidential and supervisory employees.

ADMINISTRATIVE AGENCY: Public Employment Relations Board (PERB).

UNIT DETERMINATION: PERB.

CRITERIA FOR UNIT DETERMINATION: Community of interest; wages, hours, and other working conditions; history of collective bargaining; desires of employees.

RECOGNITION: Exclusive; by voluntary designation or by election.

BARGAINING RIGHTS: Duty to bargain.

SCOPE OF BARGAINING: Direct or indirect monetary benefits, hours, vacations, sick leave, grievance procedure, and other conditions of employment.

GRIEVANCE PROCEDURE: Arbitration permitted.

EMPLOYEE RIGHTS: To form, join, and participate in unions; present grievances.

UNION SECURITY: Union and agency shop permitted; persons whose religious beliefs prohibit payment of dues or dues equivalent to a union may pay an equivalent amount to a non-religious charity or other charitable organization mutually agreed to by the union and employee.

UNFAIR LABOR PRACTICES BY EMPLOYER: Interfere with, restrain, or coerce employees; dominate unions; discriminate on account of union membership or testimony; refusal to bargain in good faith; refusal to comply with provisions of the statute; violate contract or arbitration award; refusal to reduce agreement to writing and to sign it; communicate with employees other than representatives during negotiations regarding employment relations.

UNFAIR LABOR PRACTICES BY UNION: Interfere with, restrain, or coerce employees; refusal to bargain in good faith; refusal to comply with provisions of the statute; violate contract or arbitration award; refusal to reduce contract to writing and to sign it; communicate with employer other than representatives during negotiations regarding employment relations.

IMPASSE PROCEDURE: Mediation--Either party may request or PERB may initiate mediation after reasonable period of negotiations; PERB assigns mediator from state conciliation service. Fact Finding--Either or both parties may request or PERB may initiate after 15 days of mediation; single fact finder or tripartite panel; report issued within 30 days of hearing and made public 10 days thereafter; costs shared equally by the parties. Arbitration--Mandatory for emergency telephone workers, police, fire fighters, and guards at prisons and hospitals; single mediator or tripartite panel; award due within 30 days of hearing; costs shared equally by the parties. Voluntary for all other public employees.

CRITERIA FOR ARBITRATION AWARD: Lawful authority of employer; stipulations of the parties; public interest and welfare; ability to pay; comparison with other employees doing similar work and employees in general in public and private employment in comparable communities; cost of living; overall compensation; changes in circumstances; other factors normally considered.

STRIKE POLICY: Prohibited for emergency telephone workers, police, fire fighters, and guards at prisons and hospitals; permitted for all other employees after use of mediation and fact finding provided 10 days' notice is given and 30 days have elapsed since report was made public; employer may seek injunction where there is a clear and present danger to public health, safety, and welfare; court may order dispute to be submitted to arbitration; strikes in violation of injunction are subject to fines. ULP is not a defense for a prohibited strike; employees may not strike unless union is recognized by employer or certified by PERB or where there is an interest arbitration provision; employees other than those engaged in a non-prohibited strike who refuse to cross a picket line are deemed to be engaged in a prohibited strike.

NOTE: Local ordinances in effect on Oct. 5, 1973, not in conflict with statute may remain in force after PERB determination; three student representatives may be designated to attend and observe negotiation sessions involving public postsecondary institutions; arbitration awards are not subject to legislative approval.

## PENNSYLVANIA

**There are three public employee bargaining laws in the State of Pennsylvania. One statute covers state, county, and municipal employees in general and grants the right to strike after mediation and fact finding. Police and fire fighters are covered by a second statute that provides for compulsory arbitration of bargaining disputes. A third statute covers municipal transit employees.**

## *PUBLIC EMPLOYEES IN GENERAL*

AUTHORITY: Act 195, Section 101 et seq. (1970) as last amended effective May 20, 1976.

EXCLUSIONS: Police and fire fighters; elected or appointed officials; managerial or confidential employees; clergy or employees of church offices.

ADMINISTRATIVE AGENCY: Pennsylvania Labor Relations Board (PLRB).

UNIT DETERMINATION: PLRB.

CRITERIA FOR UNIT DETERMINATION: Community of interest; avoidance of over-fragmentation; majority of professionals must vote for inclusion in nonprofessional units; prison and mental hospital guards, court employees, and security guards must form their own units; security guards may not affiliate with unions representing other job classifications; statewide units for statewide bargaining; supervisors must form own units.

RECOGNITION: Exclusive; by voluntary designation or by election.

BARGAINING RIGHTS: Duty to bargain; meet and discuss for supervisors.

SCOPE OF BARGAINING: Wages, hours, and other terms and conditions of employment; meet and discuss on the impact of decisions made on issues within management rights.

GRIEVANCE PROCEDURE: Arbitration required.

EMPLOYER RIGHTS: Functions and programs of employer; standards of service; budget; technology; direct personnel and organizational structure; hire or discharge employees for just cause.

EMPLOYEE RIGHTS: To organize, form, join, or assist unions; engage in lawful concerted activities; refrain from doing so; present grievances.

UNION SECURITY: Maintenance of membership permitted.

UNFAIR LABOR PRACTICES BY EMPLOYER: Interfere with, restrain, or coerce employees; dominate unions; discriminate on account of union membership or testimony; refusal to bargain in good faith, including grievance processing; refusal to reduce agreement to writing and to sign it; violate PLRB rules and regulations regarding conduct of representation elections; refusal to implement arbitration award; refusal to meet and discuss.

UNFAIR LABOR PRACTICES BY UNION: Restrain or coerce employees or employer's representative; refusal to bargain in good faith; violate PLRB rules and regulations regarding conduct of representation elections; refusal to reduce agreement to writing and to sign it; strike or boycott for jurisdictional reasons; secondary boycott; refusal to implement arbitration award; refusal to meet and discuss.

IMPASSE PROCEDURE: Mediation--If no agreement is reached within 21 days of negotiations or 150 days prior to budget submission date, Pennsylvania Bureau of Mediation must be called in; if no agreement after 20 days or 130 days prior to budget submission date, Bureau of Mediation notifies PLRB. Fact Finding--PLRB may name a single or tripartite panel; report due within 40 days of Bureau of Mediation notice to PLRB; state pays one half the cost, parties each pay one fourth. Arbitration--Mandatory for prison and mental hospital guards and court employees; voluntary for all other employees; tripartite panel; PLRB pays for neutral, parties pay for their own representative; any part of the award requiring legislation is advisory.

STRIKE POLICY: Prohibited for prison and mental hospital guards and court employees; other employees may strike after mediation and fact finding; employer may seek injunction where there is a clear and present danger to public health, safety, and welfare; employee may not be paid for period of strike; court may punish violation of injunction with fines and imprisonment; employees other than those on strike who refuse to cross picket lines are deemed to be engaged in a prohibited strike; ULP is not a defense to an illegal strike.

## POLICE AND FIRE FIGHTERS

AUTHORITY: Act 111, Section 1 et seq. effective June 24, 1968.

RECOGNITION: Exclusive; by 50 percent showing.

BARGAINING RIGHTS: Duty to bargain.

SCOPE OF BARGAINING: Compensation, hours, working conditions, retirement, pensions, and other benefits, and terms and conditions of employment.

EMPLOYEE RIGHTS: To bargain and settle grievances.

IMPASSE PROCEDURE: Arbitration--Upon request of either party; impasse exists if no agreement after 30 days of bargaining or if legislature has not approved an agreement within one month after settlement (local government) or within six months (state government); tripartite panel; award due within 30 days of appointment of neutral chairperson; union pays for its panel member, employer pays all other costs.

NOTE: Arbitration awards are not subject to legislative approval.

## TRANSIT EMPLOYEES

AUTHORITY: Act 288, Section 1 (1967).

EXCLUSIONS: Executive and administrative officers.

BARGAINING RIGHTS: Duty to bargain.

SCOPE OF BARGAINING: Wages, salaries, hours, working conditions, and pension or retirement provisions.

IMPASSE PROCEDURE: Arbitration--Tripartite panel; final and binding decision; costs shared equally by the parties.

## RHODE ISLAND

**There are six public employee bargaining laws in the State of Rhode Island. Separate statutes cover state employees, state police, nonuniform municipal employees, and teachers. In addition, two nearly identical statutes grant bargaining rights to municipal police and fire fighters and provide for compulsory binding arbitration to resolve bargaining disputes.**

## STATE EMPLOYEES

AUTHORITY: Rhode Island General Laws, Section 36-11-1 et seq. (1958) as last amended effective May 19, 1980.

EXCLUSIONS: State police having rank of lieutenant or higher; casual or seasonal employees.

ADMINISTRATIVE AGENCY: State Labor Relations Board (SLRB).

UNIT DETERMINATION: SLRB.

CRITERIA FOR UNIT DETERMINATION: Supervisors must be in separate units.

RECOGNITION: Exclusive; by voluntary designation or by election.

BARGAINING RIGHTS: Duty to bargain.

SCOPE OF BARGAINING: Wages, hours, and working conditions.

EMPLOYEE RIGHTS: To organize and choose a bargaining representative.

UNION SECURITY: Agency shop mandatory; service fees are to be equivalent to membership dues.

UNFAIR LABOR PRACTICES: Discriminate on account of union membership.

IMPASSE PROCEDURE: Fact Finding--If no agreement within 30 days of bargaining, parties must submit disputed issues to SLRB; SLRB appoints a fact finder; report due within 10 days. Arbitration--Mandatory; all unresolved issues submitted to arbitration; single arbitrator; hearing concluded within 20 days and report issued within 10 days; award is advisory as to wages and binding on all other issues; costs of transcripts borne by the state, all other costs shared equally by the parties.

CRITERIA FOR ARBITRATION AWARD: Comparison with public and private sector employees doing similar work in the region; interest and welfare of the public; comparison of peculiarities with other trades or professions such as work hazards, physical, educational, and mental qualifications, job training, and skills.

STRIKE POLICY: Prohibited.

---

## STATE POLICE

AUTHORITY: Rhode Island General Laws Chapter 311, Section 28-9.5-1 et seq. effective May 9, 1979.

UNIT DETERMINATION: All full-time state police from rank of trooper up to and including sergeant.

RECOGNITION: Exclusive; by election.

BARGAINING RIGHTS: Duty to bargain.

SCOPE OF BARGAINING: Wages, rates of pay, hours, working conditions, and all other terms and conditions of employment.

EMPLOYEE RIGHTS: To organize, be represented, and bargain collectively.

IMPASSE PROCEDURE: Arbitration--Mandatory; all unresolved issues are submitted to arbitration after 30 days of bargaining; tripartite panel; hearing must be concluded within 20 days; award issued within 10 days; award binding on all issues; costs shared equally by the parties.

CRITERIA FOR ARBITRATION AWARD: Comparison with building trades and industry in the state; comparison with state police departments in other states; interest and welfare of the public; comparison of peculiarities with other trades or professions, including work hazards, physical, educational, and mental qualifications, job training, and skills.

STRIKE POLICY: Prohibited.

NOTE: Contract duration may not exceed three years.

## MUNICIPAL EMPLOYEES

AUTHORITY: Rhode Island General Laws, Section 28-9.4-1 et seq. (1967) as last amended 1984.

EXCLUSIONS: Elected or administrative officials; members of commissions and boards; certified teachers; police; fire fighters; part-time employees; supervisors.

ADMINISTRATIVE AGENCY: State Labor Relations Board (SLRB).

UNIT DETERMINATION: SLRB.

RECOGNITION: Exclusive; by election; requires 20 percent to petition and 15 percent to intervene.

BARGAINING RIGHTS: Duty to bargain.

SCOPE OF BARGAINING: Hours, salaries, working conditions, and all other terms and conditions of employment.

GRIEVANCE PROCEDURE: Arbitration permitted.

EMPLOYEE RIGHTS: To organize, be represented, negotiate and bargain collectively; freedom to join or not to join any employee organization.

UNFAIR LABOR PRACTICES BY EMPLOYER: To spy or keep surveillance on employees or their representatives; blacklist; dominate unions; discriminate on account of union membership or testimony; require employee to join "company union" or any other union as a condition of employment; refusal to discuss grievances; interfere with, restrain, or coerce employees; refusal to bargain in good faith. (Employer ULPs are cross-referenced to the State Labor Relations Act, Section 28-7-13.)

UNFAIR LABOR PRACTICES BY UNION: Refusal to bargain in good faith.

IMPASSE PROCEDURE: Mediation--Either party may request mediation and conciliation after 30 days of bargaining. Arbitration--Voluntary; if mediation or conciliation fail or after 30 days of negotiations, either party may request arbitration; tripartite panel; hearings concluded within 20 days; award issued within 10 days; award is binding on all non-monetary issues; costs shared equally by the parties.

STRIKE POLICY: Prohibited.

NOTE: Contract duration may not exceed three years.

## *TEACHERS*

AUTHORITY: Rhode Island General Laws Chapter 149, Section 28-9.3-1 et seq. (1966) as last amended effective June 27, 1986.

EXCLUSIONS: Superintendents, assistant superintendents, principals, assistant principals, and other supervisors above rank of assistant principal.

ADMINISTRATIVE AGENCY: State Labor Relations Board (SLRB).

UNIT DETERMINATION: All teachers in any city, town, or school district.

RECOGNITION: Exclusive; by election; requires 20 percent to petition and 15 percent to intervene.

BARGAINING RIGHTS: Duty to bargain.

SCOPE OF BARGAINING: Hours, salaries, working conditions, and other terms and conditions of professional employment.

EMPLOYEE RIGHTS: To organize, be represented, negotiate and bargain collectively; refrain from doing so.

UNION SECURITY: Agency shop mandatory; service fees are to be equivalent to membership dues.

UNFAIR LABOR PRACTICES BY UNION: Refusal to bargain in good faith.

UNFAIR LABOR PRACTICES BY EMPLOYER: To spy or keep surveillance on employees or their representatives; blacklist; dominate unions; discriminate on account of union membership or testimony; require employee to join a "company union" or any other union as a condition of employment; refusal to discuss grievances; interfere with, restrain, or coerce employees; refusal to bargain in good faith. (Employer ULPs are cross-referenced to the State Labor Relations Act, Section 28-7-13.)

IMPASSE PROCEDURE: Mediation--Either party may request if no agreement after 30 days of negotiations. Arbitration--If mediation or conciliation fail or after 30 days of negotiations, either party may request arbitration; tripartite panel; hearings concluded within 20 days; award issued within 10 days; award binding on all non-monetary items; costs shared equally by the parties. *Note: If no agreement is reached 30 days before last day money can be appropriated to cover first year of contract, unresolved issues shall be submitted to director of labor for compulsory mediation until date when money is scheduled to be appropriated; director may waive requirement upon mutual agreement of the parties; if no agreement is reached within 10 days of school opening, unresolved issues shall be submitted to director of labor for compulsory mediation; if parties cannot agree on mediator within 24 hours, director of labor selects mediator; parties must attend all meetings deemed necessary until dispute is resolved.*

STRIKE POLICY: Prohibited.

NOTE: Contract duration may not exceed three years.

---

## *MUNICIPAL POLICE*

AUTHORITY: Rhode Island General Laws Title 28, Chapter 9.2, Section 28-9.2-2 (1963) as last amended 1985.

UNIT DETERMINATION: All full-time police in any city or town.

RECOGNITION: Exclusive; by election.

BARGAINING RIGHTS: Duty to bargain.

SCOPE OF BARGAINING: Wages, rates of pay, hours, working conditions, and all other terms and conditions of employment.

EMPLOYEE RIGHTS: To organize, be represented, and bargain collectively.

IMPASSE PROCEDURE: Arbitration--Mandatory; all unresolved issues are submitted to arbitration after 30 days of negotiations; tripartite panel; hearings must be concluded within 20 days; award issued within 10 days; award binding on all issues; costs shared equally by the parties.

CRITERIA FOR ARBITRATION AWARD: Comparison with building trades and industry in local area; comparison with police departments in cities of comparable size; interest and welfare of the public; comparison of peculiarities with other trades or professions, including work hazards, physical, educational, and mental qualifications, job training, and skills; ability to pay.

STRIKE POLICY: Prohibited.

NOTE: Contract duration may not exceed three years.

---

## FIRE FIGHTERS

AUTHORITY: Rhode Island General Laws, Title 28, Chapter 9.1, Section 28-9.1-2 et seq. as last amended effective May 23, 1986.

UNIT DETERMINATION: All uniformed members and all employees of any paid fire department in any city or town.

RECOGNITION: Exclusive; by election.

BARGAINING RIGHTS: Duty to bargain.

SCOPE OF BARGAINING: Wages, rates of pay, hours, working conditions, and all other terms and conditions of employment.

EMPLOYEE RIGHTS: To organize, be represented, and bargain collectively.

IMPASSE PROCEDURE: Arbitration--Mandatory; unresolved issues are submitted to arbitration after 30 days of bargaining; tripartite panel; hearings must be concluded within 20 days; award issued within 10 days; award binding on all issues; costs shared equally by the parties.

CRITERIA FOR ARBITRATION AWARD: Comparison with building trades and industry in local area; comparison with other employees with same or similar skills in local area; comparison with other fire departments in cities of comparable size; interest and welfare of the public; comparison of peculiarities with other trades or professions, including work hazards, physical, educational, and mental qualifications, job training, and skills; ability to pay.

STRIKE POLICY: Prohibited.

NOTE: Contract duration may not exceed three years.

---

## SOUTH DAKOTA

**The single public employee bargaining statute in the State of South Dakota covers employees of the state and its political subdivisions, including public school teachers. Unions convicted of inciting a strike may be fined up to $50,000, while striking employees may be fined up to $1,000 or jailed for up to one year or both.**

## *ALL PUBLIC EMPLOYEES*

AUTHORITY: South Dakota Compiled Laws Chapter 88, Section 3-18-1 et seq. (1969) as last amended effective July 1, 1985.

EXCLUSIONS: Elected or appointed officials; members of boards or commissions; administrators, except elementary and secondary school administrators; supervisors; students working part-time; temporary employees; National Guard; judges and employees of unified court system; legislators and full- and part-time employees directed by legislative branch of government.

ADMINISTRATIVE AGENCY: Department of Labor (DOL).

UNIT DETERMINATION: DOL.

CRITERIA FOR UNIT DETERMINATION: Principles of efficient administration; position classification and compensation plans; history and extent of organization; occupational classification; administrative and supervisory levels of authority; geographical location; recommendations of the parties.

RECOGNITION: Exclusive; by voluntary designation or by election.

BARGAINING RIGHTS: Duty to bargain.

SCOPE OF BARGAINING: Rates of pay, wages, hours of employment, or other conditions of employment.

GRIEVANCE PROCEDURE: Each employer shall enact a grievance procedure; if employer does not enact a grievance procedure, DOL establishes procedure; DOL hears appeals, conducts hearings, and renders a binding decision on appeals under either procedure.

EMPLOYEE RIGHTS: To form and join unions; refrain from doing so; present grievances.

UNFAIR LABOR PRACTICES BY EMPLOYER: Interfere with, restrain, or coerce employees; dominate unions; discriminate on account of union membership or testimony; refusal to bargain in good faith; failure or refusal to comply with statute.

UNFAIR LABOR PRACTICES BY UNION: Restrain or coerce employees or employer's representative; cause or attempt to cause employer to discriminate; refusal to bargain in good faith.

IMPASSE PROCEDURE: Either party may request intervention of DOL; Sections 60-10-1 to 60-10-3 of state laws authorize DOL to perform conciliation services and, if impasse continues, to make recommendations for settlement; parties may adopt their own procedure for settlement.

STRIKE POLICY: Prohibited; union found guilty of inciting or urging a strike may be fined up to $50,000; employees who incite or urge a strike may be fined up to $1,000 or jailed for up to one year or both; employer may seek an injunction.

## TENNESSEE

**The two public employee bargaining statutes in the State of Tennessee cover teachers and transit employees. Teachers may bargain over salaries, working conditions, and fringes, excluding pensions or retirement benefits. Strike penalties include dismissal and forfeiture of tenure for three years. Transit employees may bargain over wages, health insurance, and pensions.**

### *TEACHERS*

AUTHORITY: Tennessee Code Title 49, Chapter 570, Section 49-5501 et seq. (1978).

EXCLUSIONS: Managerial employees may not be considered part of the bargaining unit (maximum allowable number of managerial personnel determined by pupil attendance).

RECOGNITION: Exclusive; by election.

BARGAINING RIGHTS: Duty to bargain.

SCOPE OF BARGAINING: Salaries or wages, grievance procedure, insurance, fringe benefits (excluding pensions or retirement), working conditions, leave, student discipline procedure, payroll deductions; cannot violate federal or state law or municipal charter, employee rights, or board of education rights.

GRIEVANCE PROCEDURE: Arbitration permitted.

EMPLOYEE RIGHTS: To organize, form, join, or assist unions; engage in other concerted activities; refrain from doing so.

UNFAIR LABOR PRACTICES BY EMPLOYER: Threaten or discriminate against employees; interfere with, restrain, or coerce employees; refusal to bargain in good faith or execute a written memorandum; deny access at reasonable times to union; discriminate on account of union membership or testimony; dominate unions; refusal to participate in impasse procedure in good faith.

UNFAIR LABOR PRACTICES BY UNION: Cause or attempt to cause employer to violate statute; refusal to bargain in good faith or execute a written memorandum; interfere with, restrain or coerce employees or employer; refusal to participate in impasse procedure in good faith; strike; urge, coerce, or encourage others to engage in unlawful acts; enter work area that will interfere with normal operations.

IMPASSE PROCEDURE: Mediation--Either party may request the services of FMCS; if such service is not available, mediator shall be selected by tripartite panel; costs borne by party requesting mediation. Fact Finding--If mediation fails, either party may request fact finding; either party may request that AAA designate a neutral; neutral shall not be same person as mediator without parties' consent; report due within 30 days of appointment; costs borne by party requesting fact finding.

STRIKE POLICY: Prohibited; employer may seek an injunction; employees may be dismissed or forfeit tenure for three years.

NOTE: Contract duration may not exceed three years; initial recognition shall be for 24 months.

---

### *TRANSIT EMPLOYEES*

AUTHORITY: Tennessee Code Chapter 160, Section 6-3802 (1971).

BARGAINING RIGHTS: Duty to bargain.

SCOPE OF BARGAINING: Wages, salaries, hours, working conditions, health benefits, pensions, retirement allowances.

GRIEVANCE PROCEDURE: Arbitration required.

IMPASSE PROCEDURE: Arbitration with consent of both parties; tripartite panel; final and binding award.

---

## TEXAS

**The one public employee bargaining statute in the State of Texas covers police and fire fighters, but applies only in jurisdictions where voters petition their municipal governments for a referendum and adopt the law by a majority vote. Sanctions against strikes for unions include fines up to $20,000 per day and suspension of dues deductions for one year.**

### *POLICE AND FIRE FIGHTERS*

AUTHORITY: Vernon's Annotated Consolidated Statutes Article 5154e-1, Section 1 et seq. (1973). *Note: Statute covers police and/or fire fighters in cities, towns, and political subdivisions where collective bargaining has been approved by a majority of voters.*

EXCLUSIONS: Chief of police and fire department; volunteer fire fighters.

UNIT DETERMINATION: Fire and police departments in any city, town, or other political subdivision shall constitute separate units.

RECOGNITION: Exclusive; by voluntary designation or by election.

BARGAINING RIGHTS: Duty to bargain.

SCOPE OF BARGAINING: Wages, hours, working conditions, and other terms and conditions of employment.

EMPLOYEE RIGHTS: To organize and bargain.

IMPASSE PROCEDURE: Mediation--Provided mediator can be appointed by agreement of the parties or by an appropriate agency of the state. May be invoked by either party when impasse is reached or if employer's legislative body fails to approve a contract; impasse exists after 60 days of bargaining. Arbitration--Voluntary, within five days of impasse; tripartite panel; hearing must be concluded within 20 days; award issued within 10 days; costs of arbitration hearing and neutral arbitrator shared equally by the parties; either party may request appointment of arbitration board; neutral arbitrator will not be same person as mediator unless both parties consent; award may be enforced in a state district court; award may be reviewed under certain stipulations by district courts.

CRITERIA FOR ARBITRATION AWARD: Hazards of employment; physical qualifications; educational qualifications; mental qualifications; job training; skills.

STRIKE POLICY: Prohibited; court shall enjoin lockout and/or impose on individual violator a fine up to $2,000; union may be fined $2,500 to $20,000 per day and have dues deduction suspended for one year; court may reduce fine if employer provoked strike; employees may not receive a wage increase for one year and are on probation for two years.

NOTE: Joint police and fire negotiations are permitted; party may not request arbitration more than once during any fiscal year; bargaining sessions are open to public.

---

## VERMONT

**There are three public employee bargaining statutes in the State of Vermont. The laws cover state employees, including state college personnel; municipal workers, including police and fire fighters; and teachers.**

### STATE EMPLOYEES

AUTHORITY: Vermont Statutes Annotated Title 6, Chapter 27, Section 901 et seq. (1969) as last amended effective July 1, 1986.

EXCLUSIONS: Exempt or excluded employees under state classified service, Title 3, Section 311 (except state police in the Department of Public Safety); employees of the lieutenant governor; legal assistants to the attorney general; department heads and their deputies; managerial employees; private secretaries; employees of the personnel department; certain budget department employees; employees with conflict of interest; confidential employees; legislative and judicial employees.

ADMINISTRATIVE AGENCY: State Labor Relations Board (SLRB).

UNIT DETERMINATION: SLRB determines appropriate unit.

CRITERIA FOR UNIT DETERMINATION: Authority of employer to take positive action on matters subject to negotiation; community of interest; desires of employees; avoidance of over-fragmentation; extent of organization is not controlling; supervisors must be in separate units.

RECOGNITION: Exclusive; by election.

BARGAINING RIGHTS: Duty to bargain.

SCOPE OF BARGAINING: Wages, salaries, and benefits; minimum hours; working conditions; overtime; leave; reduction in force procedures; grievance procedure; insurance programs; personnel rules, excluding classified service under Section 311; merit system; matters controlled by statute.

GRIEVANCE PROCEDURE: SLRB prescribes procedure, conducts hearing and makes final determination; nonmembers must pay service fee if using exclusive representative for grievance procedure.

EMPLOYEE RIGHTS: To organize, form, join, or assist unions; bargain; engage in concerted activities; refrain from doing so; present grievances.

EMPLOYER RIGHTS: Carry out statutory mandate and goals of agency; use personnel, methods, and means in most appropriate manner; take necessary actions in cases of emergency.

UNION SECURITY: Union or agency shop prohibited.

UNFAIR LABOR PRACTICES BY EMPLOYER: Interfere with, restrain, or coerce employees; dominate unions; discriminate on account of union membership or testimony; refusal to bargain; discriminate on account of race, color, creed, sex, or national origin; boycott any other product or person by agreement with union.

UNFAIR LABOR PRACTICES BY UNION: Restrain or coerce employees or employer's choice of representatives; cause or attempt to cause employer to discriminate; refusal to bargain; strike or boycott; threaten, restrain, coerce, or require employees to join a union or participate in secondary boycotts or jurisdictional disputes; cause or attempt to cause employer to pay for services not rendered; picket for recognitional purposes; engage in unlawful activities under Section 903 [Employee's rights and duties; prohibited acts] of the Act.

IMPASSE PROCEDURE: Mediation--Either party may request mediator from SLRB. Fact Finding--Either party may request fact finding from SLRB; tripartite panel; fact finding panel may mediate; panel issues report; mutually incurred costs shared equally by the parties. *Note: If impasse continues 15 days after fact finder report is issued, each party shall submit its last offer as a single package to SLRB; SLRB shall select between the last offers within 30 days and make recommendations to the general assembly; recommendations become effective subject to appropriation; general assembly may enact laws amending provisions of any collective bargaining agreement.*

CRITERIA FOR FACT FINDING REPORT: Prevailing rate for comparable work within the state; employees' needs and public's requirement for continuous service; generally accepted safety standards and working conditions within the state.

STRIKE POLICY: Prohibited.

NOTE: Contract duration may not exceed two years (except higher education).

## *MUNICIPAL EMPLOYEES*

AUTHORITY: Vermont Statutes Annotated Title 21, Chapter 20, Section 1721 et seq. (1973) as last amended effective July 1, 1984.

EXCLUSIONS: Elected officials; members of boards and commissions; executive officers; supervisors; probationary, part-time, seasonal, or temporary employees; confidential employees; certified employees of school districts.

ADMINISTRATIVE AGENCY: State Labor Relations Board (SLRB).

UNIT DETERMINATION: SLRB.

CRITERIA FOR UNIT DETERMINATION: Community of interest; majority of professionals must vote for inclusion in nonprofessional unit; avoidance of over-fragmentation; extent of organization is not controlling; desires of employees.

RECOGNITION: Exclusive; by voluntary designation or by election.

BARGAINING RIGHTS: Duty to bargain.

SCOPE OF BARGAINING: Wages, hours, and conditions of employment; excluding managerial prerogatives.

GRIEVANCE PROCEDURE: Arbitration permitted.

EMPLOYEE RIGHTS: To form, join, or assist unions; present grievances.

UNION SECURITY: Union or agency shop permitted.

UNFAIR LABOR PRACTICES BY EMPLOYER: Interfere with, restrain, or coerce employees; dominate unions; discriminate on account of union membership or testimony; refusal to bargain in good faith; refusal to appropriate sufficient funds to implement an agreement; discriminate on account of race, color, religion, creed, sex, national origin, age, or political affiliation; discriminate against employees for nonpayment of service fee or for nonmembership if membership is not available uniformly or is denied for reasons other than nonpayment of dues and initiation fees.

UNFAIR LABOR PRACTICES BY UNION: Restrain or coerce employees or employer's representative; cause or attempt to cause employer to discriminate; refusal to represent all employees; refusal to bargain in good faith; strike or boycott; charge excessive initiation fees; cause employer to pay for services not rendered; picket for recognitional purposes; discriminate against employee for nonpayment if membership is not available uniformly or is denied for reasons other than nonpayment of dues and initiation fees; discriminate on account of race, color, religion, creed, sex, national origin, age, or political affiliation; penalize employee for exercising rights guaranteed by constitution or laws of United States or State of Vermont; cause or attempt to cause discharge because of religious beliefs, refuse membership dues therein.

IMPASSE PROCEDURE: Mediation--Either party may petition or Commissioner of Labor and Industry may initiate mediation; Commissioner may act as mediator or appoint one; costs shared equally by the parties. Fact Finding--Either party may request fact finding after 15 days of mediation; fact finder may mediate; report due within 30 days of conclusion of hearings; costs shared equally by the parties. Arbitration--Voluntary unless made compulsory by referendum; initiated 20 days after fact finder's report is made public; tripartite panel; award due within 30 days.

CRITERIA FOR FACT FINDING AND ARBITRATION AWARD: Lawful authority of employer; stipulations of the parties; interest and welfare of the public; ability to pay; comparison with public and private sector employees doing similar work in comparable communities; cost of living; overall compensation.

STRIKE POLICY: Limited right to strike; prohibited if (1) it occurs within 30 days of fact finder's report (2) occurs after parties have agreed to arbitration or award has been issued (3) endangers public health, safety, and welfare; employer may seek injunction for strikes in violation of limitations.

NOTE: Fact finding hearing shall be open to public at request of any party; arbitration is exclusive procedure for resolving controversy over tenure.

---

## TEACHERS

AUTHORITY: Vermont Statutes Annotated Title 16, Chapter 57, Section 1981 et seq. (1969).

EXCLUSIONS: Superintendent and assistant superintendent.

UNIT DETERMINATION: If disputed, unit limited to all teachers in school district.

CRITERIA FOR UNIT DETERMINATION: Principals, assistant principals, and administrators may join administrators' union or form separate unit of any teachers' union.

RECOGNITION: Exclusive; by voluntary designation or by election.

BARGAINING RIGHTS: Duty to bargain.

SCOPE OF BARGAINING: Salaries, related economic conditions of employment, procedures for processing complaints and grievances and any mutually agreed upon matters not in conflict with statutes of Vermont.

EMPLOYEE RIGHTS: To join, assist, or participate in unions; refrain from doing so.

UNFAIR LABOR PRACTICES: As prescribed for municipal employees.

IMPASSE PROCEDURE: Mediation--Upon mutual agreement of the parties; costs shared equally by the parties. Fact Finding--Either party may request fact finding if mediation fails or is not requested; tripartite panel; report due within 30 days of panel appointment; made public within 10 days of issue; costs shared equally by the parties.

## WASHINGTON

**There are seven public employee bargaining statutes in the State of Washington. Four separate laws cover municipal employees, teachers, academic employees in community college districts, and classified personnel in institutions of higher education. Three additional statutes cover port district employees, marine employees (state ferries system), and utility district workers.**

### *MUNICIPAL EMPLOYEES*

AUTHORITY: Revised Code of Washington, Section 41.56.010 et seq. (1967) as last amended effective July 27, 1985. Includes any county or municipal corporation or any political subdivision of the state.

EXCLUSIONS: Elected or appointed officials; confidential employees; state ferry and toll bridge systems employees; teachers; port district employees; public utility employees.

ADMINISTRATIVE AGENCY: Public Employment Relations Commission (PERC).

UNIT DETERMINATION: PERC.

CRITERIA FOR UNIT DETERMINATION: Duties, skills, and working conditions of employees; history of collective bargaining; extent of organization; desires of employees.

RECOGNITION: Exclusive; by voluntary designation, election, or cross-check of cards.

BARGAINING RIGHTS: Confer and negotiate.

SCOPE OF BARGAINING: Wages, hours, and working conditions.

GRIEVANCE PROCEDURE: Arbitration permitted.

EMPLOYEE RIGHTS: To organize, bargain, present grievances.

UNION SECURITY: Dues deduction mandatory. Closed shop prohibited; all other forms of union security are permitted provided that persons whose religious beliefs prevent membership must be permitted to donate equivalent amount to non-religious charities.

UNFAIR LABOR PRACTICES BY EMPLOYER: Interfere with, restrain, or coerce employees; dominate unions; discriminate against employees on account of filing an unfair labor practice charge; refusal to bargain.

UNFAIR LABOR PRACTICES BY UNION: Interfere with, restrain, or coerce employees; induce employer to commit an unfair labor practice; discriminate against employees on account of filing an unfair labor practice charge; refusal to bargain.

IMPASSE PROCEDURE: Mediation--For non-uniformed employees, either party may request mediation by PERC; for uniformed employees (police in cities with populations over 15,000, counties of second class or larger, and all fire fighters) either party may request PERC mediation after 60 days of negotiations. Arbitration--For uniformed employees, tripartite panel created if no settlement within reasonable period of negotiations and mediation; award due 30 days after conclusion of hearings; each party pays for its panel member; if neutral member is selected by parties, costs shared equally; if neutral member is appointed by PERC, costs borne by PERC.

CRITERIA FOR ARBITRATION AWARD: Constitutional and statutory authority of employer; stipulations of the parties; comparison with uniformed personnel in comparable cities and counties on the West Coast; cost of living; changes in circumstances; other factors normally considered.

STRIKE POLICY: For non-uniformed employees, prohibited under common law. For uniformed employees; prohibited and a fine up to $250 per day.

NOTE: Contract duration may not exceed three years.

## *TEACHERS*

AUTHORITY: Revised Code of Washington, Section 41.59.010 et seq. (1975) as last amended effective July 14, 1983.

EXCLUSIONS: Chief executive and administrative officers; confidential employees.

ADMINISTRATIVE AGENCY: Public Employment Relations Commission (PERC).

UNIT DETERMINATION: PERC.

CRITERIA FOR UNIT DETERMINATION: Duties, skills, and working conditions; history of bargaining; extent of organization; desires of employees; all nonsupervisory employees are to be in a single unit; unit of only supervisors is appropriate upon vote of majority; unit of only principals and assistant principals is appropriate upon vote of majority; unit of principals and assistant principals and other supervisory employees is appropriate upon vote of both groups; unit that includes supervisors and/or principals and assistant principals and nonsupervisory employees is considered appropriate upon vote of each group; vocational, technical, or occupational skill center employees may have a separate unit if history of bargaining so justifies.

RECOGNITION: Exclusive; by voluntary designation or by election.

BARGAINING RIGHTS: Duty to bargain.

SCOPE OF BARGAINING: Wages, hours, and terms and conditions of employment; units of supervisors and/or principals and assistant principals limited to compensation, hours, and number of days of work per year.

GRIEVANCE PROCEDURE: Arbitration permitted.

EMPLOYEE RIGHTS: To organize, form, join, or assist unions; bargain; present grievances; refrain from doing so.

UNION SECURITY: Dues deduction mandatory. Closed and union shop prohibited; agency shop permitted provided that persons whose religious beliefs prevent membership must be permitted to donate equivalent amount to non-religious charities; PERC designates charity if employee and union do not agree.

UNFAIR LABOR PRACTICES BY EMPLOYER: Interfere with, restrain, or coerce employees; dominate unions; discriminate on account of union membership or testimony; refusal to bargain.

UNFAIR LABOR PRACTICES BY UNION: Restrain or coerce employees or employer's representative; cause or attempt to cause employer to commit an unfair labor practice; refusal to bargain.

IMPASSE PROCEDURE: Mediation--Either party may request PERC to appoint a mediator; costs borne by PERC. Fact Finding--Either party may request after 10 days of mediation; single fact finder; mediator may not be fact finder without parties' consent; report due within 30 days of appointment and may be made public five days thereafter if dispute is not settled; costs borne by PERC.

## COMMUNITY COLLEGE DISTRICTS (ACADEMIC EMPLOYEES)

AUTHORITY: Revised Code of Washington, Section 28B.52.010 et seq. (1971) as last amended effective Jan. 1, 1976.

EXCLUSIONS: Chief administrative officer and administrators in each community college district.

ADMINISTRATIVE AGENCY: Public Employment Relations Commission (PERC).

UNIT DETERMINATION: Academic employees within a community college district; supervisors may be in nonsupervisory units upon majority vote of both groups.

RECOGNITION: Exclusive; by election.

BARGAINING RIGHTS: Meet, confer, and negotiate.

SCOPE OF BARGAINING: Including, but not limited to, curriculum, textbooks, in-service training, student teaching programs, personnel, hiring and assignment practices, leaves of absence, salary and salary schedules, and noninstructional duties.

EMPLOYEE RIGHTS: Employee may appear in his own behalf.

IMPASSE PROCEDURE: Mediation--PERC mediates upon consent of both parties. Fact Finding--PERC conducts fact finding upon consent of both parties. Other--If no agreement by means provided, parties may request assistance from PERC.

NOTE: Contract duration may not exceed three years.

## CLASSIFIED PERSONNEL (HIGHER EDUCATION)

AUTHORITY: Revised Code of Washington, Section 28B.16.100 et seq. (1971) as last amended effective Aug. 23, 1983.

ADMINISTRATIVE AGENCY: Higher Education Personnel Board.

UNIT DETERMINATION: Higher Education Personnel Board.

CRITERIA FOR UNIT DETERMINATION: Duties, skills, and working conditions; history of bargaining; extent of organization; desires of employees.

RECOGNITION: Exclusive; by election.

SCOPE OF BARGAINING: Grievance procedure and personnel matters over which the institution may lawfully exercise discretion.

GRIEVANCE PROCEDURE: Permitted on matters within institution authority.

UNION SECURITY: Union shop permitted upon referendum of employees in unit; persons whose religious beliefs prevent membership must be permitted to pay agency fee; dues deduction permitted.

UNFAIR LABOR PRACTICES BY EMPLOYER: Interfere with, restrain, or coerce employees; dominate unions; discriminate against employees on account of filing an unfair labor practice charge; refusal to bargain.

UNFAIR LABOR PRACTICES BY UNION: Interfere with, restrain, or coerce employees;

induce employer to commit an unfair labor practice; discriminate against employees on account of filing an unfair labor practice charge; refusal to bargain.

STRIKE POLICY: Prohibited.

## PORT DISTRICT EMPLOYEES

AUTHORITY: Revised Code of Washington, Section 53.18.010 et seq. (1967) as last amended effective Jan. 1, 1976.

EXCLUSIONS: Managerial, professional, and administrative personnel; confidential

ADMINISTRATIVE AGENCY: Public Employment Relations Commission (PERC).

UNIT DETERMINATION: PERC.

SCOPE OF BARGAINING: Includes, but not limited to, wages, salaries, hours, vacation, sick leave, holiday pay, and grievance procedures.

EMPLOYEE RIGHTS: Maximum freedom to exercise right of self-organization.

EMPLOYER RIGHTS: To hire and to secure regular employees from the local community.

NOTE: Security and supervisory personnel shall not be included in same agreement.

## MARINE EMPLOYEES (FERRY SYSTEM, TOLL BRIDGE AUTHORITY)

AUTHORITY: Revised Code of Washington, Section 47.64.010 et seq. (1961) as last amended effective Aug. 31, 1979. Covers employees aboard ferries, wharves, or terminals acquired or constructed under authority of the Washington toll bridge authority.

ADMINISTRATIVE AGENCY: Public Employment Relations Commission (PERC).

EMPLOYEE RIGHTS: Association, self-organization, and designation of representatives of own choosing.

IMPASSE PROCEDURE: PERC prescribes rules.

NOTE: PERC surveys wages, hours, and working conditions and considers prevailing practices for similarly skilled trades in area in which employee is employed.

## UTILITY DISTRICTS

AUTHORITY: Revised Code of Washington, as added to  Section 54.04  (1963).

NOTE: Any public utility district may enter collective bargaining relations with its employees as a private employer might do and agree to be bound by the result of such collective bargaining.

## WISCONSIN

**There are three public employee bargaining laws in the State of Wisconsin. One statute covers state employees, while the second law extends bargaining rights to**

**municipal employees, including teachers. A third statute provides for arbitration of disputes concerning policemen and fire fighters.**

## STATE EMPLOYEES

AUTHORITY: Wisconsin Statutes Annotated, Chapter 111, Subchapter V, Section 111.80 et seq. (1966) as last amended effective July 1, 1986.

EXCLUSIONS: Limited term, seasonal, and project employees; supervisory, managerial, and confidential employees; employees of the Wisconsin Employment Relations Commission (WERC).

ADMINISTRATIVE AGENCY: Wisconsin Employment Relations Commission (WERC).

UNIT DETERMINATION: The following state-wide units are established by statute: clerical and related; blue collar and non-building trades; building trades crafts; security and public safety; technical; professional (nine separate units). For employees in unclassified service, units are structured for program, project, and teaching assistants in the University of Wisconsin system. *Note: Statewide units of professional supervisors in the classified service may be certified if representatives are not affiliated with unions representing employees in the statutory units.*

CRITERIA FOR UNIT DETERMINATION: To avoid excessive fragmentation.

RECOGNITION: Exclusive; by election.

BARGAINING RIGHTS: Duty to bargain.

SCOPE OF BARGAINING: Wage rates (including general salary schedules and temporary assignments), fringe benefits, hours and conditions of employment; excludes employer rights, mission and goals of agency, merit system, and matters related to employee occupancy of houses or other lodging provided by the state.

GRIEVANCE PROCEDURE: Arbitration permitted.

EMPLOYEE RIGHTS: To organize, form, join, or assist unions; bargain; engage in lawful concerted activities; present grievances; refrain from doing so.

EMPLOYER RIGHTS: To carry out statutory goals using most appropriate means and personnel; manage employees; hire, promote, transfer, assign, or retain; establish work rules; discipline employees; initiate layoffs because of lack of work, funds, or where continued work would be inefficient and nonproductive.

UNION SECURITY: Dues deduction mandatory; agency (fair share) shop permitted with at least two-thirds vote of eligible employees voting in favor; maintenance of membership permitted with at least majority of eligible employees voting in favor; maintenance of membership authorized if less than two thirds but more than one half of eligible employees vote in favor of *fair share* agreement; agency shop and maintenance of membership can be rescinded by vote if union discriminates on basis on race, color, sexual orientation, or creed. *Note: If employee has religious convictions against dues payments, he shall on request to union have dues paid to charity mutually agreeable to employee and union. Disputes may be submitted to WERC for adjudication.*

UNFAIR LABOR PRACTICES BY EMPLOYER: Interfere with, restrain, or coerce employees; dominate unions; discriminate on account of union membership; refusal to bargain; violation of any collective bargaining agreement, agreement to arbitrate, or arbitrator's award.

UNFAIR LABOR PRACTICES BY UNION: Coerce or intimidate employees; induce employer to commit an unfair labor practice; refusal to bargain; violation of any collective bargaining agreement, agreement to arbitrate, or arbitrator's award; strike; coerce or intimidate supervisors to join union.

IMPASSE PROCEDURE: Mediation--Either party may request or WERC may assign mediator. Fact Finding--Parties may jointly petition WERC to initiate; if WERC decides in favor of fact finding, it shall appoint single fact finder or three-member panel when jointly requested by parties; fact finder may mediate; costs shared equally by the parties.

CRITERIA FOR FACT FINDING REPORT: Efficient and economical administration.

STRIKE POLICY: Prohibited; employer may seek injunction, file unfair labor practice charge, or both; employer may discipline strikers, cancel reinstatement eligibility, request fines, or file suit for damages from union or strikers.

NOTE: Tentative agreements must be submitted to the legislative joint committee on employment relations, which holds public hearing before determining approval or disapproval. If committee does not approve a tentative agreement, it shall be returned to the parties for renegotiation.

## MUNICIPAL EMPLOYEES, INCLUDING TEACHERS

AUTHORITY: Wisconsin Statutes Annotated, Chapter 111, Section 111.70 et seq. (1959) as last amended effective May 6, 1986.

EXCLUSIONS: Independent contractors; supervisors; confidential, managerial, or executive employees.

ADMINISTRATIVE AGENCY: Wisconsin Employment Relations Commission (WERC).

UNIT DETERMINATION: WERC.

CRITERIA FOR UNIT DETERMINATION: Avoid fragmentation; separate units for professionals and nonprofessionals unless majority of professional employees vote for inclusion in nonprofessional unit; separate units for craft and noncraft employees unless majority of craft employees vote for inclusion; desires of employees.

RECOGNITION: Exclusive; by election.

BARGAINING RIGHTS: Duty to bargain.

SCOPE OF BARGAINING: Wages, hours, and conditions of employment.

GRIEVANCE PROCEDURE: Arbitration permitted.

EMPLOYEE RIGHTS: To organize, form, join, or assist unions; bargain; engage in lawful concerted activities; present grievances; refrain from doing so.

UNION SECURITY: Dues deduction mandatory; agency shop permitted; rescinded if less than majority of unit supports continuation in an election or if union refuses membership on basis of race, color, sexual orientation, creed, or sex.

UNFAIR LABOR PRACTICES BY EMPLOYER: Interfere with, restrain, or coerce employees; dominate unions; refusal to bargain; violate any collective bargaining agreement; deduct dues without authorization; discriminate on basis of membership in a union.

UNFAIR LABOR PRACTICES BY UNION: Coerce or intimidate employees; coerce, intimidate, or induce employer to commit an unfair labor practice; refusal to bargain; violate any collective bargaining agreement; coerce or intimidate an independent contractor, supervisor, confidential, managerial, or executive employee to join the union.

IMPASSE PROCEDURE: Mediation–Either or both parties may request or WERC may initiate. Arbitration–Voluntary; either or both parties may request WERC to initiate; final offer by package; WERC appoints single arbitrator or tripartite panel at both parties' request; cost shared equally by the parties. Fire fighters, police: Mediation–Either or both parties may request or WERC may initiate. Fact Finding–Either or both parties may request WERC to initiate; WERC appoints single fact finder or parties may jointly request tripartite panel; fact finder may mediate; costs shared equally by the parties.

CRITERIA FOR ARBITRATION AWARD: Lawful authority of the employer; stipulations of the parties; interests and welfare of the public; ability to pay; comparison with other employees performing similar services; comparison with other public and private employees in same and in comparable communities; cost of living; overall compensation; changes in circumstances; other factors normally considered.

*Arbitration procedure for Milwaukee police only: Either party may request WERC to appoint arbitrator; hearing 14 days after appointment; in determining compensation, arbitrator shall use U.S. Labor Department BLS statistics of urban family budgets and increases in Consumer Price Index; for noncompensatory items, arbitrator considers employee-employer relationships between technical and professional employees and employers in public and private sectors in established labor agreements; award 30 days after hearing; costs shared equally by the parties; within 60 days of award, either party may petition Milwaukee County circuit court to set aside or enforce the decision.*

STRIKE POLICY: Prohibited; court may enjoin strikes; union may have dues check-off agreement suspended for one year and be fined up to $10,000 per day; individuals shall be fined $10 with each day constituting separate offense; municipal employees absent because of illness are presumed to be on strike unless physician verifies illness.

NOTE: Presentation of initial proposals along with supporting rationale shall be open to public; contract duration may not exceed three years.

---

## POLICE AND FIRE FIGHTERS

AUTHORITY: Wisconsin Statutes Annotated, Chapter 111, Section 111.77 (1971) as last amended effective Jan. 1, 1978.

EXCLUSIONS: Cities of 500,000 population or more and towns of 2,500 population or less.

ADMINISTRATIVE AGENCY: Wisconsin Employment Relations Commission (WERC).

BARGAINING RIGHTS: Duty to bargain.

IMPASSE PROCEDURE: Mediation--Mandatory if requested by WERC. Arbitration--Mandatory if agreed to between the parties; binding arbitration; either party may petition WERC to order final and binding arbitration; single arbitrator; costs shared equally by the parties. Alternate forms of arbitration--(1) arbitrator determines all issues in dispute involving wages, hours, and conditions of employment, (2) arbitrator selects final offer of one of the parties. Alternate form 2 is used unless parties agree prior to hearing to form 1.

CRITERIA FOR ARBITRATION AWARD: Lawful authority of employer; stipulations of the parties; interest and welfare of the public; ability to pay; comparison with employees in public and private sectors doing similar work in comparable communities; cost of living; overall compensation; changes in circumstances; other factors normally considered.

STRIKE POLICY: Prohibited.

## WYOMING

**The one public employee bargaining statute in the State of Wyoming covers fire fighters. The law permits bargaining over pay rates, working conditions, and all other terms and conditions of employment.**

## *FIRE FIGHTERS*

AUTHORITY: Wyoming Revised Statutes, Section 27-10-101 et seq. (1965).

RECOGNITION: Exclusive; by election.

BARGAINING RIGHTS: Meet and confer.

SCOPE OF BARGAINING: Wages, rates of pay, working conditions, and all other terms and conditions of employment.

EMPLOYEE RIGHTS: To bargain and be represented by a bargaining agent.

IMPASSE PROCEDURE: Arbitration--Mandatory if no agreement is reached within 30 days of bargaining; tripartite panel; arbitration shall proceed pursuant to provisions of the state Uniform Arbitration Act (Section 1-36-101 et seq.).

NOTE: Contract duration may not exceed one year.

# Appendix B

# State Open Meeting and Freedom of Information (Public Record) Laws*

| STATE | OPEN MEETING** | FREEDOM OF INFORMATION** |
|---|---|---|
| Alabama | 13A-14-2 | 36-12-40, 41 (1982) |
| Alaska | 44.62.310–44.62.312 | 09.25.110–09.25.125 |
| Arizona | 38-431 | 39-121, 41-135 |
| Arkansas | 12-2801–2807 | 12-2801–2807 |
| California | 11120–11131 | 6250–6265 |
| Colorado | 24-6-401-02, 29-9-101 | 24-72-201–206 |
| Connecticut | 1-15–1-21k | 1-15–1-21k |
| Delaware | Title 29, 10001–10005 | Title 29, 10001–10005 |
| District of Columbia | 1-1504 | 1-1521–1-1528 |
| Florida | 286.0105–286.26 | 119.01–119.12 |
| Georgia | 50-14-1–50-14-4 | 50-18-70–50-18-74 |
| Hawaii | 92-1–92-13 | 92-21–92.71 |
| Idaho | 67-2340–67-2347 | 9-301–9-302 |

*For more detailed information, contact the Society for Professional Journalists, 840 N. Lake Shore Drive, Suite 801 W, Chicago, Illinois 60611.
**Citations are to state codes.

191

| | | |
|---|---|---|
| Illinois | Chap 102, Secs. 41–46 | Chap 116, Secs. 201–211 |
| Indiana | 5-14-1.5-5–5-14-1.5-7 | 5-14-3-1–5-14-3-9 |
| Iowa | 28A.1–28A.9 | 68A.1–68A.9 |
| Kansas | 75-4317–75-4320a | 45-205–45-213 |
| Kentucky | 61.805–61.845 | 61.870–61.884 |
| Louisiana | 42:4.1–42:4.12 | 44:1–44:37 |
| Maine | Title 1, Sec. 401–410 | Title 1, Sec. 401–410 |
| Maryland | 76A, 7-15 | 76A, 1-6 |
| Massachusetts | C.30A, 11A-11A 1/2; C.20, 23A-24 | C.66, 10-18 |
| Michigan | 4.1800 (11)–4.1800 (23) | 4.1801(1)–4.1801(13a) |
| Minnesota | 471.705 | 13.01–13.87 |
| Mississippi | 25-41-1–25-41-7 | 25-6-1–25-61-17 |
| Missouri | 610.010–610.120 | 610.010–610.120 |
| Montana | 2-3-201; Art. 2. Sec. 9 of 1972 Const. | 2-6-103; Art. 2, Sec. 9 of Const. |
| Nebraska | 84-1409–84-1414 | 84-712–84-712-09 |
| Nevada | 241.010–241.040 | 239.005–239.330 |
| New Hampshire | 91-A:1–91-A:8 | 91-A:1–91-A:8 |
| New Jersey | 10:4-6–10:4-21 | 47:1A-1–47:1A-4 |
| New Mexico | 10-15-1–10-15-4 | 14-2-1–14-2-3 |
| New York | (Public Officers) 95–106 | (Public Officers) 84–90 |
| North Carolina | 143-318.9–143-318.16 | 132-1–132-9 |
| North Dakota | 44-04-19–44-04-21 | 44-04-18; Art. XI, Sec. 6 of Const. |

| | | |
|---|---|---|
| Ohio | 121.22 | 149.43; 149.43.1 |
| Oklahoma | Title 25, 301–314 | Title 51, 24 |
| Oregon | 192.610–192-690 | 192-410 |
| Pennsylvania | Title 65, 261–269 | Title 65, 66.1–66.4 |
| Rhode Island | 42-46-1–42-46-10 | 38-2-1–38-2-12 |
| South Carolina | 30-4-10–30-4-110 | 30-4-10–30-4-110 |
| South Dakota | 1-25-4 | 1-27-1–1-27-19 |
| Tennessee | 8-44-101–8-44-106 | 10-7-501–10-7-509 |
| Texas | 6252-17 | 6252-17a |
| Utah | 52-4-1–52-4-9 | 63-2-66 |
| Vermont | Title 1, 311–315 | Title 1, 315–320 |
| Virginia | 2.1-341–2.1-346.1 | 2.1-341–2.1-346.1 |
| Washington | 42.30.010–42.30.920 | 42.17.250–42.17.340 |
| West Virginia | 6-9A-1 | 29B-1-1–29B-1-6 |
| Wisconsin | 19.81–19.98 | 19.31–19.39 |
| Wyoming | 16-4-401–16-4-407 | 16-4-201–16-4-205 |

# Appendix C

# Budgets and Proposals

## AFSCME's Public Sector Budget Guide

A jurisdiction's budget, although it usually looks very thick and complex, is little more than the combination of many departmental budgets. Analyzing how the money is allocated requires the repetitive task of reviewing each department budget for the same factors, and only simple math skills are necessary.

In general, budget documents consist of two sections: estimated revenues for the coming year by source of revenue, and estimated expenditures broken down by department and item. On the revenue side, the analysis should concentrate on receipts which appear to be underestimated based on actual collections for the current fiscal year, or have been ignored entirely. On the expenditure side, actual spending should be compared with appropriations to find if the budget overestimates expenditures in specific department or categories (wages, contractual services, etc.).

### Revenue Estimates

#### Annualizing Revenue Figures

The current year's *actual* revenue, last year's *actual* revenue and next year's *estimated* revenue should be compared. Since the budget is drafted before the end of the current year, the only actual revenue figures available will be for part of a year, probably six or nine months; therefore, the actual revenue receipts will have to be put on an annual

*Authors' Note:* Reprinted by permission of the AFSCME Research Department, Washington, D.C.

basis for comparison with the estimates for next year. This is done by taking the most recent year-to-date actual figures available and determining how many months of the current fiscal year these figures represent. Next, the revenue figure should be multiplied by 12, and the product divided by the number of months the year-to-date figure represents, to give the anticipated end of year revenue estimate. For example, if $25,000 has been collected in nine months, then $25,000 × 12 = $300,000 and $300,000 ÷ 9 would yield an end-of-year estimate of revenues of $33,333. This figure may vary significantly from estimates in the current budget which were made prior to the beginning of the year. This annualized current revenue figure should be compared to estimates of next year's revenue and any decreases noted. Obviously, every type of revenue is not received over the year in 12 equal segments. Many items such as the property tax or ice skating rink fees are collected during specific seasons and common sense must be used to determine if there is a valid criticism of any decrease in the projections.

## Federal Funds

Federal money continues to account for a large portion of many jurisdictions' total funds. Many programs, such as Community Development Block Grants, place restrictions on how the money should be spent, while others such as General Revenue Sharing do not. The Research Department can provide information on how much federal money a locality can expect to receive under a specific program and what spending restrictions exist. Many times this source of revenue is dramatically underestimated or not even listed in the budget.

## Property Tax

The property tax is the major source of local funds for many governmental units. Revenue from this tax should increase steadily because of property reevaluations and new construction. However, most areas receive less than 100 percent of this tax because of 1) abatements offered to business and 2) failure to collect delinquent taxes. Both of these reductions in property tax collections can be criticized.

As communities attempt to slow the erosion of their tax bases, there is a great temptation to offer subsidies and tax abatements to businesses for building or remaining in the city. Most of these schemes take the form of tax "holidays" or a reduction in the assessed value of the property below fair market value for a given number of years.

While tax abatements reduce the amount of revenue to the city, they force a higher proportion of the property tax burden onto individuals. Moreover, there is growing evidence that while firms will take abatements when offered, the business tax structure is not a very important consideration in the development plans of businesses. Of greater concern is the availability of a skilled labor force, access to raw material and consumer markets, and the quality of the transportation network—conditions which the jurisdiction can work to improve instead of creating tax giveaways.

The tax revenue portion of the budget will often contain an entry for uncollectable taxes. If this does not appear, the jurisdiction may have reduced its revenue estimate by some percent which it does not expect to collect. Although a collection rate of 100 percent may not be realistic, a jurisdiction collecting less than 98 percent of its taxes should be criticized as inefficient. If a jurisdiction is collecting $25 million from property taxes and has a collection rate of 95 percent, an increase of only 2 percent will add another $500,000 to available revenue! The collection rate can be improved by a "get tough" policy—including publishing the names of delinquents in the local newspaper, phone calls and elimination of services if all else fails and the amount of back taxes warrants it.

## Surplus

The prior year's actual revenue and expenditures should be compared to determine if there was a surplus. If so, this surplus should have been carried forward as available revenue into the current fiscal year and not transferred to a separate fund or used for early debt retirements. The current year annualized revenue estimates should also be compared with the current year's annualized expenditures to see if there will likely be a surplus going into the new budget year.

If the jurisdiction has established separate funds for various functions (streets, sewers, airport, revenue sharing, etc.), each of these funds must also be reviewed for surpluses.

## Interest on Investments

While high interest rates have made it more difficult for state and local governments to borrow, they have also meant unprecedented revenues from interest earnings. Many localities receive state and federal aid in lump sums, or retain large fund balances, while expenditures are evenly spaced throughout the year. The jurisdiction should invest its idle resources, striving to achieve the maximum return at the minimum risk, while allowing for ready access to invested funds. Short-term U.S. Treasury Notes and Money Market Funds are two common investments. A new innovation, especially for small local governments, is to pool the idle balances of local governments into larger amounts of investible funds.

## Summary

A budget analysis of revenue items should highlight:

(1) questionable decreases in individual revenues for the new year,
(2) any history of underestimated revenues,
(3) underestimates of federal revenues or failure to include them in budget,
(4) the failure to collect a high enough proportion of property taxes,
(5) large increases in tax abatement programs,
(6) surpluses hidden in separate funds which should be included in the general fund,
(7) the possibility of additional revenue from interest on investment,
(8) any other items which appear questionable.

## Expenditure Projections

### Comparing Expenditure Figures

The analysis of this section should include a comparison of the current year's actual expenditures (which will probably have to be annualized) to proposed appropriations. Large percent increases should be noted even though the total dollar appropriation may be small. These increases in similar items can later be grouped together (such as travel line items that appear in every agency appropriation throughout the budget), and the resulting dollar amounts may be quite large.

The percentage increase as well as dollar increase from the current year to the proposed year should be calculated. *Actual*, rather than the *proposed*, expense figures for the past or current year should be used if possible since the jurisdiction may have spent less than it expected.

As you review the expenditure side of the budget, keep in mind that a budget is a *political* document which embodies a certain set of priorities. As the financial difficulties facing state and local governments grow, the union will have to examine those priorities to see if they are reasonable. For example, it may be necessary to criticize the continued existence of appointed boards and commissions (Regional Development Boards, Beautification Commissions, etc.) or contributions to non-governmental organizations and activities, while direct services to the public are cut back. Items such as management travel, membership dues and periodical subscriptions are difficult to justify if layoffs are being proposed or wage concessions are demanded.

## Contingency Fund

Contingencies are created to allow some flexibility in meeting unforeseen and unbudgeted expenses, but are usually overestimated and unnecessary. A comparison should be made between the projected appropriation of the contingency funds and actual expense in the current and past years.

The jurisdiction may place several contingency funds throughout the budget which can be called a variety of names—Reserve, Departmental Executive Reserve, Emergency Authorization, Unallocated Appropriations and Unappropriated Expenditures.

## Salary Savings

The appropriation for salaries will often ignore the dollar savings that result from attrition and turnovers. Positions may go unfilled and experienced workers are replaced with new hires at lower rates over the year. This amount will vary, but a savings of 3–5 percent of total personnel cost may be anticipated. The jurisdiction's assumptions about the number of positions *budgeted* versus those actually *filled* and the history of turnover rates in the past several years should be examined. If wage expenditures have not been adjusted for the savings, then too much money has been reserved.

## Vacant Positions

As mentioned above, budget estimates are usually based on the assumption that all authorized positions will be filled. If the number of personnel is not listed in the budget, it should be requested and compared to positions actually filled during the year.

## Padding

Reserving more money than is actually necessary to support an activity serves two purposes. First, management appears more efficient when service is provided at less than ''projected'' cost. Second, if budget cuts become a necessity, enough "fat" exists to allow for cuts. Comparing actual expenses from last year, or annualized current expenses, to the new year's estimates will usually show some very large increases over actual expenses. Any increase above the current inflation rate should be questioned.

## Capital Projects

The budget is an operating guide for the upcoming fiscal year and should only contain revenues and expenses for the year. Expenditures that will benefit the jurisdiction for more than one year are often incorrectly charged against a single year's revenue. Items such as road resurfacings, park and recreation improvements, sewer line installations or computer purchases will benefit the jurisdiction for more than one to two years and should be financed over their useful lifespan. This concept also should be applied to many vehicle purchases, especially large vehicles. These long-term expenses may be financed as long-term debts such as general obligation bonds or short-term notes, depending on the useful life of the item. Most of these appropriations properly belong in one of the jurisdiction's capital improvement funds.

## Consulting Services

The expense of contracting with private firms to provide public services is always questionable. Many agencies may store large amounts of funds in this line item because they seldom have to justify the expense. Increases in all contracted services from year to year should be viewed with special caution.

## Transfers

A jurisdiction may establish a fund independent of the general fund for a specific activity (water, sewer, airport, etc.). These special funds should be self-sufficient with revenues covering expenses, and transferring money from the general fund to them should be unnecessary. Self-sufficient funds may accumulate large surpluses and the jurisdiction may decide to retain these surpluses. If the transfer of funds is legally prohibited and a large surplus has accumulated, two options still exist—abolishing the fund and transferring all activities back to the general fund, or transferring functions from the general fund to the special fund which will free up general fund monies for other purposes.

*Summary*

A budget analysis of the proposed expenditures should highlight:

(1) questionable increases in expenditure items for the new year,
(2) any monies appropriated in the current year but not actually spent,
(3) appropriations for agencies which do not provide direct services to the public,
(4) any contingency funds which appear,
(5) any overestimates of wage costs because of turnover and attrition savings,
(6) any padding of expenditures,
(7) long-term purchases paid for out of current revenues rather than through longer term financing,
(8) consulting costs,
(9) transfers from the general fund to funds which should be self-sufficient,
(10) surpluses accumulated in self-sufficient funds,
(11) any other items which appear questionable.

## AFSCME's Guide for Negotiators: Justifying Proposals

### Collecting Facts From the Local and/or Council

The following information should be available locally or from employer's records:

(1) Description of the bargaining unit
   —Number of employees in each department by job title
   —Seniority list and ages of those in unit
   —Wages and fringe benefits paid to employees

(2) Experience over the past contract
   —Amount of overtime, call-in pay, shift differentials, etc., actually paid
   —Average wage of employee in unit
   —Cost of fringe benefits to employer (sick leave, vacations, etc.)
   —Problems with management practices and/or working conditions (stewards should be consulted)

(3) Consultation with the membership
   —After basic facts are assembled, a membership meeting should be held to discuss proposals.

—A questionnaire or checklist may be helpful.

—Attention should be paid to specific departments or classification proposals in addition to those covering the entire unit.

(4) Analysis of recent grievances and arbitrations
   —Where does contract language need to be changed?
   —Where are there problems which need to be solved (for example, a poor supervisor)?

## Preparing Proposals

The language of the current agreement should be carefully analyzed.

(1) Is the language clear? Does it work? Does it cover all necessary subjects? Does it reflect what was decided at the last negotiations?

(2) Sample clauses from other contracts may be useful for comparison and to use as a basis for drafting new language.

(3) Each new or changed section should be reviewed to see what facts and agreements are necessary to justify the proposal.

(4) Comparisons with language in other AFSCME contracts in the area or covering similar jurisdictions and also local industrial union contracts should be made.

(5) Sample contracts and clauses on particular subjects are available from local and/or council offices and the Research Department.

The basic economic data on wage rates, salary schedules and fringes already collected must be considered with the local area conditions and what is happening nationally.

(1) Justification for union economic demands is required more and more these days because of increasing public awareness of negotiations. Some unions propose a "substantial" or "equitable" raise rather than a specific amount which allows some time and flexibility to see how negotiations proceed. It is best to avoid extreme demands which may lead to headlines in the local newspapers.

(2) Arguments on which to base proposals for increased wage and fringe benefits include:
   (a) Comparable wages
   (b) Comparable settlements
   (c) Increases in cost of living.

## Justifying the Proposals—Wage Comparisons

Information on wages, rates, salary schedules and fringes has already been collected for the unit and must be placed in perspective. Wage comparisons should be prepared to justify an increase.

(1) Key jobs called "benchmarks"—classifications common throughout many jurisdictions which have a substantial number of members—should be selected for comparison since comparisons for all jobs are not available in different jurisdictions. For example, all cities will not have a Photolithographer but will have a substantial number of employees in the Clerk I classification. Benchmarks should be picked to represent grades throughout the salary schedule and also to represent the different types of jobs in the unit such as blue-collar, clerical, professional, health care, etc.

(2) Comparisons of rates for the benchmark jobs should be made with other public employees in:
—Other like jurisdictions similar in population and/or geographic location—for example, the city with other large cities in the state
—Other jurisdictions in the area—for example, the county with the cities within the county
—Federal facilities in the area.

(The Research Department will be able to provide relevant comparisons in addition to the information already available at the local and/or council office.)

(3) Comparisons of rates for the benchmark jobs should be made with private employers in the areas, but employers should be selected with a similar number of employees and who are unionized; management will often present area wage surveys which include rates from many small and non-union employers.

(4) Information on recent settlements should also be compiled—for comparable like jurisdictions with similar populations, for other public jurisdictions in the area and for private industry in the area.

(The Research Department can provide information on recent AFSCME settlements and nationwide trends in the private sector.)

## Justifying the Proposals—Cost of Living

Information on the cost of living is important to show that an increase is necessary to maintain purchasing power and provide an adequate standard of living.

(1) The effect of an increase in the Consumer Price Index (CPI) on the member's wages should be analyzed. A comparison of the percentage wage increases over the contract with the increases in the CPI will usually show the members losing in terms of purchasing power.

(2) The CPI shows how fast prices are rising but does not show how much money it takes to maintain a certain standard of living. The Urban Family Budgets, published each year by the Bureau of Labor Statistics, estimate what it costs to maintain a typical family of four in metropolitan areas throughout the United States at three different levels—Low, Medium and High.

(Information on the CPI and Union Family Budgets is available from the Bureau of Labor Statistics or the Research Department.)

## Justifying the Proposals—Fringe Benefits

Comparisons are also very important in justifying demands for additional holidays, vacation days, health insurance benefits, etc. Again, as on the wage issues, relevant comparisons may be made with other like jurisdictions (city versus city), other jurisdictions in the same geographic area (county versus city and federal) and private industry in the same area.

Surveys listing fringe benefits in states and large municipalities can be obtained from the Research Department in addition to information on file at the local and/or council office.

## Justifying the Proposals—Language

Documentation must also be prepared where possible to substantiate the need for an addition or a change in language. Examples of problems should be listed and comparative language should be available to show what other relevant contracts contain.

## The Employer's Response of Inability to Pay

It is becoming necessary to be actively involved in the budget process since so many employers are claiming they have no money.

The proposed budgets should be examined closely by committee members, and questionable expenditure and revenue items should be brought to management's attention and perhaps publicized. The Research Department will provide an analysis of the budget for jurisdictions, but adequate time should be given for the response. Any analysis should be carefully reviewed before presentation to the employer. Local committee members may know some explanation for a questionable item and must also be able to discuss and defend the analysis.

### *Legal Considerations*

Different laws will apply in each bargaining situation, but the impact on contracts of laws in the following areas should be considered:

(1) *For the private sector*—National Labor Relations Act, Fair Labor Standards Act

(2) *For both public and private sectors*—Civil Rights Act, Equal Pay Act, Fair Labor Standards Act, Pregnancy Disability Act, Equal Employment Opportunity Act, Occupational Safety and Health Act, if applicable.

## Appendix D

# Guide to Costing Out Public Sector Wage and Benefit Packages

### Introduction

During the collective bargaining process, one of the most useful pieces of information the parties can possess is the effect of present demands on future costs of operation. Not only does it aid each party during negotiations but also it helps to prepare for future management of the workplace. The process by which costs for a future contract may be computed is commonly referred to as "costing out."

The *Midwest Monitor* has developed a method by which either party may cost out demands and which is adapted from a 1978 U.S. Department of Labor publication, *The Use of Economic Data in Collective Bargaining*. This method of costing out entails calculating the average compensation costs for the unit and determining the true value of increased demands made during negotiations.*

### Calculating Compensation Costs

During bargaining, one of the most important statistics that may be used is the bargaining unit's *average compensation* or the *weighted average compensation*. This is the employer's *average expense* for each person on the payroll. When a settlement proposal is offered, the

_____

*Authors' Note*: Reprinted by permission of the *Midwest Monitor*, Bloomington, Indiana. Although the salary figures in this guide are not current, the method of costing out wage and benefit packages remains unchanged and is useful to the public sector organizer.

205

average compensation figure will help in reaching a decision regarding the proposal.

In order to compute the average compensation costs, the following information is necessary:

- salary scales and benefit programs;
- the distribution of employees in the unit according to pay steps, shifts, and length of service; and
- each employee's coverage status for each of the benefits.

These figures need not be a year's compilation, rather they may be chosen from a fixed point in time. The time should be as close to the beginning of collective bargaining as possible.

If these three figures are known, almost all costs of compensation and increases in compensation can be computed. The only exception is overtime costs. Because these may vary from week to week, overtime costs generally cannot be computed with any degree of certainty.

The first step in computing compensation costs is to develop the base or *existing* compensation figure. The base compensation figure varies from unit to unit, thus a $500 increase means something different to a unit whose base compensation is $20,000 and something else to a unit whose base compensation is $10,000. The base compensation figure is essential in determining the percentage value of a requested increase in compensation. For the unit with a base compensation of $20,000, a $500 increase represents a 2½% increase while for the unit with a base compensation of $10,000, the $500 represents a 5% increase.

A sample firefighter bargaining unit will be used to illustrate the process for computing the base compensation figure and for costing out a contract settlement.

## Computing Base Compensation

With the information in the table it is possible to compute a base compensation figure. Given the distribution of employees according to each classification and each of their salaries, one can obtain the *weighted salary* for each classification. The weighted salary is then divided by the total number of employees, and the result is the *average annual base salary*.

## Sample Bargaining Unit

(a) Employment and Salaries

| Classification | Number of Firefighters | Salary |
|---|---|---|
| Probationary | | |
| Step 1 | 5 | $10,100 |
| Step 2 | 10 | 11,100 |
| Private | 65 | 12,100 |
| Lieutenant | 15 | 13,500 |
| Captain | 5 | 14,500 |
| | 100 | |

(b) Longevity Payments

| Longevity Step | Number of Firefighters | Longevity Pay |
|---|---|---|
| Step 1 | 20 Privates | $ 500 |
| Step 2 | 10 Privates | 1,000 |
| Step 2 | 15 Lieutenants | 1,000 |
| Step 2 | 5 Captains | 1,000 |

(c) Hours of Work

The scheduled hours consist of one 24-hour shift every three days (one on; two off), or an average of 56 hours per week and a total of 2,912 hours per year.

(d) Overtime Premium

All overtime hours are paid at the rate of time-and-one-half. The sample bargaining unit worked a total of 5,000 overtime hours during the preceding year.

(e) Shift Differential

The shift differential is 10 percent for all hours between 4 p.m. and 8 a.m. However, 10 members of the unit work exclusively on the day shift, from 8 a.m. to 4 p.m. They are 1 Captain, 3 Lieutenants, 3 Privates at Longevity Step 2, and 3 Privates at Step 1.

(f) Vacations

15 employees–(probationers) 5 shifts
35 employees—(privates) 10 shifts
50 employees—(all others) 15 shifts

(g) Holidays

Each firefighter is entitled to 10 paid holidays, and receives 8 hours pay for each holiday.

(h) Cothing Allowance

$150 per employee per year.

(i) Hospitalization

| Type of Coverage | Number of Firefighters | Employer's Monthly Payment |
|---|---|---|
| Single Coverage | 15 | $20.00 |
| Family Coverage | 85 | 47.00 |

(j) Pensions

The employer contributes an amount equal to six percent of the payroll (including basic salaries, longevity, overtime and shift differentials).

This method will also produce an average annual cost for longevity pay.

The combined average salary cost and average longevity cost amount to $12,630 per year. On an hourly basis, this comes to $4.337

**Average Annual Base Salary**

| (1)<br>Classification | (2)<br>Number<br>of Fire-<br>fighters | (3)<br>Salary | (4)<br>Weighted<br>Salaries<br>(2) × (3) |
|---|---|---|---|
| Probationary | | | |
| Step 1 | 5 | $10,100 | $ 50,500 |
| Step 2 | 10 | 11,100 | 111,000 |
| Private | 65 | 12,100 | 786,500 |
| Lieutenant | 15 | 13,500 | 202,500 |
| Captain | 5 | 14,500 | 72,500 |
| | 100 | | $1,223,000 |

Average Annual Base Salary =

$1,223,000 ÷ 100; or $12,230 per year

**Longevity Pay**

| (1)<br>Longevity<br>Step | (2)<br>Number<br>of Fire-<br>fighters | (3)<br>Longevity<br>Pay | (4)<br>Total<br>Longevity<br>Pay<br>(2) × (3) |
|---|---|---|---|
| Step 1 | 20 | $ 500 | $10,000 |
| Step 2 | 30 | 1,000 | 30,000 |
| | | | $40,000 |

Average Annual Longevity Pay =

$40,000 ÷ 100;* or $400 per year

*Since the unit is trying to determine its average base compensation—that is, all the salary and fringe benefit items its members receive collectively—the total cost of longevity pay must be averaged over the entire unit of 100.

($12,630 ÷ 2,912 hours). This hourly rate is needed to compute the cost of some fringe benefits. It is now possible to calculate the cost of overtime, shift differential, vacations, paid holidays, insurance and pensions.

*Note*: In this example, overtime, shift differential, vacations, paid holidays, and pensions are all computed using an hourly pay rate which includes *both salary and longevity pay*. This is an important factor when determining the effect of a salary increase on these benefits.

**Overtime**

Overtime work for the Sample Bargaining Unit is paid for at the rate of time-and-one-half. This means that part of the total overtime costs is an amount paid for at straight-time rates and part is a premium payment.

| (1) | (2)<br>Annual<br>Cost | (3)<br>Number of<br>Firefighters | (4)<br>Average Annual Cost<br>(1) ÷ (2) |
|---|---|---|---|
| Straight-time cost<br>($4.337 × 5,000<br>overtime hours)* | $21,685.00 | 100 | $216.85 |
| Half-time premium cost<br>(½ × $21,685.00) | 10,842.50 | 100 | 108.43 |
| Total Overtime Cost | $32,527.50 | | $325.28 |

*Based on preceding year's total overtime hours.

**Shift Differential**

The Sample Bargaining Unit receives a shift differential of 10 percent for all hours worked between 4 p.m. and 8 a.m. But 10 members of the unit who work in headquarters work hours that are not subject to the differential. This leaves 90 employees who receive the differential.

Since the differential is paid for hours worked between 4 p.m. and 8 a.m., it is applicable to only two-thirds of the normal 24-hour shift. It, therefore, only costs the employer two-thirds of 10 percent for each 24 hours. That is the reason for column (5) in the following calculation. Each employee receives the differential for only two-thirds of his 24-hour tour.

| (1) | (2) | (3) | (4) | (5) | (6) |
| | No. on | | 10% of | .667 of | Total Cost |
| Classification | Shift Pay | Salary | Col. (3) | Col. (4) | (2) × (5) |
| Probationary | | | | | |
| Step 1 | 5 | $10,100 | $1,010 | $ 674 | $ 3,370 |
| Step 2 | 10 | 11,100 | 1,110 | 740 | 7,400 |
| Private | | | | | |
| Longevity-0 | 35 | 12,100 | 1,210 | 807 | 28,245 |
| Longevity-1 | 17 | 12,600* | 1,260 | 840 | 14,280 |
| Longevity-2 | 7 | 13,100* | 1,320 | 880 | 6,160 |
| Lieutenant | 12 | 14,500* | 1,450 | 967 | 11,604 |
| Captain | 4 | 15,500* | 1,550 | 1,034 | 4,136 |
| | 90 | | | | $75,195 |

Average Annual Cost of Shift Differential = $75,195 ÷ 100;** or $751.95 per year

*Base salary plus longevity pay ($500 for Step 1 and $1,000 for Step 2).
**Since the unit is trying to determine its average base compensation—that is, all the salary and fringe benefit items its members receive collectively—the total cost of the shift differential must be averaged over the entire unit of 100.

**Vacations**

Vacation costs for the unit are influenced by (a) the amount of vacations received by the employees with differing lengths of service, and (b) the pay scales of those employees.

| (1)<br>Classification | (2)<br><br>Number of<br>Firefighters | (3)<br><br>Hourly<br>Rate* | (4)<br>Hours<br>of<br>Vaca-<br>tion** | (5)<br>Total Vaca-<br>tion<br>Hours<br>(2) × (4) | (6)<br>Total Vaca-<br>tion<br>Costs<br>(3) × (5) |
|---|---|---|---|---|---|
| Probationary | | | | | |
| Step 1 | 5 | $3.468 | 120 | 600 | $  2,080.80 |
| Step 2 | 10 | 3.812 | 120 | 1,200 | 4,574.40 |
| Private | | | | | |
| Longevity-0 | 35 | 4.155 | 240 | 8,400 | 34,902.00 |
| Longevity-1 | 20 | 4.327 | 360 | 7,200 | 31,154.40 |
| Longevity-2 | 10 | 4.499 | 360 | 3,600 | 16,196.40 |
| Lieutenant | 15 | 4.979 | 360 | 5,400 | 26,886.60 |
| Captain | 5 | 5.323 | 360 | 1,800 | 9,581.40 |
|  | 100 | | | 28,200 | $125,376.00 |

Average Annual Vacation Cost = $125,376 ÷ 100; or $1,253.76 per year

*Derived from annual salaries (including longevity pay), divided by 2,912 hours (56 hours × 52 weeks). The 10 firefighters who do not receive shift differential would be on a regular 40-hour week and would, therefore, have a different hourly rate and vacation entitlement. The impact on cost, however, would be minimal. It has, therefore, been disregarded in this computation.

**Since each firefighter works a 24-hour-shift, the hours of vacation are arrived at by multiplying the number of work shifts of vacation entitlement by 24 hours. For example, the figure of 120 hours is obtained by multiplying 5 shifts of vacation × 24 hours (one work shift).

**Paid Holidays**

Unlike vacations, the number of holidays received by an employee is not typically tied to length of service. Where the level of benefits is uniform, as it is with paid holidays, the calculation to determine its average cost is less complex.

In the Sample Bargaining Unit, each firefighter receives 8 hours of pay for each of his 10 paid holidays, or a total of 80 hours of holiday pay:

Average Annual Cost of Paid Holidays = $346.96 (80 hours × $4.337 average straight-time hourly rate derived from average salary cost plus average longevity cost.

---

**Hospitalization Insurance**

| (1)<br>Type of<br>Coverage | (2)<br>Number<br>of Fire-<br>fighters | (3)<br>Yearly<br>Premium<br>Cost to<br>Employer | (4)<br>Total<br>Cost to<br>Employer<br>(2) × (3) |
|---|---|---|---|
| Single | 15 | $240 | $ 3,600 |
| Family | 85 | 564 | 47,940 |
|  | 100 |  | $51,540 |

Average Annual Cost of Hospitalization Insurance =

$51,540 ÷ 100; or $515.40 per year

**Other Fringe Benefits**

(1) Pensions cost the employer six percent of payroll. The payroll amounts to $1,370,723 (salary cost of $1,223,000; longevity cost of $40,000; overtime cost of $32,528; and shift differential cost of $75,195). Six percent of this total is $82,243 which, when divided by 100, yields $822.43 as the average cost of pensions per firefighter, per year.

(2) The yearly cost of the clothing allowance is $150 per firefighter.

---

The nine figures may then be grouped together to provide a total figure for annual compensation:

| Base salary | $12,230.00 |
|---|---|
| Longevity pay | 400.00 |
| Overtime | 325.28 |

| (1)<br>Number of<br>Firefighters | (2)<br>Hours of<br>Increased<br>Vacation | (3)<br>Total Hours<br>(1) × (2) | (4)<br>Existing<br>Hourly Rates* | (5)<br>Cost of<br>Improvement<br>(3) × (4) |
|---|---|---|---|---|
| 10 Privates | 48 | 480 | $4.499 | $2,159.52 |
| 15 Lieutenants | 48 | 720 | 4.979 | 3,584.88 |
| 5 Captains | 48 | 240 | 5.323 | 1,277.52 |
|  |  |  |  | $7,021.92 |

*See the vacation table for derivation of hourly rates.

With no increase in salaries, the increase in vacation days would cost $7,021.92. The next step is to compute the total cost of the 4.8% increase.

| (1) | (2) | (3) | (4) | (5) | (6) |
|---|---|---|---|---|---|
| | | | | | Increased |
| | Existing | | Adjusted | | Cost from |
| | Vacation | Increase | Base Costs | Roll up | Roll up |
| Classification | Costs* | in Cost** | (2) + (3) | Factor | (4) × (5) |
| Probationary | | | | | |
|   Step 1 | $  2,080.80 | — | $  2,080.80 | 0.048 | $   99.88 |
|   Step 2 | 4,574.40 | — | 4,574.40 | 0.048 | 219.57 |
| Private | | | | | |
|   Longevity-0 | 34,902.00 | — | 34,902.00 | 0.048 | 1,675.30 |
|   Longevity-1 | 31,154.40 | — | 31,154.40 | 0.048 | 1,495.41 |
|   Longevity-2 | 16,196.40 | $2,159.52 | 18,355.92 | 0.048 | 881.08 |
| Lieutenant | 26,886,60 | 3,584.88 | 30,471.48 | 0.048 | 1,462.63 |
| Captain | 9,581.40 | 1,277.52 | 10,858.92 | 0.048 | 521.23 |
| | $125,376.00 | $7,021.92 | $132,397.92 | 0.048 | $6,355.10 |

*The base (or existing) vacation costs are from the vacation table and derived from average annual salary (base salary plus longevity).
**From data in preceding table.

Thus, there are two added costs to the vacation benefit; the $7,021.92 that represents the increase in benefits and the $6,355.10 which is a result of the increase in wages. When the two are totalled and divided by the number of firefighters in the unit, the total average cost of the new vacation benefit is $133.77 ($13,377.02 ÷ 100 employees).

Had the vacation improvement been granted across-the-board, to everyone in the unit, the calculation would have been different—and considerably easier. If the entire unit were to receive an additional 48 hours of vacation, the total additional hours would than be 4,800 (48 hours × 100 employees). These hours would then be multiplied by the unit's old average straight-time rate ($4.337), in order to arrive at the cost of the additional vacation improvement which, in this case, would have come to $20,817.60 (4,800 hours × $4.337). And, in that case, the total cost of vacations—that is the across-the-board improvement, plus the impact of the 4.8 percent average annual salary increase—would have been computed as follows:

    (a) Roll up of old vacation costs      = $ 6,018.05
          ($125,376 × 0.048)
    (b) Cost of vacation improvement      = $20,817.60
    (c) Roll up cost of improvement      = $   999.24
          ($20,817.60 × 0.048)

These pieces total to $27,834.89. When spread over the entire Sample Bargaining Unit, the increase in the average cost of vacations would have been $278.35 per year ($27,834.89 ÷ 100 employees).

This latter method of calculation does not apply only to vacations. It applies to any situation where a salary-related fringe benefit is to be improved equally for every member of the unit. An additional paid holiday would be another good example.

| | |
|---|---:|
| Shift differential | 751.95 |
| Vacations | 1,253.76 |
| Holidays | 346.96 |
| Hospitalization | 515.40 |
| Clothing allowance | 150.00 |
| Pension | 822.43 |
| Total | $16,795.78 |

## Computing the Costs of Increases

Once the *base compensation costs* have been determined, *increases* in those costs can be computed. Computing these new costs is commonly referred to as "costing out."

Assume that the Sample Bargaining Unit negotiates a settlement which contains the following changes:

- a five percent increase in base salaries,
- two additional vacation days for all employees at the second step of longevity, and
- an improvement in the benefits provided by the hospitalization program, which amounts to an additional $4.00 a month per family coverage and $2.50 for single coverage.

The objective in costing out this increase is to obtain the *average cost* (per firefighter) of the increase per year.

To compute the average annual increase, the base salary ($12,230.00) is multiplied by the percent increase (5%). This results in an increase of $611.50. There is no increase in longevity pay for this example. Had the longevity pay been tied to the base salary on a percentage basis there then would have been an increase in that amount also. As a result, the increase in the unit's *average annual salary* (base salary and longevity payments) is not 5% but 4.8%. This is determined by dividing the increase ($611.50) by the base salary plus longevity payments ($12,630).

Computing the cost of an increase is important because of the impact on the cost of fringe benefits. This impact on benefits is often referred to as the *roll up*. As salary increases, so does the cost of fringe benefits such as vacations, holidays, and overtime premiums. The *cost* of the benefits increases even if the *level* of benefits does not go up. In the example on longevity pay, the roll up did not come into play because the longevity pay was a fixed amount. Other types of benefits which are often exempt from the roll up are shift differentials, clothing allowances, and most group insurance plans. Any of these examples might be affected by the roll up if their cost is tied to the base salary amount.

Using the Sample Bargaining Unit, what items will not be affected? It has already been determined that there will be no change in longevity pay because it is a fixed dollar amount. The hours of work are not affected, nor the clothing allowance.

The remaining items in the budget will be affected in some manner. The next step is to identify in what manner they are changed. There are some items whose cost will be changed because of the roll up affect. In the sample bargaining unit, those items include:

- overtime premiums
- shift differentials
- holidays
- pensions

These benefits are tied to the original average annual salary (base salary plus longevity). The 4.8% increase in the average annual salary will increase the cost of these benefits.

| (1)<br>Fringe Benefit | (2)<br>Base<br>Average<br>Annual<br>Cost* | (3)<br><br>Roll up<br>Factor | (4)<br><br>Increased<br>Cost<br>(2) × (3) |
|---|---|---|---|
| Overtime | $325.29 | 0.048 | $ 15.61 |
| Shift differential | 751.95 | 0.048 | 36.09 |
| Holidays | 346.96 | 0.048 | 16.65 |
| Pensions | 822.43 | 0.048 | 39.48 |
| | | | $107.83 |

*See previous tables for derivation of these costs.

Once it has been determined which items have been changed by the roll up effect, the next step is to identify which items are changed by an increase in benefits. Items may be changed by either the roll up effect or an increase in benefits, or *both*. In the sample bargaining unit, the hospitalization benefit costs are changed because of an increase in benefits. The cost is a fixed dollar amount and thus is not subject to an increase in benefits because of the roll up. Costing out this benefit for the new contract entails multiplying the cost of the new program by the employees receiving the benefits:

| (1)<br>Type of<br>Coverage | (2)<br>Number<br>Covered | (3)<br>Annual<br>Cost of<br>Improvement | (4)<br>Total New<br>Cost<br>(2) × (3) |
|---|---|---|---|
| Single | 15 | $30 | $  450 |
| Family | 85 | 48 | 4,080 |
| | | | $4,530 |

The unit's average hospitalization cost will be increased by $45.30 per year ($4,530 ÷ 100 employees).

Finally, one item is affected by both the roll up *and* an increase in benefits. This is the vacation program. All vacation days will be increased by the cost increase in base salaries plus an increase of two shifts (48 hours) for all employees at the second step of longevity. The first step is to compute the cost of the two additional shifts prior to the 4.8% salary increase.

## The Total Increase in the Average Cost of Compensation

At this point, the increase in the costs of all the items of compensation which will change because of the Sample Bargaining Unit's newly-negotiated package have been calculated. All that is left is to combine these individual pieces in order to arrive at the total increase in the unit's *average cost of compensation*.

Increase in Average Annual Cost of
Compensation for Sample Bargaining Unit

| | |
|---|---|
| Base salary | $611.50 |
| Longevity pay | — |
| Overtime | 15.61 |
| Shift differential | 36.09 |
| Vacations | 133.77 |
| Holidays | 16.65 |
| Hospitalization | 45.30 |
| Clothing allowance | — |
| Pensions | 39.48 |

Total Increase in Average Annual
Cost of Annual Compensation = $898.40

*There remains one final computation that is really the most significant—the percent* increase that all of these figures represent. The unit's average base compensation per year was $16,796. The total dollar increase amounts to $898. The percent increase, therefore, is 5.3 percent ($898 ÷ $16,796), and that is the amount by which the unit's package increased the employer's average yearly cost per firefighter.

## Computing the Hourly Cost of Compensation

The increase in the cost of compensation per *hour* will be the same. The approach to the computation, however, is different than that which was used in connection with the cost per year. In the case of the hourly computation, the goal is to obtain the cost per hour of *work*. This requires that a distinction be drawn between hours worked and hours paid for. The difference between the two is leave time.

In the Sample Bargaining Unit, for example, the employee receives an annual salary which covers 2,912 regularly scheduled hours (56 hours per week, times 52). In addition, each works an average of 50 hours of overtime per year. The sum of these two—regularly scheduled hours and overtime hours, or 2,962—are the total hours paid for.

But they do not represent hours worked, because some of those hours are paid leave time. The Sample Bargaining Unit, for example, receives paid leave time in the form of vacation and holidays. The number of hours actually worked by each employee is 2,600 (2,962 hours paid for, minus 362 hours of paid leave).

Each firefighter receives 80 hours in paid holidays per year. The average number of hours of vacation per year was derived as follows:

| | |
|---|---|
| 15 firefighters × 120 hours (five 24-hour shifts) | = 1,800 hours |
| 35 firefighters × 240 hours (ten 24-hour shifts) | = 8,400 hours |
| 50 firefighters × 360 hours (fifteen 24-hour shifts) | = 18,000 hours |
| | 28,200 hours |

This averages out to 282 hours of vacation per firefighter (28,200 ÷ 100) which, together with 80 holiday hours, totals 362 paid leave hours.

The paid leave hours are hours paid for above and beyond hours worked. Thus, in order to obtain the hourly cost that they represent the annual dollar cost of these benefits is divided by the annual hours *worked*.

So it is with *all* fringe benefits, not only paid leave. In exchange for those benefits the employer receives hours of work (the straight-time hours and the overtime hours). Consequently, the hourly cost of any fringe benefit will be obtained by dividing the annual cost of the benefit by the annual number of hours *worked*. In some instances that cost is converted into money that ends up in the employee's pocket, as it does in the case of fringe benefits like shift differentials, overtime premiums and clothing allowances. In other instances—such as hospitalization and pensions—the employee is provided with benefits in the form of insurance programs. And in the case of paid leave time— holidays, vacations, sick leave, etc.—the return to the employee is in terms of fewer hours of work.

The average annual costs of the fringe benefits of the Sample Bargaining Unit were developed earlier in connection with the computations of the unit's average annual base compensation.

In order to convert the costs of these fringe benefits into an average hourly amount, they are divided by 2,600—the average hours worked during the year by each employee in the unit. As can be seen, the hourly cost of all fringe benefits amounts to $1.518.

| (1)<br><br>Cost<br>Fringe Benefit | (2)<br>Average<br>Annual<br>Cost | (3)<br>Average<br>Hours<br>Worked | (4)<br>Average<br>Hourly<br>(2) ÷ (3) |
|---|---|---|---|
| Overtime Premium* | $  108.43 | 2,600 | $0.042 |
| Shift Differential | 751.95 | 2,600 | 0.289 |
| Vacations | 1,253.76 | 2,600 | 0.482 |
| Holidays | 346.96 | 2,600 | 0.133 |
| Hospitalization | 515.40 | 2,600 | 0.198 |
| Clothing Allowance | 150.00 | 2,600 | 0.058 |
| Pensions | 822.43 | 2,600 | 0.316 |
|  | $3,948.93 |  | $1.518 |

*Includes only the premium portion of the pay for overtime work.

In addition to the fringe benefit costs, compensation includes the base pay. For our Sample Bargaining Unit this is $12,630 per year (average salary plus average cost of longevity payments). On a straight-time hourly basis, this comes to $4.337 ($12,630 ÷ 2,912 hours). Even with the straight-time portion for the year's overtime included ($216.85), the average straight-time hourly rate of pay will still remain at $4.337 ($12,846.45 ÷ 2,962 hours).

A recapitulation of these salary and fringe benefit cost data produces both the average *annual* base compensation figure for the Sample Bargaining Unit and the average *hourly* figure:

|  | Yearly | Hourly |
|---|---|---|
| Earnings at Straight-time | $12,846.85 ÷ 2,962 = $4.337 |  |
| Fringe Benefits | 3,948.93 ÷ 2,600 = $1.519 |  |
| Total Compensation | $16,795.78 | $5.856 |

Essentially the same process is followed if the *increase* in compensation is to be measured on an hourly (instead of an annual) basis.

The five percent pay increase received by the Sample Bargaining Unit would be worth 21 cents ($12,230 × 0.05 = $611.50 ÷ 2,912 = $0.21). The annual increase in the unit's fringe benefit costs per firefighter—$276.49 for all items combined (overtime-premium only, shift differential, vacations, holidays, hospitalization, pensions, and clothing allowance)—works out to 10.6 cent per hour ($276.49 ÷ 2600 hours).

Together, these represent a gain in average compensation of 31.6 cents per hour, or 5.4 percent ($0.316 ÷ $5.856). This is one-tenth of a percentage point off from the amount of increase (5.3 percent) reflected by the annual data—a difference due to the rounding of decimals during the computation process.

## Conclusion

If the data that were used for the Sample Bargaining Unit in our discussion is available for an actual unit, almost all demands can be evaluated in terms of future costs. Costing out requires careful documentation and thorough record keeping. But in return, either of the parties will have the ability to see what effect the increases will have on the budget. Costing out prepares the parties for realistic negotiations; offers and demands are supported by the facts obtained through costing out. Finally, because costing out is a clearly defined method, it reduces the discrepancies and disagreements over budget items. Although it will not provide answers to every question that arises, it will provide important, pertinent information for the parties' use during collective bargaining.

# Appendix E

# Sample Dues Deduction Authorization Form

## Authorization of Voluntary Deduction
## For Payment Of Employee Organization Dues

*To Be Completed by Employee*

Names: _____
(Please Print)

Social Security Number: _____

Agency (or other Identifying Information: _____

Payroll Code: _____

Effective Date: _____

I hereby authorize a deduction from my pay each pay period, to be forwarded to the employee organization named herein, in the amount certified by said employee organization:

Name of Organization
_____

| | |
|---|---|
| _____ | _____ |
| Signature of Employee | Date |

219

## To Be Completed by Employee Organization

Name of Organization: _____

Address: _____

I hereby certify that the regular dues for the above-named individual are currently established at $_____ per pay period.

_____    _____
Signature and Title of Authorized Official          Date

# Appendix F

# Sample Representation Election Agreement

The undersigned parties hereby enter into this agreement for the purpose of conducting a representation election for certain employees of the [agency] in accordance with the following terms and conditions:

*Secret Ballot Election*: An election by secret ballot will be conducted under the direction and supervision of [fill in], hereinafter referred to as the Election Judge. The Election Judge shall make the final decision regarding the conduct of the election in accordance with this agreement. Within two (2) days of the tally of the ballots, the Election Judge shall certify the results to the parties.*

*Appropriate Unit*: The unit of employees among whom the question concerning representation exists and among whom the election shall be conducted is as follows:

[Describe the unit]

*Excluded Employees:*

[Describe]

*Date, Time and Place:*

The election will be conducted on [date] at

[place]

[time]

---

*If an impartial agency exists, like a public employee relations board, the results would be certified to that agency.

221

*Voter Eligibility*: Those employees eligible to vote in the secret ballot election are limited to those employed and working in the appropriate unit during the payroll period which ended [date], and employed on the date of the election.

*Notices of Election*: Notices of this election shall be posted on all employee bulletin boards where other notices to employees in the appropriate unit are customarily posted as well as any other places voluntarily selected by the signatory parties or specified by the Election Judge provided that there shall be no obligation to supply notices of election to eligible voters individually. Notices of the election shall include the date, place, and time of election; the appropriate unit; the eligibility rules specified above; and a sample of the ballot to be used. The notices of election shall be posted for at least 7 consecutive days prior to the date of the election, and shall remain posted until after the election.

*Observers*: Each party to this agreement will be allowed to station two observers at the polling station to assist in its conduct, to challenge for good cause the eligibility of voters, and to verify the tally. The Union shall designate in writing to the agency and the Election Judge the names of observers at least two days prior to the election to allow for any necessary adjustment of work schedules.

*Wording on the Ballot*: The choices on the ballot will appear in the wording indicated below:

OFFICIAL SECRET BALLOT
For Certain Employees of the [Agency]

Do you desire to be represented for the purpose of exclusive representation by

[Name of Union]

MARK AN "X" IN THE SQUARE OF YOUR CHOICE
YES ☐          NO ☐

DO NOT SIGN THIS BALLOT:
Fold and Deposit in the Ballot Box Provided

*Tally of Ballots*: Immediately following the election, the Election Judge shall count the ballots and issue a tally. Ballots which contain identifying markings or which are unmarked or do not otherwise clearly reveal the intent of the voter shall be declared void provided that ballots shall be liberally construed in favor of validity.

*Election Results*: The choice on the ballot receiving a majority of the valid ballots cast shall be certified to the [agency].

*Electioneering*: There shall be no electioneering in or about the polling area during the course of the election and supervisory personnel will not be allowed in or around the polling area during the course of the election.

*Challenges*: Any party, by its appointed observer, may challenge the eligibility of a voter for good cause. All challenges are to be made to the Election Judge before the ballot is cast. Before counting the unchallenged ballots, the agent in charge shall attempt to resolve such challenges. Challenges not resolved by the Election Judge shall be resolved [describe procedure].

*Objections*: Objections concerning the procedural conduct of the election or to conduct which improperly affected the results of the election must be filed with [the agency] within five (5) calendar days of the date of counting of ballots. A copy of objections to the election shall be sent to all parties simultaneously. Only employees and signatory parties to this agreement may file objections concerning the conduct of the election.

*Approval of Agreement*: This agreement shall be effective on the date of approval by the Election Judge and the parties. Once approved, all signatory parties will be furnished a copy of the agreement. After approval of this agreement, no party will be permitted to withdraw from the agreement after seventy-two hours prior to the scheduled date of the election.

Signatory parties certify that they have notified all individuals, groups, or organizations known to them who may have an interest in becoming a party to this agreement of the existence of this agreement. Any provision herein declared void or unlawful by a competent court of law or other governmental agency shall not cause the remaining provisions to be void or unlawful.

_____     _____

UNION                                    EMPLOYER

_____     _____

DATE                                     DATE

_____

ELECTION JUDGE

_____

DATE

Appendix G

# AFL-CIO Public Sector Bargaining Law Report

## ONE COUNTRY...
## TWO DIFFERENT WORLDS

**How the Absence of Collective Bargaining Laws
Limits Public Employee Bargaining Rights**

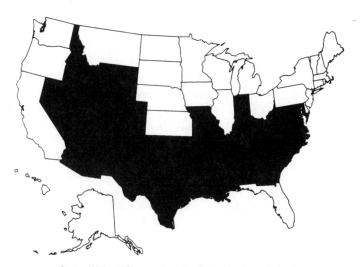

**States Without Comprehensive Collective Bargaining Laws**

**February 1987**

**Public Employee Department
of the AFL-CIO**

225

## Introduction

There are approximately ten and one-half (10.5) million state and local government employees in the United States who are in jobs that are generally considered to be eligible for collective bargaining. But, because employees of our states and local governments have been traditionally excluded from the protection of national labor laws, it has been left to the individual states to determine whether to extend such rights to the public workers within the states. Today, twenty-seven (27) states and the District of Columbia have enacted comprehensive collective bargaining laws for their public employees. Six and one-half (6.5) million employees in these states are protected. There are four (4) million employees in the twenty-three (23) states without such laws, amounting to forty (40) percent of the ten and one-half (10.5) million total.

To determine the extent to which employees in the "bargaining" versus "non-bargaining" states have opted in favor of collective bargaining, our study focused on the years 1976 through 1982, the most recent years for which accurate and comprehensive data are available. Inasmuch as two of our "bargaining" states—Ohio and Illinois—implemented new laws in 1984, we made a special effort to collect data for those states for 1985.

The figures are dramatic. In the "bargaining" states, where public employees have the protected right to join unions of their own choosing, fully seventy-one (71) percent were represented for collective bargaining in 1982. On the other hand, in the twenty-three (23) "non-bargaining" states, only fourteen (14) percent were represented in 1982. There has been a consistent rise in the "bargaining" states and an equally consistent decline in the "non-bargaining" states.

In "bargaining" states, a general examination of bargaining unit composition, incidence of unfair labor practices and consummation of first contracts reveals that units encompass a wide range of occupations from blue collar to professional. Cases of employer interference in the representation election process are infrequent, and first contracts are usually negotiated promptly. Further, decertification elections are almost always instigated by competing unions and not by employer initiative. Specific data in these areas will require another, much more detailed study.

*Authors' Note*: Research performed by Paula D. Lucak, Public Employee Department, AFL-CIO. A publication of the Public Employee Department, AFL-CIO, 815 16th Street, N.W., Room #308, Washington, D.C. 20006, 202/393-2820. Reprinted by permission of the AFL-CIO Public Employee Department, Washington, D.C.

While the trend in "bargaining" states is encouraging, we detect a disturbing parallel between the gradual decline in public employee unionization in the "non-bargaining" states and among unionized workers in the private sector generally. Both hover in the teens. For both the question may be the same: How protected are they in their right to collective bargaining?

## Public Employee Bargaining Laws in the States

Twenty-seven (27) states and the District of Columbia have enacted comprehensive collective bargaining laws covering the vast majority of their public employees. While some states have a single law covering all these employees, many states achieve comprehensive coverage with several laws. For example, the state of Washington covers its state and local employees through seven (7) separate statutes covering municipal employees, teachers, community college academics, higher education employees, marine employees, and employees of port and utilities districts. The following chart summarizes public employee bargaining laws in the states with comprehensive bargaining laws.

### SUMMARY OF STATES' PUBLIC EMPLOYEE BARGAINING LAWS
### States with Comprehensive Laws

| | Number of Laws | Groups Covered | Original Enactment |
|---|---|---|---|
| Arkansas | 2 | —State & Local Employees | 1972 |
| | | —Teachers | 1970 |
| California | 5 | —State Civil Service and Teachers | 1977 |
| | | —State Non-Civil Service | 1971 |
| | | —Local Employees | 1961 |
| | | —Public School Employees | 1975 |
| | | —Higher Ed. Employees | 1978 |
| Connecticut | 3 | —State Employees | 1975 |
| | | —Municipal Employees | 1965 |
| | | —Teachers | 1958 |
| Delaware | 4 | —State, County & Local Employees | 1965 |
| | | —Teachers | 1969 |
| | | —Transit Employees | 1968 |
| | | —Police and Fire Fighters | 1986 |

## SUMMARY OF STATES' PUBLIC EMPLOYEE
## BARGAINING LAWS—*Cont'd*

| | Number of Laws | Groups Covered | Original Enactment |
|---|---|---|---|
| District of Columbia | 1 | —Municipal Employees | 1978 |
| Florida | 1 | —State & Local Employees | 1974 |
| Hawaii | 1 | —State & Local Employees | 1970 |
| Illinois | 2 | —State & Local Employees | 1984 |
| | | —Educational Employees | 1984 |
| Iowa | 3 | —State & Local Employees | 1974 |
| | | —Fire Fighters | 1974 |
| | | —Judicial Employees | 1985 |
| Kansas | 2 | —State & Local Employees | 1971 |
| | | —Teachers | 1970 |
| Maine | 4 | —State Employees | 1974 |
| | | —Municipal, County, School and Turnpike Employees | 1969 |
| | | —University Employees | 1975 |
| | | —Judicial Employees | 1984 |
| Massachusetts | 2 | —State & Local Employees | 1973 |
| | | —Police & Fire Fighters | 1977 |
| Michigan | 2 | —State & Local Employees | 1947 |
| | | —Police & Fire Fighters | 1969 |
| Minnesota | 1 | —State & Local Employees | 1971 |
| Montana | 2 | —State & Local Employees | 1973 |
| | | —Nurses | 1969 |
| Nebraska | 2 | —State & Local Employees | 1947 |
| | | —Teachers in School Dist. | 1967 |
| New Hampshire | 1 | —State & Local Employees | 1975 |
| New Jersey | 2 | —State & Local Employees | 1968 |
| | | —Police & Fire Fighters | 1977 |
| New York | 1 | —State & Local Employees | 1967 |
| N. Dakota | 2 | —State & Local Employees | 1951 |
| | | —Teachers | 1969 |
| Ohio | 1 | —State & Local Employees | 1984 |
| Oregon | 1 | —State & Local Employees | 1963 |
| Pennsylvania | 3 | —State & Local Employees | 1970 |
| | | —Police & Fire Fighters | 1968 |
| | | —Transit Employees | 1967 |
| Rhode Island | 6 | —State Employees | 1958 |
| | | —State Police | 1979 |

## SUMMARY OF STATES' PUBLIC EMPLOYEE
## BARGAINING LAWS—*Cont'd*

| | Number of Laws | Groups Covered | Original Enactment |
|---|---|---|---|
| Rhode Island *cont.* | | —Municipal Employees | 1967 |
| | | —Teachers | 1966 |
| | | —Municipal Police | 1963 |
| | | —Fire Fighters | 1961 |
| S. Dakota | 1 | —State & Local Employees | 1969 |
| Vermont | 3 | —State Employees | 1969 |
| | | —Municipal Employees | 1973 |
| | | —Teachers | 1969 |
| W. Virginia | 7 | —Municipal Employees | 1967 |
| | | —Teachers | 1975 |
| | | —Community College Academics | 1971 |
| | | —Higher Ed. Employees | 1971 |
| | | —Port Dist. Employees | 1967 |
| | | —Marine Employees | 1961 |
| | | —Utility Dist. Employees | 1963 |
| Wisconsin | 3 | —State Employees | 1966 |
| | | —Municipal Employees | 1959 |
| | | —Police & Fire Fighters | 1971 |

## Bargaining Unit Representation in the States: An Overview

Overall, state and local public employees represented in bargaining units grew from 44.72 percent (1976) to 49.42 percent (1982) of all public employees that were eligible for coverage under state and local collective bargaining laws. While this is a relatively high rate of representation as compared to the private sector, in the twenty-seven (27) states and the District of Columbia that have comprehensive bargaining laws, the level of representation has been significantly stronger, growing from 60.09 percent in 1976 to 71.19 percent in 1982. The overall figures also show a dramatic gulf between the level of bargaining unit membership in states with comprehensive bargaining laws as compared to states without such laws. Bargaining unit representation among eligible public employees in states with no comprehensive laws, in fact, steadily decreased over the six year period from 16.12 percent in 1976 to 13.99 percent in 1982.

## STATE AND LOCAL PUBLIC EMPLOYEES REPRESENTED IN BARGAINING UNITS, 1976–1982
### (in thousands—000)

| | 1976 | 1977 | 1978 | 1979 | 1980 | 1982 |
|---|---|---|---|---|---|---|
| *All States* | | | | | | |
| Eligible Public Emplys. | 9,375 | 10,212 | 10,195 | 10,482 | 10,652 | 10,395 |
| In Bargaining Units | 4,354 | 4,726 | 4,816 | 4,980 | 5,122 | 5,137 |
| Percent | 44.72 | 46.27 | 47.23 | 47.51 | 48.09 | 49.42 |
| *States with Comprehensive Laws* | | | | | | |
| Eligible Public Emplys. | 6,221 | 6,379 | 6,427 | 6,587 | 6,668 | 6,438 |
| In Bargaining Units | 3,787 | 4,128 | 4,275 | 4,407 | 4,539 | 4,582 |
| Percent | 60.09 | 64.72 | 66.52 | 66.91 | 68.07 | 71.19 |
| *States with No Comprehensive Laws* | | | | | | |
| Eligible Public Emplys. | 3,514 | 3,833 | 3,767 | 3,895 | 3,984 | 3,956 |
| In Bargaining Units | 566 | 598 | 540 | 573 | 583 | 554 |
| Percent | 16.12 | 15.59 | 14.34 | 14.70 | 14.64 | 13.99 |

(*Note*: Numbers may not add up due to rounding.)

### *Bargaining Unit Representation in States With Comprehensive Laws*

Among the twenty-seven (27) states and the District of Columbia which have enacted comprehensive collective bargaining laws for public employees, representation in 1982 ranged from a low of 18.19 percent in North Dakota to a high of 98.61 percent in New York.

In 1982, only three (3) states: Kansas, North Dakota and South Dakota, represented less than 40 percent of their eligible public employees. State and local public employees in these three states, it should be noted, made up only 3.15 percent of all eligible public employees in states with comprehensive laws. Sixteen (16) states, employing 52.69 percent of all eligible public employees in states with comprehensive laws, represented in bargaining units from 40 to 80 percent of their state and local public employees. Seven (7) states and the District of Columbia, who employed 44.16 percent of all eligible public employees in the comprehensive law states, had a bargaining unit representation rate from 80 to 100 percent. The following chart presents rates of bargaining unit representation in states with comprehensive laws.

## STATE AND LOCAL PUBLIC EMPLOYEES REPRESENTED IN
## BARGAINING UNITS, 1972–1986
### (States with Comprehensive Bargaining Laws)

| | 1976 | 1977 | 1978 | 1979 | 1980 | 1982 |
|---|---|---|---|---|---|---|
| Alaska | 83.99% | 99.89% | 86.14% | 75.48% | 77.53% | 75.81% |
| California | 51.94 | 61.61 | 66.15 | 63.81 | 64.99 | 83.62 |
| Connecticut | 59.50 | 83.29 | 86.75 | 90.29 | 89.35 | 81.74 |
| Delaware | 59.90 | 56.04 | 62.15 | 69.34 | 60.14 | 61.74 |
| Dist. of Col. | 76.57 | 80.54 | 88.50 | 90.25 | 88.17 | 95.99 |
| Florida | 41.91 | 46.52 | 56.72 | 55.26 | 66.57 | 59.54 |
| Hawaii | 86.93 | 45.50 | 84.42 | 85.23 | 88.90 | 88.90 |
| Illinois* | 40.12 | 43.51 | 36.80 | 42.76 | 44.00 | 45.46 |
| Iowa | 37.49 | 48.82 | 46.57 | 46.89 | 49.28 | 63.62 |
| Kansas | 28.77 | 36.75 | 34.86 | 32.92 | 35.91 | 35.55 |
| Maine | 32.95 | 48.83 | 52.14 | 50.20 | 57.49 | 66.32 |
| Massachusetts | 83.39 | 83.75 | 85.03 | 86.26 | 87.13 | 84.73 |
| Michigan | 66.23 | 64.83 | 65.41 | 70.95 | 66.22 | 66.56 |
| Minnesota | 57.87 | 55.58 | 61.85 | 62.65 | 65.42 | 65.07 |
| Montana | 41.07 | 38.21 | 48.96 | 44.13 | 46.65 | 46.33 |
| Nebraska | 31.33 | 36.69 | 35.17 | 37.73 | 38.95 | 41.78 |
| New Hampshire | 24.09 | 41.72 | 49.58 | 47.61 | 51.50 | 55.02 |
| New Jersey | 72.21 | 72.09 | 72.30 | 72.49 | 74.39 | 83.95 |
| New York | 96.51 | 92.22 | 99.33 | 96.78 | 98.53 | 98.61 |
| North Dakota | 14.74 | 18.48 | 19.97 | 22.08 | 21.09 | 18.19 |
| Ohio*† | 45.35 | 50.67 | 48.44 | 50.16 | 49.11 | 41.18 |
| Oregon | 69.75 | 73.58 | 73.05 | 73.18 | 72.61 | 72.52 |
| Pennsylvania | 75.80 | 76.11 | 77.16 | 75.48 | 75.38 | 78.32 |
| Rhode Island | 85.64 | 89.38 | 90.34 | 91.30 | 85.70 | 86.96 |
| South Dakota | 29.19 | 27.74 | 26.88 | 28.70 | 28.87 | 30.10 |
| Vermont | 43.36 | 50.14 | 50.22 | 55.09 | 49.26 | 48.90 |
| Washington | 64.17 | 65.70 | 69.26 | 68.23 | 69.82 | 71.43 |
| Wisconsin | 53.41 | 63.78 | 66.12 | 64.00 | 60.59 | 50.66 |
| Average | 60.09% | 64.72% | 66.52% | 66.91% | 68.07% | 71.19% |

*Comprehensive law implemented in 1984. Illinois' representation rate in 1985 was 79.98%. Ohio's representation rate was 51.55% in 1986.

†Figures for Ohio bargaining unit membership provided by the Bureau of Census are overstated for the years 1976–80. Data collection in the state prior to the consideration of the new 1984 law proved unreliable. The reliability of data improved for 1982 as the state considered the new law.

## *Bargaining Unit Representation in States With No Comprehensive Laws*

The twenty-three (23) states with no comprehensive bargaining laws covering state and local public employees present a dramatically different and lower rate of bargaining unit membership among their public employees. In 1982, the rates ranged from a low of zero percent (North Carolina) to a high of 54.18 percent (Nevada).

For 1982, fully 52.78 percent of all eligible public employees in these states were employed in the nine (9) states with a representation rate of less than 10 percent. Those states are: Alabama, Arkansas, Georgia, Mississippi, North Carolina, South Carolina, Texas, Virginia and West Virginia. Twelve (12) states, employing 41.59 percent of the non-bargaining law states' eligible employees, had representation rates of between 10 and 40 percent. Two (2) states, Maryland and Nevada, had representation rates of 53.10 and 54.18 percent, respectively. These two states, it should be noted, have relatively extensive local bargaining laws, although coverage of state employees is non-existent.

In general, if one focuses on only state employees in the 23 states with no comprehensive laws, representation rates drop even further, with sixteen (16) of them showing zero bargaining unit representation. The following chart presents rates of bargaining unit representation in states with no comprehensive bargaining laws.

## STATE AND LOCAL PUBLIC EMPLOYEES REPRESENTED IN BARGAINING UNITS, 1976–1982
### (States with no comprehensive laws.)

|  | 1976 | 1977 | 1978 | 1979 | 1980 | 1982 |
|---|---|---|---|---|---|---|
| Alabama | 6.29% | 6.17% | 8.94% | 8.41% | 6.73% | 4.77 |
| Arizona | 28.13 | 28.49 | 31.88 | 29.65 | 30.34 | 31.89 |
| Arkansas | 6.29 | 5.80 | 6.07 | 7.32 | 7.14 | 7.10 |
| Colorado | 26.46 | 28.96 | 28.26 | 30.73 | 28.95 | 28.68 |
| Georgia | 2.07 | 3.71 | 2.60 | 2.28 | 3.72 | 1.80 |
| Idaho | 22.87 | 25.35 | 27.69 | 25.38 | 25.07 | 25.47 |
| Indiana | 32.69 | 34.17 | 34.12 | 32.88 | 31.98 | 32.77 |
| Kentucky | 8.93 | 9.54 | 11.30 | 12.43 | 12.84 | 12.25 |
| Louisiana | 15.63 | 15.39 | 14.45 | 12.25 | 12.86 | 12.38 |
| Maryland | 50.75 | 53.59 | 54.23 | 51.09 | 51.76 | 53.01 |
| Mississippi | 1.42 | 1.19 | 1.23 | .98 | 1.23 | .20 |
| Missouri | 54.90 | 50.56 | 56.80 | 59.67 | 55.00 | 54.18 |
| New Mexico | 27.71 | 32.87 | 29.91 | 27.03 | 26.79 | 27.83 |
| Nevada | 19.57 | 24.17 | 21.07 | 25.52 | 28.20 | 25.17 |
| North Carolina | .16 | — | — | — | — | — |
| Oklahoma | 19.01 | 20.87 | 20.93 | 20.75 | 20.47 | 18.48 |
| South Carolina | 1.37 | 1.30 | .54 | .47 | .48 | .14 |
| Tennessee | 16.70 | 15.40 | 16.75 | 21.44 | 21.85 | 22.01 |

### STATE AND LOCAL PUBLIC EMPLOYEES REPRESENTED IN
### BARGAINING UNITS, 1976–1982—*Cont'd*
#### (States with no comprehensive laws.)

|               | 1976   | 1977   | 1978   | 1979   | 1980   | 1982   |
|---------------|--------|--------|--------|--------|--------|--------|
| Texas         | 10.38  | 12.26  | 1.49   | 1.47   | 2.15   | 1.22   |
| Utah          | 47.84  | 43.59  | 32.22  | 47.88  | 37.92  | 36.13  |
| Virginia      | 13.05  | —      | —      | —      | —      | .05    |
| West Virginia | 6.04   | 5.08   | 3.52   | 3.80   | 3.84   | 2.91   |
| Wyoming       | 25.61  | 26.24  | 26.54  | 20.50  | 19.04  | 20.79  |
| Average       | 16.12% | 15.59% | 14.34% | 14.70% | 14.64% | 13.99% |

## *Bargaining Unit Representation Since 1982*

Data for the years since 1982 are generally unavailable. We were, however, able to develop 1985 numbers for a few of the states through consultations with the appropriate state labor relations board officials. They are as follows:

|                      | 1982   | 1985    |
|----------------------|--------|---------|
| District of Columbia | 95.99% | 96.38%  |
| Hawaii               | 88.90  | 88.11   |
| Illinois             | 45.46  | 79.98   |
| New Hampshire        | 55.02  | 63.72   |
| Ohio                 | 41.18  | 51.55*  |
| Washington           | 71.43  | 70.53   |
| Wisconsin            | 50.66  | 63.35   |

*Data are for 1986.

Overall, for these states bargaining unit representation remained stable. Significant increases since 1982 were indicated in four (4) states: Illinois (+34.52%), New Hampshire (+8.7%), Ohio (+10.37%) and Wisconsin (+12.69%). We note, particularly, the increases experienced in Ohio and Illinois since they represent the effect that passage of comprehensive bargaining laws in 1984 has had on bargaining unit representation in these two states.

## Definitions and Sources

*Bargaining Unit*: A group of employees recognized as appropriate for representation by an employee organization for the purpose of collective bargaining. The number of state and local public employee bargaining unit members in the states for the years 1976 through 1982 are from the Bureau of Census' reports *Labor-Management Relations in State and Local Governments* for those years. Bargaining unit membership numbers for 1985 were determined through consultation with appropriate labor relations board officials. The numbers include full and part-time employees.

*Comprehensive Bargaining Law States*: States whose bargaining laws provide effective bargaining rights to the majority of public employees at both the state and local levels.

*Eligible Public Employees*: For the years 1976–82 the Bureau of Census provides numbers for total state and local public employees in the states in their reports, *Labor-Management Relations in State and Local Governments*. For 1985 the Bureau of Census provides total numbers in its report *Public Employment in 1985*. The Bureau defines public employees as all persons gainfully employed by and performing services for a government. This includes all full and part-time persons paid for services performed including paid elected officials; persons paid on a "per meeting," annual, semi-annual or quarterly basis; as well as supervisors, managers, administrators and confidential employees who are normally excluded from coverage under state collective bargaining laws. We adjusted the Bureau's total numbers, reducing them by twenty (20) percent, in order to eliminate ineligible employees. The appropriateness of a 20 percent reduction was confirmed through discussions with state and local labor relations board officials and state and local public employee unions.

# Index

# About the Authors

**Michael T. Leibig** is a partner in the firm of Zwerdling, Paul, Leibig, Kahn and Thompson, P.C., where he specializes in labor, pension, employee benefits, and related areas of the law. He is an adjunct professor at the Georgetown University Law Center where he teaches courses in labor policy, state and local labor law, and termination of employment. He serves as General Counsel to the International Union of Police Associations, AFL-CIO; as General Counsel to Virginia Public Employees Council 30, AFSCME; as Counsel to the Alexandria (Virginia) Firefighters' Local 2141, AFL-CIO; as Counsel to the AFSCME Employees' Pension Plan; as National Secretary to the National Resource Center for Consumers of Legal Services. He has served on the special advisory committee of the Citizen's Commission on Pension Policy and has advised the Pension Rights Center and the President's Commission on Pension Policy. He is past Co-Chair of the Labor Relations Division of the District of Columbia Bar. He is a member of the District of Columbia Bar and the Virginia Bar. He was an associate counsel with Zwerdling and Maurer (1974–1980) in the Office of the General Counsel of the American Federation of State, County and Municipal Employees, AFL-CIO. He served as Counsel to United States Senator Walter "Dee" Huddleston in 1973–1974.

Mr. Leibig attended Georgetown University (B.A. 1967), the Ohio University Graduate School (1967–1968), the University of Virginia School of Law (J.D. 1971); and participated in graduate law programs at Georgetown and George Washington Universities, and the U.S. Army Judge Advocate General School. He has published numerous articles including, "The Surprising Conservative Preference for the Government as Labor's Protector," in the *Journal of Law and Contemporary Problems*; *The Fair Labor Standards Act in Policing*, published by The Institute for Police Research; and *Mandating Social Prudence: A Handbook for Pension Investments*, published by the Conference on Alternative State and Local Policies.

PUBLIC EMPLOYEE ORGANIZING AND THE LAW

**Wendy L. Kahn** is a partner in the firm of Zwerdling, Paul, Leibig, Kahn and Thompson, P.C., where she specializes in labor law and employment discrimination law. She is an adjunct professor at the Georgetown University Law Center where she has, since 1978, taught labor relations in state and local government in the graduate labor law program.

Ms. Kahn was an attorney with Zwerdling and Maurer in the Office of the General Counsel of the AFSCME, AFL-CIO from 1973–1980. Since then, in private practice, she has represented unions in the private sector as well as in the public sector. She has been active since 1973 on the ABA Labor and Employment Law Section's Committee on State and Local Government Collective Bargaining and is a past Chair of the Labor Law Division of the District of Columbia Bar. She is a past board member of the Women's Legal Defense Fund and of the National Committee on Pay Equity, and has just completed a three-year appointment to the Montgomery County, Maryland, Commission for Women.

Ms. Kahn is author of articles on public sector labor law and on pay equity. She is a graduate of the University of Michigan (1966) and the New York University School of Law (J.D. 1973). She is a member of the District of Columbia Bar and the Maryland Bar, in addition to various federal court bars.